CL

Advanced Contemplation

The Peace Within You

THE NOTEBOOKS OF PAUL BRUNTON

(VOLUME 15)

ADVANCED CONTEMPLATION

THE PEACE WITHIN YOU

PAUL BRUNTON

(1898–1981)

An in-depth study of
categories twenty-three and twenty-four
from the notebooks

Published for the
PAUL BRUNTON PHILOSOPHIC FOUNDATION
by Larson Publications

International Standard Book Number (cloth) 0-943914-42-6
International Standard Book Number (paper) 0-943914-43-4
International Standard Book Number (series, cloth) 0-943914-17-5
International Standard Book Number (series, paper) 0-943914-23-X
Library of Congress Catalog Card Number: 84-47752

Manufactured in the United States of America

Published for the
Paul Brunton Philosophic Foundation
by
Larson Publications
4936 Route 414
Burdett, New York 14818

2   4   6   8   10   9   7   5   3

The works of Paul Brunton

A Search in Secret India
The Secret Path
A Search in Secret Egypt
A Message from Arunachala
A Hermit in the Himalayas
The Quest of the Overself
The Inner Reality
(*also titled* Discover Yourself)
Indian Philosophy and Modern Culture
The Hidden Teaching Beyond Yoga
The Wisdom of the Overself
The Spiritual Crisis of Man

Published posthumously

Essays on the Quest

The Notebooks of Paul Brunton

volume 1: Perspectives
volume 2: The Quest
volume 3: Practices for the Quest
          Relax and Retreat
volume 4: Meditation
          The Body
volume 5: Emotions and Ethics
          The Intellect
volume 6: The Ego
          From Birth to Rebirth
volume 7: Healing of the Self
          The Negatives
volume 8: Reflections on My
            Life and Writings
volume 9: Human Experience
          The Arts in Culture
volume 10: The Orient

(continued next page)

CONTENTS

EDITORS' INTRODUCTION

In this volume we encounter another major turning point of the quest: the point at which the ego relinquishes the practices and pace to the Overself. On the Long Path we initiate our development through our own effort. For guidance on the Long Path we must rely on our own intelligence and feelings, strengthened by the external influence of friends, teachers, and sacred literature. This point of view is established in volume three and is continued in the volumes that follow, dealing with the nature of this quest, the structure of the ego, the experiences of mysticism, the study of philosophy, and the understanding of mentalism. All these work toward weakening our identification with the ego and strengthening our awareness of the Overself. The present volume deepens this contact with the Overself until the ego must surrender to its guidance both in daily life and in meditation. Here we begin the quest anew, with a direct comprehension of the goal for the first time. At last we come to know that nothing else matters, that there is nothing outside the quest. Up to this point the quest may be an intermittent affair, a confusing journey through the misconceptions and misdirections of the ego; hereafter, the student moves in light along the mysterious path of spiritual attainment. This is because the quester is no longer primarily concerned with battling the ego; the focus is now on living always in the presence of the Overself. Part 1 of this volume, *Advanced Contemplation*, explores the nature of this redirection of attention from ego to Overself and shows us how it can be done; Part 2, *The Peace Within You*, shows us how to live inside the quest, inside the stillness of the Overself, once this transition has occurred.

As we look through the topics in *The Notebooks*, we can see that P.B. considers the quest as ascending through three levels: the physical, the subtle, and the mental. As P.B. examines each level, he alternates between objective understanding and subjective awareness. For example, in *The Sensitives* (volume eleven) P.B. acquaints us with the misconceptions and ignorance about the psychic realm, which prepares the way for *The Reverential Life* (in volume twelve), where we turn our hearts toward the image of the Overself in the subtle plane of interior feeling. P.B. repeats this pattern in volumes thirteen and fourteen, first defining the characteristics with which mind imbues experience and the nature of the mind itself (volume thirteen), and then lifting our awareness beyond the mental plane into the intuitive awareness of the Overself (volume fourteen).

This pattern of alternating objective and subjective perspectives reaches its conclusion in Part 1 of the present volume. On a first reading, it may appear to have two sections: the first five chapters, which include the definitions of the Short Path and its combination with the Long Path, and the last three chapters, which describe various techniques for advanced meditation, including contemplations of the Void. However, a closer reading will show that this category is a whole. The difference between the extroverted state of mind, treated in the first five chapters, and the introverted mind, treated in the last three chapters, must become very slight if this stage of the quest is to be successful. In fact, in Part 2, this difference vanishes as completely as it can. This blending of the objective and subjective perspectives is a central point for this volume. In the opening chapter of *Advanced Contemplation*, P.B. tells us to begin and end with the goal, to turn 180 degrees around—not away from the ego, but toward the Overself—to face the Overself always, and in all ways: to orient our daily life and activities towards the achievement of its presence, and to devote our meditations not to its symbols or signs but to itself alone. This single-minded focus on the transcendent Overself naturally draws the extroverted mind and the introverted mind more closely together, since the primary content in either mode is now the same for both. When P.B. describes the Void as a contemplative state, he makes clear that no sort of subject or object can exist in that state, and that the stillness it generates cannot be accurately described in either context alone.

Another point P.B. clearly makes in Part 1 is that the Short Path gets its name neither from its speed of attainment nor from its ease of accomplishment, but from the directness of its approach to the quest. Like a solitary ascent of a challenging cliff-face, the Short Path keenly focuses the mind on the demands of spiritual development. This approach is a necessary stage of the quest, and one whose dangers are real if we make the assault unreadied and unaware. The nature of these risks and remedies is discussed in the second and third chapters. Having made the challenge and the warnings clear, in chapter four P.B. describes exactly how we can make the changeover to the Short Path. Then, in chapter five, P.B. adds his wonderful sense of balance to the picture, pointing out the place of the Long Path's milder approach—as first separate, then interwoven with, and finally combining with the Short Path to become the philosopher's way of life. So P.B. begins by presenting the Short Path as a challenge to the quester, but concludes by stating that the Short Path, when balanced by the Long Path, becomes the "way" of living in the radiant presence of the Overself.

In Part 1, the chapters are arranged as a development from simple to more advanced stages of practice. However, the fundamental stages are only briefly described here, having been fully discussed in earlier volumes. We would recommend that the reader review *Practices for the Quest* (in volume three), and *Meditation* (in volume four) as a part of studying the present volume. Volume three gives a full consideration of the Long Path; it may be helpful to read chapters one and nine of Part 1 there before reading chapters four and five of the present volume. Volume four, Part 1, covers what P.B. calls elementary meditation. It is especially important to review the section titled "Levels of Absorption" in the first chapter there before reading the meditation exercises and experiences in chapters six through eight of the present volume. That earlier section defines and describes all the stages of meditation, right up through advanced contemplation, and gives some indication of how they can be recognized. For the reader who has already studied volume four, we have repeated nine paras from that section as a reference guide to P.B.'s description and definition of the various stages of meditation and contemplation; see paras 52–60 on pages 175–178 in chapter seven of the present volume.

We should also mention that chapter three, "The Dark Night of the Soul," is not a topic originally assigned to this volume by P.B. These paras were originally scattered throughout the various categories. However, we felt that having all this material in one place would be useful to individuals confronted with this difficult experience, and that the subject—while not exactly belonging in Part 1 of this volume—does depend upon ideas and practices first described here. This artificial gathering of a topic into one place by the editors is very rare in the *Notebooks* series—almost all topics were originally given their placement into specific categories by P.B.

The chapter titles of *The Peace Within You*, Part 2 of this volume, summarize nearly all that can be said about it: The Search for Happiness; Be Calm; Practise Detachment; and Seek the Deeper Stillness. Here we meet the Great Silence of the Overself and the Peace that motivates our desire for happiness, the same Peace that we ultimately find underlying even our greatest sorrows. The difference between Part 1 and Part 2 of this volume is that the quester is *seeking* the stillness of the Overself in every part of life in the first half, while in the second half the quester is learning to *live inside* the stillness, so the practices in Part 2 are designed to create a way of living that doesn't disturb the delicate presence of the Overself. This difference can be seen by comparing the paras on the Witness exercise in Part 1, chapter six, to the paras titled "Becoming the Witness" in Part 2, chapter three. In the first group the quester is shown how to bring about the Witness attitude, while in the second the quester is shown how to apply this attitude to the practice of detachment.

The Peace Within You provides a sort of contemplative pause between the revolutionary enterprise of the Short Path and the final challenge of the Enlightenment Which Stays (to be found in volume sixteen, Part 1). Although Part 2 is only 103 pages long, marking but a short distance in print between these two stages, the actual length of time between them may prove to be quite long. This is because much of the growth of the quester now occurs in silence, and really can't be expressed in thought. So it is fitting that this volume end with the section titled "The Great Silence."

Volume fifteen is penultimate in the *Notebooks* series, but it turned out to be the last one prepared for publication, and we feel that the last para is an appropriate way to end our seven years of work on these books: *"Truth may be written or spoken, preached or printed, but its most lasting expression and communication is transmitted through the deepest silence to the deepest nature in man."* These written pages may not always be available to us, nor can we hear the subtle, quiet voice of P.B.; but the P.B. that inspired these words, that empowered that voice, that Self, in its eternal peace, can always be found within the inner stillness of the heart.

Editorial conventions with regard to quantity and structuring of material, spelling, capitalization, and other copy-editing practices for this volume are the same as those outlined in previous introductions. As in earlier volumes, (P) at the end of a para indicates that the para also appears in *Perspectives*, volume one of the *Notebooks* series.

With this last volume to reach publication, we are especially grateful to the many special individuals whose stamina and dedication have made the completion of this seven-year project possible. We would like to acknowledge the unique gift our teacher, Anthony Damiani, gave us in creating the community of friends that Wisdom's Goldenrod has become, and in giving us the education needed to recognize P.B. for what he is, and what his writings are. In the end, we thank P.B. for his willingness to share his universal wisdom with us all, through his writings, his life, and his presence.

For more information about the *Notebooks* series and other publications and ongoing activities of the Paul Brunton Philosophic Foundation, please write to the

Paul Brunton Philosophic Foundation
P.O. Box 89
Hector, New York 14841

Part 1:
ADVANCED
CONTEMPLATION

Evolution is only an idea within the mind, hence it has the value of something imagined. The reality is that one has *never* left the heavenly being, but ignorance prevents him from realizing this. To get rid of this ignorance, he must sharpen the mind by constant effort, tranquillize it by meditation, and guide it through the help of a teacher.

Whatever path a man starts with, he must at the end of it come to the entrance of this path—the destruction of the illusion of the ego and giving up identification with it.

1

ENTERING THE SHORT PATH

Begin and end with the goal itself

This notion that we must wait and wait while we slowly progress out of enslavement into liberation, out of ignorance into knowledge, out of the present limitations into a future union with the Divine, is only true if we let it be so. But we need not. We can shift our identification from the ego to the Overself in our habitual thinking, in our daily reactions and attitudes, in our response to events and the world. We have thought our way into this unsatisfactory state; we can unthink our way out of it. By incessantly remembering what we really are, here and now at this very moment, we set ourselves free. Why wait for what already is?

2

All other approaches to the goal depend on a dualistic principle, which puts them on a lower plane. But the Short Path is nondual: it begins and ends with the goal itself; its nature is direct and its working is immediate.

3

Consciousness appearing as the person seeks itself. This is its quest. But when it learns and comprehends that it is itself the object of that quest, the person stops not only seeking outside himself but even engaging in the quest itself. Henceforth he lets himself be moved by the Overself's flow.

4

All these substitutes for the truth may appear to be useful stepping-stones to it but in fact they keep him from it, for there is no end to the number of steps he will be able to take since there is no end to the number of ways the human mind can spin out its ideas and fancies. Unless he begins with the end first, he will get lost on the way to it.

5

Are we to reject the plain statements of these enlightened men—that is, statements of the Short Path that you are divine? Do we know more and better about divine things than they do? Why can we not accept the idea that they describe not a theory but a discovery?

6

This then is the ultimate truth—that in our inmost nature we are anchored in God, inseparable from God, and that the discovery of this heavenly nature is life's loftiest purpose. Even now, already, today, we are as divine as we ever shall be. The long evolutionary ladder which by prophets and teachers, gurus and guides we are bidden to climb toilsomely and slowly and painfully need not be climbed at all if only we heed this truth continually, if we refuse to let it go, if we make it ours in all parts of our being—in thought, feeling, faith, and action.

7

For if we are divine and timeless beings now (and who can gainsay it that has had a glimpse of that starry state memorably vouchsafed to him?) then we have always been such. How can we evolve who are already self-existent, perfect beings? Does it not seem more probable that something alien has accreted around us, covering up the sublimer consciousness; that Time's work is not to raise us but to free us; that our search is not for a loftier state but for our *pristine* state, to recover our former grandeur? What we need is not to grow but to know. Evolution cannot help us, but *self*-knowledge can.

8

This is the concept which governs the Short Path: that he is in the Stillness of central being all the time whether he knows it or not, that he has never left and can never leave it. And this is so, even in a life passed in failure and despair.(P)

9

The man on the Short Path moves forward directly to fulfil his objective. Instead of working by slow degrees toward the control of thoughts, he seeks to recollect the fact that the sacred Overself is present in his mind at this very moment, that It lives within him right now, and not only as a goal to be attained in some distant future. The more he understands this fact and holds attention to it, the more he finds himself able to feel the great calm which follows its realization, the more his thoughts automatically become still in consequence.(P)

10

What it asserts is that the real truth already exists in the pithy core of man's mind, that it can be seen by anyone who will undo the illusions which cover it so thickly, the passions which obscure it so agitatedly, and, above all, the egoism which fears it so greatly. This does not imply the development of new things: it implies the removal of old ones. It is concerned with the discovery of what we really are, not what we shall one day become.

11

Pascal said in *Le Mystère de Jesus*: "Thou wouldst not seek Me, if thou didst not possess Me. Be not therefore anxious."

12

We cannot attain reality, for we already are in it; but we can attain consciousness of it. And such consciousness arises naturally the moment we know appearance as being appearance. This knowledge may be nothing more than a second's glimpse, before old habit powerfully reasserts itself again, but it will be enough to tell us the truth.

13

Ibn ul Farid, the thirteenth-century adept in practical and theoretical mysticism, lived in Cairo. He attained to permanent union with his real self (the Beloved) by getting rid of the dualistic illusion of two selves. "It is like a woman possessed by a spirit," he said. By casting off his self-existence he had found the Beloved to be his real self. "Naught save otherness marred this high estate of thine," the Beloved said to him, "and if thou wilt efface thyself thy claim to have achieved it will be established indeed!" (Among Sufis otherness is equivalent to thinking of one's self as something other than God.)

14

How far is it true that the limitations of one's capacity to understand truth are illusion, and that the constant suggestion to oneself that one is divine in attributes and qualities produces the realization of it?

15

It is the paradox of the Short Path that it begins with the end, in order to arrive at the end!

16

The finest of all experiences is to perceive that he need no longer pursue experiences because the pursuer and the Pursued are one and the same Being. Inner experiences are all in time, doomed to pass away; but he, the Consciousness behind them, behind the ego's consciousness, is out of time, hence Immortal.

17

The divine presence is there, its power is consequently there too. He may avail himself of it by Grace. Let him *look* to it then. But where is he to see it? Jesus provides the clearest answer: "The kingdom of heaven is within you." His hope of help can find its realization coming from one direction only—from the deeper part of his own self.

18

Wang Yang-ming: "Our original nature is purely good. It is not possible to add anything to this original state. The knowledge of the superior man merely serves to clear away the obscuration, and thus to show forth the shining virtue." And again, "The mind of man is heaven but because of the obscurations caused by selfishness, that state is not manifested. When all of them are cleared away, the original nature is restored."

19

What has never been lost can never be found. If a quester fails to find the Overself, it is not because of faults or weaknesses in the ego but because he is himself that which he seeks. There is nothing else to be found than understanding of this fact. Instead of seeking Overself as something above, beyond, or apart from himself, he should stop seeking altogether and recognize *i am* as *I AM*!

20

The moment the questing attitude is taken, with the Overself as its sought-for goal, in that moment the ego and the Overself are put apart as two separate things and cannot be brought together again. But by letting such thoughts go, and all thoughts subside, mind may enter the Stillness and know itself again as Mind. Yet even this is useless if the understanding that the seeker is really the sought is lacking.

21

If you will not accept the saving truth that you are now as divine as you ever will be, and follow the ultimate path, then you rank yourself with those men who, as Jesus said, "love darkness rather than light," however much you may protest against such a classification.

22

Once we can grasp this psychic fact that tomorrow exists today—as precognition has finally grasped it—we are ready to mount up to the higher philosophic fact that the spiritual goal is already within our reach, and only needs claiming.

23

Believe implicitly that the divinity is within you, a *knowing* divinity, and—if you will harmonize yourself with it intuitively—a guiding divinity. As a Far Eastern poet has put it: "Your rice has been cooked from the very beginning."

24

So long as the aspirant takes the attitude that *he* aspires to unite with the Overself, that *he* wants permanent spiritual illumination, he is merely adding another desire to those which his ego already possesses. He is still turning round inside the closed circle of the little self. There is no way out except to forget himself, to turn away from the ego and regard, fixedly and constantly, the Overself.

25

The idea that we have to wait for liberation from the ego and enlightenment by the Overself, to evolve through much time and many reincarnations, is correct only if we continue to remain mesmerized by it, but false if we take our stand on reality rather than appearance: we are now as divine as we ever shall be—but we must wake up from illusion and see this truth.

26

Because it is impossible for the questing ego to *become* the Overself, the quester must recognize that he *is* the Overself and stop thinking in egoistic terms of progress along a path, or attainment of a goal.

27

Of what use is unrealized divinity to anyone? If he is unconscious of his higher self, is a man any better off? The link of being linked with God potentially is not enough. It must also be personally discovered, felt, known, and demonstrated in living activity.

28

Because what we seek is ours already, because the Overself is always here and now, there is in reality no quest to follow, no path to travel, and no goal to reach.

29

Job carried the answer to his own question, "Oh that I knew where I might find Him," within himself all the time, but he did not know it.

30

We suffer under the delusion that we must struggle, centimetre by centimetre, all the long way to the kingdom of heaven. We stare, astonished and sceptical, when a Sage—Indian, Chinese, Japanese—tells us that we are already in it.

31

There is really nothing to be achieved here; only something to be accepted—the fact of your own divinity.

32

Why go on hoping for a far-off day when peace and truth will be attained? Why not drastically strip off all the illusions of self-identification with ego and recognize that the true identity is already fulfilled?

33

The divine is actually within us and has been there all along—if we set out to gain knowledge of it. What then really happens should we succeed in doing so? A recognition and a remembrance! Why then all this fuss of studies and practices, exercises and meditations, flocking to gurus and labouring at self-improvements? Is it not enough to be our own teachers and to remember our own long-held wisdom?

34

On the Short Path he does away with the duality of thought which sets up two ruling powers—good and evil, God and Adverse Force—and recognizes GOD as the only real existence.

35

If the Long Path begins and ends with ego, the Short Path begins with a 180 degree turnaround, opens up a vista of the infinite Overself.

36

This identification with the Overself is the real work set us, the real purpose for which human life in the world serves us. All else is merely a comfortable way of escape, a means of keeping us busy so that conscience need not be troubled by the central duty to which we are summoned.

37

Here he turns about-face, toward the sun, and releases himself from the old thought-constructions based on the belief that he is a sinner. Too much emphasis on that belief may have harmed him, and certainly depressed him. Looking too often and too long at his defects may cause him to become obsessed by them. A more positive and less restraining attitude is available on the Short Path.

38

The Long Path methods and attitudes, ideas and principles—admirable in their place and time—have to be got rid of; otherwise the Short Path truths cannot be brought in. For the one is dualistic and objective, whereas the other is nondualistic and nonobjective. The aspirant has to turn around and take a totally opposite direction.

39

At this point he must turn round on all that he has believed and done because of his beliefs and withdraw for a while from the Long Path because it is occupied solely with the pairs of opposites. Otherwise it will become his goal.

40

Without any preparation, training, or effort, without even any intention to seek God, Simone Weil was swiftly plunged into the mystical union. Unforeseen and improbable though this event must seem to Long Path eyes, yet it is dramatic testimony that the Short Path is not claiming the impossible in claiming less, and that Grace is a leading agent in bringing about this union.

41

The changeover to the Short Path calls for a tremendous leap from his present standpoint—whatever that may happen to be—to the highest possible one.

42

Is it not a psychological absurdity to say that what conscious effort cannot bring forth may be brought forth by unconscious effort? No—the deeper mind must not be deprived of its own kind of consciousness merely because we cannot bring its operation within the range of imagination.

43

What he had formerly to accomplish by a series of separate steps, he is now able to accomplish by a single step.

44

There *is* hope if only he is determined to wake up and begin afresh, to supplant negatives with positives, and to give more of himself to the Short Path.

45

If, in his earlier days when on the Long Path, he practised daily checking his personal feelings where they were negative, hostile, or condemnatory in the relationship with others, or when they interrupted his inner calm in the relationship with himself, now on the Short Path he abandoned this training. It was no more the really important thing, for it had been just a preparation of the ego for that thing—which was to forget and transcend the ego by transferring attention to the remembrance of his divine being, his Overself.

46

The Long Path man's thoughts are too often with his personal self, too seldom with his Overself. The blessed turning point will be reached when he looks away from himself with persevering faith.

47

He must now throw himself up in the air and perform a somersault. This is the transition from Long to Short Path. Working up to it is slow, actually doing it is sudden.

48

The Long Path man who is worried about his sins and content with his virtues gives place to the Short Path man who is preoccupied with neither—because both are facets of the ego—but seeks to understand, revere, and contemplate the Overself.

49

He comes up against the inevitable limitation of his personal ego and, both in meditation exercise and in practical life, turns away from it, opens his eyes, and recognizes the Presence of the Overself as his never-absent guardian angel. With that act of seeing he also receives its Grace. One after another the virtues drop into his hands as easily as ripened fruits.

50

This progress through a series of attitudes leads in the end to something transcending them altogether—a shift of consciousness from ego to Overself.

51

From the gloom and groaning of the Long Path at its worst—the Dark Night of the Soul—to the radiance and joy of the Short Path at its best, the change is startling, dramatic, and revolutionary.

52

It is at such a time that he needs to go straight to the source of divine grace, to break his mental alliance with the ego and begin a joyful reliance on the Overself.

53

While a man's mind is full of himself, he shuts out the influx of the Overself. This remains just as true of meditation times as of ordinary times. He must empty out all these earthly interests, all these personal concerns, and even, in the end, all these egoistic spiritual aspirations by transferring his attention to that which is beyond the ego. He must think only of the Overself—of its nature and attributes, of its tokens and signs of presence, of its reality and eternity.

54

He can repudiate the man that he was in the past: the fool who committed grave errors of judgement; the sinner who fell into trap after trap; the seeker who was preoccupied with his own advancement, his own condition. He can liberate himself from all the old images of himself and assume a new one, become a new man. For he can turn his back on all these ego-regarding attitudes and transfer his thoughts, his self-identification, to the Overself.

55

It is not good to live in unwholesome memories of what we ought not to have done but did do, and never put a period to them. Such repeated self-flagellation keeps the ego immersed in its own little circle. It is better to turn away from them and live in the sunshine of the Overself.

56

To bring about insight into the Overself requires an inner revolution, a psychological burrowing beneath the entire ego-consciousness to that secret place from where it arises.

57

All pruning of the ego is of little use, for as one fault is removed a new one springs out of latency. Why? Because the ego *is*. The Short Path is the only genuine approach to truth, the only one offering real possibility of liberation. It is endorsed by Atmananda and Krishnamurti and Ramana Maharshi. Lifetimes have been spent by seekers who have travelled the Long Path but arrived nowhere, or are not much nearer the goal, whereas others have made swift advance from their first steps on the Short Path. The assertion that the Long Path is a necessary complement to or preparation for the Short one is correct only for those who are still under the thraldom of illusion, who are asleep. Its followers merely travel in a circle: they never get out of the illusion or awake from the sleep. That is why in the end it has to be given up, abandoned, understood for the egoistic effort that it really is. The entire length of the Long Path is an attempt at self-improvement and self-purification planned, managed, operated, and supervised by the ego itself. Is it conceivable that the ego will work for its own destruction? No!—it will never do that however much it pretends to do so, however subtle the bluff with which it deceives itself or others. Even when the ego rebels against itself, it is merely playing a part. It has played many different parts in the past. Appearing as a rebel is merely one more disguise in the whole series.

58

The Short Path calls for a definite change of mind, a thinking of totally new thoughts, a fastening of attention upon the goal instead of the way to it. It calls for a revolution, dethroning the ego from being the centre of attention and replacing it by the Overself.

59

The basis of Short Path practices is that the mind is like a transparent crystal which takes on the colour of what is brought into propinquity with it. By turning the mind away from the ego, even from its improvement, and towards the Overself, uplift results.

60

The Short Path offers the quickest way to the blessings of spiritual joy, truth, and strength. For since these things are present in the Overself, and since the Overself is present in all of us, each of us may claim them as his own by the direct declaration of his true identity. This simple act requires him to turn around, desert the dependence on personal self, and look to the original Source whence flows his real life and being, his true providence and happiness. Disregarding all contrary ideas that the world outside thrusts upon him, disdaining the ego's emotions and desires concerning them, he "prays without ceasing" to that Source. That is, he keeps himself concentrated within upon it until he can feel its liberating qualities and expand in its sunny glories.

61

On the Short Path he must give no backward glances at the ego, must no longer abase himself by identifying himself with that fraudulent self. He must cling to his new attitude with the ardour of a new convert.

62

Let him try to look beyond his own defects to the perfection which is in the Overself, the true image of himself in which God made man.

63

The Short Path frees him from all gnawing regrets about the past, with its sins of commission and of omission, its errors and follies, its mistakes and deficiencies. Instead it puts his mind to work upon their contraries— what is beautiful and worthy, what is truthful and serene, what is pure and noble. This is the inner work to which a man is called, this transition from long detours, painful struggles, and entrapment in self-centeredness which all form the Long Path. Let them go, turn around, turn to the Short Path and find peace—a peace which is not only felt but also understood.

64

There comes a stage, whether in meditation or in the ordinary daily experience of life, at which he has to cross over from doing, trying, and managing things by his own self alone and when he can let go and open himself to the higher force—when he can submit his ego to its ordinances, its commands, or to its whispers.

65

In the end, he gets tired of taking the world, others, and his own ego as the object of exclusive attention and turns with relief to the Void.

66

Saint John of the Cross gave the following advice: "Enter into your heart and labour in the presence of God who is always present there to help you. *Fix your loving attention upon Him without any desire to feel or hear anything of God.*" Could a beginner be asked to apply such words? A person in a well-advanced state is alone likely to respond to them. Or, those who have been told about the Short Path and have studied its nature and tried to fit it into their inner work—whether they be beginners or proficient—can also put them into practice.

67

His secret is simple. He neutralizes his ego, while at the same time he affirms the Overself.

68

He comes at last to the point where he must turn against his own constant indictment, where he must defend himself against these self-made and self-directed accusations.

69

The self-revilements of the Long Path must be abandoned: his eyes must look up at that other and higher Self.

70

Not by the acquisition of virtues and the abandonment of vices can you attain the deeper enlightenment, they assert, but by the transference of consciousness itself to an altogether different plane.

71

He thinks only of the infinite goodness at his core and ignores the human frailty of his surface.

72

He is asked to turn his back on what he gave so much of his time and thought and feeling to for so long and to give them henceforth to a totally transcendent level—the Short Path.

73

The new thinking that is needed when one enters the Short Path is not merely different from the old but totally opposite to it.

74

On this Long Path, he stands with his back to the Overself and tries to re-educate the ego. On the Short Path he turns around from this position and faces the Overself.

75

The mind must move to a higher dimension and breathe a more rarefied air.

76

The time will come when you will have to turn your back upon the Long Path in order to give full attention, the full energy and the full time, to the Short Path. For with this comes a new era when the whole concern is not with the ego, not with its improvement or betterment, but with the divine itself alone—not with the surface consciousness and all its little changes but with the very depths, the diviner depths where reality abides. At this point seek only the Higher Self, live only with positive thought, stay only for as long as you can with the holy silence within, feel only that inner stillness which belongs to the essence of consciousness. Henceforth you are not to become this or that, not to gather the various virtues, but simply to be. For this you do not have to strive, you do not have to think, you do not have to work with any form of yoga, with any method of meditation.

77

There is a certain forthright logicality in the Short Path attitude which is uncomfortably uncompromising. If each man must find out the Overself's existence for, and by, himself, by his own intuition, it will confuse him and lead him astray if he discusses his problems with others or exchanges ideas and inner experiences with them. Secondly, if that existence must be found deep within his own nature, it will be travelling in an exactly opposite direction to travel to some land or place in search of a glamorous guru.

78

If true light can come only from within a man, every outer method of bringing it to him must be in reality a method which leads him astray.

79

He sees the truth as with a jolt. There it is, within his own being, lying deep down but still in his own self. There never was any need to travel anywhere to find it; no need to visit anyone who was supposed to have it already, and sit at his feet; not even to read any book, however sacred or inspired. Nor could another person, place, or writing give it to him—he would have to unveil it for himself in himself. The others could direct him to look inwards, thus saving all the effort of looking elsewhere. But he himself would have to give the needful attention to himself. The discovery must be his own, made within the still centre of his being.

80

If he is to be true to his espousal of philosophy he will keep himself outside partisan, officially titled, and other limiting forms. And one of the best ways to approach this ideal is through the practice of self-emptying.

81

There is an element of truth in the statement—often made by Krishnamurti—that the best way to start on the Way to Truth is to discard all that previous thinking, reading, and listening have yielded.

82

The teacher of the Short Path tells men—and rightly—to beware of letting techniques, practices, or methods become new manacles on their hands, new obstructions on their way to inner freedom.

83

The Short Path man ought not to depend on authorities, scriptures, rules, regulations, organizations, gurus, or writings. His past history may outwardly force such an association on him, but inwardly he will seek to liberate himself from it. For his ultimate aim is to reach a point where no interpreter, medium, or transmitter obtrudes between him and the Overself.

84

Krishnamurti's free-thinking, idol-shattering teaching is a good counterbalance and advanced complement to the ordinary yoga teaching. It is not really a contradiction, since it is a Short Path form completing yoga's Long Path. Krishnamurti's uncompromising rigidity is also a corrective to the sectarian fanaticism and guru deification which mark the seeking of many beginners. They receive a shock when first reading or hearing him. He undermines and explodes the little attitudes they have been taught to copy, the precious beliefs they have been told to hold. From his point of view, the solemnities of religious ritual and the frivolities of theatrical revue are both on the same plane.

85

Here, on this Short Path, he is to direct his yearnings and seekings, his hopes and thoughts, solely to the Overself. Nothing and nobody, not even a guru, is to come between them.

86

In Tibet, the name "Short Path" is given to the path of complete self-reliance without any guidance from an outer master. It is understood that only exceptionally advanced aspirants are capable of entering such a path.

87

It is often advisable to be one's own guide, studying worthy books, using prayer and reflection, and following the intuitive guidance of one's Higher Self.

88

Whatever technique is adopted, in the end it cages them in, keeps them its prisoner and prevents the free search which is necessary to find truth.

89

At this stage the student ceases to be concerned with those egoistic and dualistic ideas which form so much of the concern of orthodox religious people. For their conception of God is no longer his, their desire to perpetuate the present state of the person in some eternal post-mortem heaven fades away naturally as the illusion of the person itself fades away. Yet nobody need be alarmed at these changes of outlook. All that is true and worthy in popular religion is not discarded but kept and conserved.

The practice

90

One thing about the Short Path which must be firmly impressed on the student's mind is that its success depends on how much love for its objective a man brings to it. If he has ever had a moment's Glimpse of the Overself, and has fallen more deeply in love with it than with anything else, he will be able to fulfil the basic requirement for all Short Path techniques: but without such wholehearted attachment, he is sure to fail.

91

He must bring to this formidable task an adventuresome quality which is willing to take a few risks, if only because merely negative aims, hesitant "ifs," timid "buts," and the general lack of courage to take an imperative plunge will invite what they seek to avoid.

92

What is the key to the Short Path? It is threefold. First, stop searching for the Overself since it follows you wherever you go. Second, believe in its Presence, with and within you. Third, keep on trying to understand its truth until you can abandon further thoughts about it. You cannot acquire what is already here. So drop the ego's false idea and affirm the real one.(P)

93

The Short Path teaching will only prove immediately successful with those who are ready for it. It should qualify its claims with this statement.

94

In its earlier stages, the Short Path is a continued practice of becoming aware of those moments when he slips away into forgetfulness of the Stillness.

95

The Short Path stimulates him to dynamically energetic endeavours and encourages him to make lightning-like thrusts toward Reality. This he cannot do without inexorably and resolutely crushing his ego or taking advantage of a grave circumstance and unresistingly letting it crush the ego for him.

96

From the Short Path high-altitude standpoint, no variation in doctrine to meet the needs of weaker minds, no yielding of any kind to the mass mind is to be tolerated. It is rigidly uncompromising, and therefore isolated. It is final and closed and rejects all cheap, facile, suave diplomacy for the sake of popularity.

97

The Short Path is, in essence, the ceaseless practice of remembering to stay in the Stillness, for this is what he really is in his innermost being and where he meets the World-Mind.(P)

98

The Short Path uses (a) *thinking*: metaphysical study of the Nature of Reality; (b) *practice*: constant remembrance of Reality during everyday life in the world; (c) *meditation*: surrender to the thought of Reality in stillness. You will observe that in all these three activities *there is no reference to the personal ego*. There is no thinking of, remembering, or meditating upon oneself, as there is with the Long Path.(P)

99

A part of the Short Path work is intellectual study of the metaphysics of Truth. This is needful to expose the ego's own illusoriness, as a preliminary to transcending it, and to discriminate its ideas, however spiritual, from reality.(P)

100

In the first and second stages of the Short Path, his aim is to set himself free from the egoism in which his consciousness is confined.(P)

101

This is simply a way of practice for any sincere seeker. It does not interfere with his religious creed or belief.

102

The Short Path is the real way! All else is mere preparation of the equipment for it. For with it he is no longer to direct his meditation upon the shortcomings and struggles of the personal self but up to the Overself, its presence and strength. For the consciousness of the Real, the True, the Beneficent and Peaceful comes by its Grace alone and by this practice he attracts the visitation.

103

Although he refuses to identify himself with the ego's outlook and actions, he refuses also to condemn them.

104

The Short Path calls for a discernment and intelligence which are not needed in ordinary living, which are so subtle that the truth of mentalism must first be applied to the world and allowed to permeate the understanding, for a long time, before it can be applied to the person himself.

105

The Short Path is no dryly intellectual affair or coldly unfeeling one. It nurtures beautiful, exquisite moments and richly uplifting moods. Both this path and its term are vital and dynamic aesthetic experiences.

106

He cultivates a more joyous attitude, this man on the Short Path, for remembrance of the Overself, which he practises constantly, reminds him of the glory of the Overself.

107

It is better at this stage to forget his failings and bring in the atmosphere which would make them inoperative.

108

It is not enough to learn to bear with others, to excuse and accept their shortcomings. He must also learn to bear with himself, to accept his own shortcomings.

109

To adopt the Short Path is to place oneself at a point of view where all the efforts of the Long Path are seen as a sheer waste of time and where its successes are regarded as equal in value to its failures, since both are illusory experiences of an illusory entity.

110

In its advanced phases the Short Path is no pathway at all. It has all the freedom of air and sea.

111

It is a kind of spiritual ju-jitsu, for it uses the ego's own strength to overthrow the ego!

112

It is a Short Path attitude to avoid censorious reproaches and condemnatory speech—these as a part of its larger rejection of negatives and preference for positives.

113

Reject every negative thought with implacable rigour—this is one of the important practical deductions of the Short Path.

114

Recognition is a prominent feature on the Short Path. The Overself is always there but only those on the Short Path recognize this truth and think accordingly. The world is always with us, but only those on the Short Path *recognize* the miracle that it is. In moments of exaltation, uplift, awe, or satisfaction—derived from music, art, poetry, landscape, or otherwise—thousands of people have received a Glimpse; but only those on the Short Path recognize it for what it really is.

115

To practise the Short Path is to be aware of the miracle entailed in every moment of living.

116

The Short Path concentrates thought upon the Real, deliberately forgetful of everything and everyone in the world of illusion.

117

The attitudes of reverence, even awe, devotion, worship, ought not to be eliminated just because he is practising the Short Path. It is still a technique even if it does embody the assumption of nonduality.

118

This Short Path is the path of paradox.

119

He cannot walk this Shorter Path without rejecting the world as illusion and consequently without labelling the world's evil and suffering as illusory. It is a hard test for him to pass, a narrow gate which bars successful travel on this Path to him if he persists in clinging to his old beliefs. Their sacrifice is required of him—yet not blindly as a matter of faith alone but justly as a matter of reason as well.

120

The practice of refusing to accept appearances of evil or illusion and penetrating to realities of beneficence and truth draws out and discovers the purifying and healing capabilities which can remedy those appearances.

121

A boundless faith in the Overself's power to assist him must be the possession of a Short Path votary—that is, faith in both the existence and the efficacy of its Grace.

122

The Short Path precludes impatience and forbids anxiety.

123

The attitude of pursuing an objective, of searching for a truth, however admirable in the early stages, becomes an obstruction in this the latest stage.

124

When he is established to some extent on the Short Path he may not only expect the expected, as most people do, but also expect the unexpected.

125

The Short Path accepts no other power than the divine power, no other reality than the divine reality. It recognizes no second entity and ascribes no force whatever in its own life to such an entity.

126

Eliminate religious comforts, imaginations, and illusions from inner life. They are escapes for our weakness, lower levels masquerading to remain outside God while pretending to be inside God. Suspend all thinking.

127

On the Short Path he fixes his mind on divine attributes, such as the all-pervading, ever-present, beginningless and endless nature of the One Life-Power, until he is lifted out of his little ego entirely.

128

Take the goal in view from the new beginning. This will help prevent going astray, making detours, losing discrimination.

129

If he firmly plants his feet on the Short Path, if he never lets himself forget his real being is in the Overself, then he must refuse to accept a single one of those thoughts which so often trouble the traveller on the Long Path—thoughts of anxiety, frustration, or concern about his progress. He stays well above them.

130

The Short Path tells us that the goal need not be approached grimly.

131

He does not have to think meanly of himself all the time, does not have to worry anxiously about his unworthy character. Rather should he learn to get more relaxed, more remindful of the existence of his diviner being.

132

On the Short Path, instead of attacking the lower self, he lifts himself up to the presence of the higher. The evil in him may then melt away of its own accord.

133

The Short Path shows him that it is better to take the highest model, to look for his strength rather than his weakness.

134

It is the unique contribution of the Short Path that it takes advantage of the Overself's ever-present offer of Grace.

135

When body and feeling are cleansed by disciplinary regimes, when the intellect is inspired by meditational exercises, one is ready for the Short Path.

136

Your reaction to events and persons depends on your recognition of Overself. If you see only little ego, and fail to see the Overself, there will be a negative reaction. Both are within you.

137

Not by harshly and negatively condemning others who act wrongly— which is needful at the proper time, with the proper person—does the Short Path votary correct them but by constructively, kindly suggesting the better way.

138

Just as the ancient pagan Mysteries required some amount of preparation and some form of purification before candidates were admitted, so the

Short Path ordinarily requires some Long Path work as a prerequisite. But not always and not now.

139

The Short Path techniques are available for use not only at fixed periods and special sessions for meditation but also throughout the day as a constant habit, a regular way of living.

140

The Short Path can only be travelled if faith in the Overself is fundamental and complete, and if trust in the effectiveness of its power is strong and unwavering.

141

Expect the unexpectable!

142

It is the art of being artless, spiritual without doing it consciously. It is achievement of effortless mental quiet. It is ordinary living, plus an extraordinary continuous awareness.

Benefits and results

143

This is the wonder of the Short Path—that it teaches us to refuse at once every thought which seeks to identify us with the feeble and unworthy self. This is the gladness of the Short Path—that it urges us to accept and hold only those thoughts which identify us directly with the strong and divine Overself, or which reflect its goodness and wisdom.

144

With the Short Path, one emerges into an atmosphere that is totally different in nature and quality from the Long Path's. It is like seeing the sun break through the clouds.

145

The Direct Path's influence should show itself in bringing a brighter outlook to a man and a more cheerful tone to his character. It is true that philosophy is quite aware of the Buddhistic picture of life, of the sorrows and sicknesses which drag him down at times. That is why it makes equanimity a leading item of the inner work upon himself, why it becomes so necessary. But it is also true that moments, moods, and glimpses are also possible when there is uplift, and he can confirm for himself that the human link with the higher power is a very real thing.

146

It is while working with the Short Path that the man discovers he may apply its principles to his worldly existence, his earthly fortunes too. He learns that the ultimate source of his physical welfare is not the ego but the Overself. If he looks only to the little ego for his supply, he must accept all its narrow limitations, its dependence on personal effort alone. But if he looks farther and recognizes his true source of welfare is with the Overself, with its miracle-working Grace, he knows that all things are possible to it. Hope, optimism, and high expectation make his life richer, more abundant.

147

If we turn towards our truer selves, then light will descend and dissolve the evils in our being.

148

It is not essential to enter the trance state in order to experience sufficient depth of meditation, although many do seek it in the popular belief of its necessity. The advanced Short Path treader develops the capacity without the necessity. That is to say, he can enjoy the benefits of a stilled mind in an instant whenever outer circumstances permit him to relax but without having to fall into a condition oblivious of outside scenes, sounds, and shapes.

149

The consequence of this self-training on the Short Path is that in all questions, problems, situations, and practices his first thought will be to take the matter to the Overself, identifying with Overself, and later, when he returns to the second thought, the matter will be looked at under this diviner light.

150

When he shifts the centre of his interest from the ego to the Stillness his life begins to manage itself. Happenings pertaining to it come about without his doing anything at all.

151

Put in another way, it may be said that the Short Path develops inspiration and evokes intuition.

152

The Short Path will bear fruit in several virtues, which will come of their own accord and without his trying to gain them. In this way it will help him calm his passions and discipline his ego, even though his thoughts and meditations make no reference to them.

153

The discovery—that he need not torment himself with attempts to improve, reform, correct, and purify himself—may come into his mind with joyously explosive effect. He need not fear to freely recognize and boldly use the power of the Source. There is no other with which he can come into contact which can so utterly transform him and transcend his circumstances. It is the human parallel to atomic energy.

154

His life will become more cheerful and he himself more human when he takes to the Short Path.

155

Even without making special efforts to deal with undesirable traits, some will tend to fall away through being denied attention. This is one consequence of following the Short Path.

156

Because he travels along the Short Path with a happy heart, his attitude towards other persons tends to be a loving one, or kindly, or at least emanating goodwill.

157

Such is the value of Short Path exercises, and more especially of those which give constant mindfulness and the Witness-attitude, that earnest practice of them may bring realization in as little time as one week to seven years.

158

When Jesus said, ". . . and all these things shall be added unto you," he did not primarily mean material things such as money and houses, although these were included. He meant that the moral virtues and the moral excellences for which so many seekers after perfection strive in vain would spontaneously add themselves to him as an after-effect of being "born again."

159

Since the Overself is the source of all virtues, the man who unites with it will easily and naturally be virtuous in the truest sense: all the bad in his character will be eliminated.

160

The Short Path brings joy, hope, enthusiasm and confidence, lyricism and optimism.

161

The virtues he attempted to acquire on the Long Path, and too often attempted in vain, come to him of themselves by the magical grace of the Short Path.

162

Entry on the Short Path bestows a feeling of glorious freedom.

163

Only the Short Path can turn aspiration into attainment, for only it proffers Grace.

164

The Short Path makes miracles possible because it leads through the gate of the timeless, futureless, pastless Now.

165

You will know truth and experience reality in those moments when you have freed yourself from the ego's conditioning processes, from its limiting past memories and imprisoning emotions. In such moments you will be abruptly enlightened and your whole attitude toward life will be different in consequence.

166

Just as welcome as bright sunlight pouring in through a cell-window is the hope proffered by the Short Path.

167

One advantage of the Short Path is that whoever takes to it thoroughly gets rid of guilt complexes, of sorrowing over his past, his errors, his sins.

168

In this way he does little to free himself from a weakness, a desire, or a passion. It goes, falls away of its own accord, if he looks to the Higher Self rather than to the management of his own ego for salvation. It is in this spontaneous way, too, that the attitude of detachment begins to appear in his character and little by little—but sometimes swiftly—becomes established. But a warning is needed here. Whatever purifications or strengthenings, whatever other attempts and trainings at self-betterment he has begun need not be dropped, provided they are kept in their place and not allowed to obscure the view of the primary goal or gradually sidetrack direction from its superior level.

169

This is a paradox of the Short Path, that on the one hand he practises this exercise of playing the game of being enlightened, and on the other of freely confessing his faults, limitations, and weaknesses but just as freely accepting them. Thus a curious peace of mind settles in him and becomes naturalized. But it is not a spurious peace. It rejects worry or anxiety and negates fear.

170

It takes his mind off himself and his difficulties and lifts him to the level where he can perceive that the Overself can take adequate care of him and them too. It is all-sufficient for all his needs, for clearing away old spiritual perplexities, or for providing new physical surroundings.

171

The effects of this Short Path work are sometimes miraculous and always life-giving.

172

He has entered a new and happier phase of his life. The problems of the past have disappeared. The door to inner light is always ready to open at his mere push.

173

The Short Path gives its followers gaiety of outlook and an assurance of victory.

174

If he keeps in right relation with his Overself, he will inevitably keep in right relation with everything and everyone else.

175

The question of the difficulty of dislodging the ego does not arise on the Short Path.

176

The Short Path makes it possible for the most ordinary man—unprepared, untrained though he be—to find spiritual fulfilment.

177

The Short Path frees us from the anxieties and guilts which make living more of a burden than it need be.

178

Only when it becomes natural and therefore easy, continuous and therefore well-established, does meditation become completely fruitful. But this is possible only on the Short Path.

179

Without expecting miracles from human nature, it is not unreasonable to assert that the realization of its larger possibilities is more likely to happen on the Short Path and has a better chance to be achieved.

180

The Short Path provides him with the chance of making a fresh start, of gaining new inspiration, more joy.

181

What he feels on the Short Path is confidence and peace.

182

Those mesmeric announcements of inner grandeur awaiting human beings—breathtaking in the way they sweep aside those negativities and pessimisms which beset us—belong to the Short Path.

183

Out of this altered metaphysical consciousness there emerges an altered ethical conscience. Along with the movement to a new intellectual centre there is a parallel movement to a new heart. This is miracle enough to attract all those who want a shorter easier way, or those who want to avoid the long-drawn labours of self-sculpture.

2

PITFALLS AND LIMITATIONS

The Long Path is unutterably irksome whereas the Short Path is gloriously attractive. The one is associated with toil and suffering; its emblem is the Cross. The other is associated with peace and joy; its emblem is the Sun. Yet, those who would prematurely desert the one for the other will find their hopes frustrated in the end, however enthusiastic and rapturous the experience may be in the beginning. This is because Nature, the Overself, will not let them enjoy permanently what must be taken into every part of their being, properly cleansed and prepared to absorb it, with the being itself properly equilibrated to endure the experience of absorption without stimulating the ego.

2

The introduction of the Short Path ought not to be mistimed; it ought not to be introduced until enough work has been done to prepare a moral and intellectual basis for it, and enough balance secured. Then only will its capacity to lead the seeker toward the glorious climax of his quest be actualized. If introduced too early it merely stimulates egotism, animates intellectual pride, or simulates illumination.

3

Most beginners are not usually ready for the entire Short Path. They ought not attempt more than its simpler practices, such as those concerned with recollection of the Quest and remembrance of the Overself. If they attempt the more advanced exercises, such as self-identification with the Overself or cultivation of the attitude which rejects evil's reality, they are likely to put themselves in a false, self-deceived position. That is, the attempt to ignore the ego does not eradicate it but merely alters its pattern. If it seems to be absent because the divine is present, the transformation has taken place in imagination, not in actuality. It would be better to postpone the advanced part until they have done enough preparatory work on the Long Path, and thus cleansed their emotions, developed mental controls, and balanced their temperament.

4

There is no need to think twice to understand that this is a dangerous doctrine. If a man believes that he is already divine and has nothing more to gain in that way, pitfalls lie ahead of him: first, self-deception leading to spiritual arrogance; second, indolence leading to lack of any effort to purify character and better the mind. The end could be a smug dwelling in illusion, very far from the divine reality it is supposed to be. Out of such illusions step forth the ambitious leaders of little groups or large movements, claiming special knowledge, power, vision, authority, even messiahship.

5

If the Long Path is to be utterly avoided and no self-restraints or trainings practised, in what way is this different from being an ordinary person who behaves as he pleases? Indeed, even the Zen master Ma-tsu admitted as much when he said, "If there is no discipline, this is to be the same as ordinary people."

6

Properly used—and especially at the proper time, after due preparation—the Short Path is an essential phase of every man's quest. But misunderstood and wrongly used, by the wrong person at the wrong time, regarded solely as a cheap easy and rapid way to success, an excuse for dodging labour and for evading discipline, it is turned into something meretricious.

7

The dangers inherent in the Short Path have to be noted and even proclaimed. The self-identification with the divine leads to the idea that since it is sinless the practiser is sinless, too, and whatever he does is right. Such an idea can come only to those who unconsciously seek excuses to justify the satisfaction of their desires. To them, the Long Path with its exhortations to self-control and self-discipline is something to be evaded. Another danger is the conceited belief that since the divine is ever-present, the goal has been attained and nothing further need be done—no exercises, no study, no meditation, and of course no ascetic regimes. It is such dangers which were part of the reasons why, in former times, the hidden teaching was not communicated to any persons until their character was first secretly and carefully tested for maturity and their mind was tested for fitness. This caution was as existent in Christian circles as in Hindu ones. Today, since it has largely been broken down, the results are to be seen in the West as well as in the East, among solitary obscure individuals as well as among publicized cults. They are to be seen in mental derangement and immoral licence, in parrot-like prattle and charlatanic deception.

8

Whether the ego is constantly anxious about itself, as on the Long Path, or constantly joyous in itself, as on the substitutes for the true Short Path, it is still the old ego.

9

Holding on to this awareness of the Overself automatically brings with it control over the body's appetites and desires. This is one of the benefits of success on the Short Path, but such easy spontaneous control lasts no longer than the awareness.

10

Those who use terms or utter phrases which transcend all meaning, delude themselves and mystify others to no purpose. If the experiences and insights of the Short Path are beyond intellectual comprehension, and consequently beyond intellectual communication, the proper way to consider them is in perfect silence—not in speech or writing.

11

Where the Short Path has been followed exclusively and without the guidance of a tested inner voice or a master competent in both paths, the man is bereft of the background of self-discipline and self-training which the Long Path provides. He will then have to pick his way over the stonefalls of hallucination and along the verge of precipices of paranoia.

12

The Short Path advocates who decry the need of the Long Path altogether because, being divine in essence, we have only to realize what we already are, are misled by their own half-truth. What we actually find in the human situation is that we are only potentially divine. The work of drawing out and developing this potential still needs to be done. This takes time, discipline, and training, just as the work of converting a seed into a tree takes time.(P)

13

It is as sure as the sun's rising that if the mass of people are taught that good is no better than evil, both being merely relative, or no more valuable than evil, both being concerned with the illusory ego, they will fall into immorality, wickedness, and disaster. To teach them the Short Path before they have acquired sufficient disciplinary habits from the Long one will only degrade them.(P)

14

Those who are attracted to the Short Path because apparently it makes none of the disciplinary demands which the Long Path makes, who are repelled or frightened by the self-subjugation and self-abnegation which the latter requires, will not have so easy an escape as they think.

15

To have come prematurely to this yoga would have led to confusion of planes of reference, to self-deception, unbalance, and merely verbal realization.

16

The Short Path leads to a continual happiness, for it refuses to look upon the world's sorrows and one's own troubles but cheerfully gazes beyond them toward the eternal and impersonal blessedness. But since it can do this theoretically only, for realization depends on Grace, the happiness may one day vanish when fact collides with faith.

17

Because good and bad have no meaning on the plane where there is no opposition, no struggle between them, the "enlightened" man who taught others to ignore this opposition and abandon this struggle, who told them that to do what they will is the whole of the law, would thereby prove his own lack of enlightenment. In other words, he would be a dangerous impostor or a mere intellectual.

18

Yes, the Short Path extremists, and especially the more poetic, imaginative, and artistic ones among them, may get their illuminations more quickly and more frequently. But, because they have not purified, straightened, and formed their characters, these are distorted, crooked, or adulterated illuminations.

19

Most Short Path teachings lack a cosmogony. They evade the fact that God is, and must be, present on the plane of manifestation and expressing through the entire universe. Why?

20

They consider themselves to be free from the possibility of committing sin, since they are joined to the divine consciousness. They do not regard the moral codes of society as binding upon them, since they are a law unto themselves. Whatever they do, it can only be right. The dangers here are, of course, first, that the ego's desire may only too easily be mistaken for the divine ordinance, and second, that all things are permitted to them. Since they feel that they are in a state of grace, there is no longer any controlling power to judge, criticize, or curb their acts, no outside help to warn them when they go perilously astray.

21

It would be a misconception to use the Short Path as an attempt to escape from one's own inadequacies.

22

The Short Path *describes* the consciousness to be attained but fails to *prescribe* the way to attain it.

23

The danger of Short Path, and of the "As If" exercise, is to fall into deception of oneself, or even into charlatanic deception of others.

24

If the conscious practice of self-discipline and the deliberate pursuit of virtue are discarded too soon, the practice of unscrupled selfishness and the pursuit of unworthy pleasures will take their place. The character begins to fall and a man who might have ennobled himself and helped his fellows degrades himself and abrases them.

25

To make a fetish out of freedom from dogma, from authority, from organization, from convention—as Krishnamurti does—is to worship a good idea so blindly and so fanatically that bad results follow.

26

The Short Pathers want to rush towards their goal in one all-sweeping operation. They lack the patience to move toward it step by step. They do not comprehend that to fully attain their wish a high degree of spiritual maturity is needed, that their way must have previously been prepared.

27

Men who are bundles of uncontrolled passions and grasping desires can only imagine that they are ready—much less, likely—to receive illumination because the true teaching of Sudden Enlightenment is misinterpreted by them or by their instructors.

28

It is an ancient error which makes unimportant the strivings for moral virtue provided they are replaced by strivings for ultimate knowledge.

29

It is a perilous error which besets the right and the left sides of the Short Path which lets the aspirant believe that he need no longer trouble his head with questions of what is right and what is wrong in ethics nor put upon himself the burden of any general or special discipline. If his nature has run to extremes in these matters, if he has troubled himself too long or too much with them, he will do well to relax and restore his balance. But this is no sanction to fall into self-indulgence and slackness.

30

Belief in their own perfection may follow the premature intellectual identification with Spirit. The belief that they have become incapable of sin may follow as a consequence of the first one. Nothing that they do can possibly be wrong. The end of all this is to bring disaster to themselves and to dislocate the lives of others.

31

It is understandable that aspirants would like to save themselves from the exertions demanded by the Long Path, and would prefer to receive sufficient Grace to grant them the desired higher experiences. But if they turn the existence of the Short Path into an excuse to avoid these exertions, they are unlikely to gain what they want.

32

To seek to jump to the highest level, while neglecting to improve bad ways of living or to correct the grievous weaknesses of feeling or to eliminate the faults of undisciplined thinking, is foolish and often useless.

33

Steep yourself in the pure being of Spirit; then the ego's weaknesses and faults will automatically drop away from it. This is the teaching and the truth of the Short Path. What is not told is how fleeting the purification— so magically gained—must necessarily be.

34

Elbert Hubbard was a great soul and a great man. The clear hard truth and Thoreauvian simplicity of his sentences show he was a great writer, too. But he fell into that abuse of Short Path ethics which holds that the man of understanding can do no wrong. He also failed to see the purpose and worth of asceticism. He would have become a greater soul and a greater man had he corrected those errors.

35

All stages of the quest, the advanced as well as the elementary, are forms of ambition. They are still activities of the self, continuations of its own life in different guises. All attempts to rise spiritually, to develop, to gain "better" qualities or "mystical" experiences are trying to run away from self through self-projected means. The end result is, and must be, frustration or failure.

36

Those who are impatient with the restraints, the labours, and the disciplines of the Long Path may take prematurely to the Short Path. The result, as seen in the cases of younger people, is unhealthy. They get intoxicated with their new freedom and may take unrestrictedly to drink, drugs, sex, and general slovenliness of speech, manner, and dress. The absence of the idea of sin from their outlook may produce an irresponsibility dangerous to themselves and disturbing to society.

37

Those who turn to the Short Path because they are in revolt against irksome disciplines and trying exercises, and who turn to the other extreme of letting all impulses loose, forget that if they have set themselves a purpose high above the ordinary there must be some submission of impulse to that purpose, some restraint of aimlessness by discipline. But this said, there is some wisdom in their revolt. The restraint which is imposed from outside by others is of very limited value; but that which is put upon a man by himself from within will achieve much more lasting results.

38

The Short Path follower who wrongly believes himself to be suddenly and miraculously changed will still show in his life and character the unmistakable signs of his old self's continuance.

39

Beware of losing balance in the study of metaphysical truth or in the practice of the Short Path, of imagining that you are surpassing the intellect and getting spiritually illumined. Beware of getting intellectually drunk with your own self-importance and emotionally intoxicated with your own self-glorification. Such study can be very stimulating. Beware of coming to believe that you have found the Divine in a single flash, overnight. Have you really become God? Is omnipotence really yours?

40

The wish to attain realization of the Overself becomes father to the belief that realization is actually happening!

41

The claim that if the true self is found, all the qualities and attributes which pertain to it will also be found, naturally and automatically, at the same time is a valid one. How could the qualities and attributes of the lower nature thrive or even exist in that rarefied air? They would instantly be displaced by the higher ones. But what is overlooked by, or unknown to, the makers of this claim, is that the period of such displacement would, and could, only be a temporary one. "Nature never leaps toward what she will eventually bring about," Goethe announces, and truly. As soon as the impetus which launched him into the deep waters of the Spirit exhausts itself, as it must if he is still unpurified, unprepared, and undeveloped, the man will be thrown back to the place where he belongs. His illumination will not have enough basis to be securely established and so will turn out to be only a passing glimpse.

42

Those who believe they can skip all this preparatory work and still realize their latent possibility are foolish. The obstructions will not remove themselves by themselves. They can be overwhelmed for a time, while the glimpse prevails, but they will certainly become evident again when the glimpse fades.

43

It is tempting to skip the natural order of development through various graduated stages, with all the time and patience, work and practice which that entails. But what is so cheaply gained will have a corresponding value.

44

Some of the literary statements by Short Path advocates are so extreme as to show that the writers are drunk with words, carried away into completely forgetting where they are (in a body), ignoring the difference between Being (knowing that the world is appearance, idea) and denying that the world exists.

45

Those who come to the Short Path without competent guidance or proper preparation are often either emotionally intoxicated by the prospects of easy attainment that it seems to offer or intellectually carried away into spiritual arrogance. The humility which is inbred by the difficulties of the Long Path will be thrown away to their peril.

46

The Short Path devotee who believes he has nothing to do and can leave all to the master, or to the Overself, believes wrongly. Such spiritual idleness may lull him pleasantly into a thin contentment but this is not the same as real inner peace won by grappling in the right attitude with difficulties as they come, or by keeping the personal will submissive during tests and obedient during temptations.

47

There are certain other dangers to which enthusiasts for the various Short Paths are exposed. They read books devoted to descriptions of the attainments and goals and become captivated by what they read and charmed by what they are taught. Then they begin to imitate what they can and to imagine what they cannot. In the end they fall into ego-centered fantasies and ego-fostered deceptions. They think they are more exalted in attainment than they really are. But so subtle is this disguised spiritual egoism that they are quite unaware of their peril until disaster deflates it.

48

The man who thinks of himself instead of the Overself when practising a Short Path exercise, who is unable to forget his little ego, is a traitor to that Path.

49

It is well not to be boastful about one's attainments on the Long Path, still less about one's achievements on the Short Path.

50

The person who has undergone little preparation or purification before feeling the mystic's peace in some unexpected experience does not feel what the person who has had both his preparation and purification feels. In the first case it is an unbalanced peace, whereas in the second case it is a balanced peace. This is one reason why it vanishes after a time in the first case and why the complementary work of the Long Path is needed.

51

The high-level teaching has been taken advantage of by the weak or the egotistic to defend their weaknesses or egotism. Personal freedom and self-expression are rightly sought but in the wrong way and for the wrong reasons.

52

It is a matter of simple observation that these Vedantic teachings are unfortunately not adequate to meet all the demands of a worthwhile life. They have no more useful advice to give concerning the physical body than, as I was told by one guru: "Take it to the doctor when it falls sick. Give it no attention otherwise and forget it."

53

The Short Path schools are correct in asserting that if we gain the Overself we shall also gain the purity of heart and goodness of character which go with it. But they omit to point out that such a gain will be quite temporary if we are unable to remain in the Overself.

54

They believe it is possible to attain truth without tears, without discipline, and without training.

55

The lack of clear definition of the two approaches, and the failure to make a proper distinction between them, cause much confusion, many errors, and some self-deception.

56

To begin the Short Path without ever having done some of the corrective work of the Long one, may result in the old defects being supplemented by the new ones. The desire for quick gains and shortcuts is understandable but the desire for unearned and undeserved gains, to get something for nothing, leads to deception in the spiritual as in the financial world.

57

Although the Short Path obviously offers a far more attractive picture, it balances the attraction with the danger of neglecting those self-chastening and self-disciplinary preparations which are indispensable.

58

The Short Path tries to get round the ego by ignoring it altogether!

59

Nearly everyone would most likely choose a way which evaded all the long discipline of thought and feeling, all the stern reform of bodily habits, and yet brought him swiftly to the goal and gave him in full its glorious rewards. This choice is pardonable and seemingly sensible. But observation and experience, study and research, show that such a way exists only in theory, not in factuality; that its dramatic successes are the rare cases of a very few geniuses; that those who take this seemingly easy and short road mostly arrive, if they arrive at all, at a state of intellectual intoxication and pseudo-illumination; and that where their reward for this Short Path practice is a genuine Glimpse, they wrongly believe it to be the End of the Road and cease all further effort to grow.

60

People who follow the Short Path because it seems to offer miracles are trying to escape from the irksome necessity of dealing with their lower self and overcoming it, but they try in vain. No master, no cult, no particular breathing exercise or meditation practice can take the place of this necessity. All are nothing more than another help in the struggle.

The truth about sudden enlightenment

61

Must we crawl like the worm, inch by inch, or is there really the possibility of sudden enlightenment? Must time be allowed to do its work or can some magic act abruptly? Can there be any adequate substitute for the experiences, the reflections, and the operations of many lifetimes? Or are we merely showing ignorance when we assert that immediate awareness is too good to be true?

62

The Zenist who asserts that enlightenment comes all of a sudden is correct, but the evolutionist who insists that time and development are still needed is also correct.

63

The offer of instantaneous spiritual illumination is too good to be missed. But it may also prove too good to be true. The fact is that it is true only for a very few, false for the great majority.

64

It is said by the advocates of the Short method that the power of the Spirit can remove our faults instantaneously and even implant in us the opposite virtues. That this has happened in some cases is made clear by the study of the spiritual biography of certain persons. But those cases are relatively few and those persons relatively advanced. This miraculous transformation, this full forgiveness of sins, does not happen to most people or to ordinary unadvanced people. A world-wide observation of them shows that such people have to elevate themselves by their own efforts first. When they embrace the Short method without this balancing work done by themselves upon themselves, they are likely to fall into the danger of refusing to see their faults and weaknesses which are their worst enemies, as well as the danger of losing the consciousness of sin. Those who fail to save themselves from these perils become victims of spiritual pride and lose that inner humility which is the essential price of being taken over by the Overself.(P)

65

Those who believe in the Short Path of sudden attainment, such as the sectarian following of Ramana Maharshi and the koan-puzzled intellectuals of Zen Buddhism, confuse the first flash of insight which unsettles everything so gloriously with the last flash which settles everything even more gloriously. The disciple who wants something for nothing, who hopes to get to the goal without being kept busy with arduous travels to the very end, will not get it. He has to move from one point of view to a higher, from many a struggle with weaknesses to their mastery. Then only, when he has done by himself what he should do, may he cease his efforts, be still, and await the influx of Grace. Then comes light and the second birth.

66

It is a legitimate criticism that most exponents of the Short Path make it seem just too easy: heaven is always just around the corner!

67

The notion that by the simple yet miraculous event of attaining union he can be rid of all his faults and weaknesses is an attractive one. But is it a true one? Can they all drop off at once? Some schools of religion and mysticism answer affirmatively. But philosophy says that the new kind of man he wants to become can be formed only by slow degrees, little by little.

68

That inspired and excellent little book, Brother Lawrence's *The Practice of the Presence of God*, is an example of Short Path teaching. The contemporary biographer of Lawrence writes: "He could never regulate his devotion by certain methods as some do. . . . At first, he had meditated for some time, but afterwards that went off." "All bodily mortifications and other exercises are useless," he thought, "but as they serve to arrive at the union with God by love." Now it is all very well for Brother Lawrence to decry techniques and to tell aspirants that his prayer or method was simply a sense of the presence of God. He himself needed nothing more than to attend to what was already present to, and existing in, him. But how many average aspirants are so fortunate, how many possess such a ready-made sense or feeling? Is it not the general experience that this is a result of long previous toil and sacrifice, an effect and not itself a cause?

69

Can we justify the Short Path Sudden Enlightenment school by the sudden, instantaneous character of spiritual healing of the body when it includes a spiritual conversion or moral "cure"? If the latter is possible, why not the former, as both are of the same family?

70

We would all like some magic formula which could be applied in a few minutes, at the end of which time we would be different persons. The evil, the ineffectual, and the unattractive traits in us will be dramatically shed; the good, the dynamic, and the charming ones will be strikingly enhanced. But alas! life is not so easy as that.

71

Whether it be through Existentialism in France or through Zen Buddhism in the United States, the attraction towards metaphysical nihilism among young men and women of the postwar world has drawn attention in cultural circles. In the States, they became known under their own title of "The Beat Generation." John C. Holmes, one of their literary leaders, said in a New York newspaper interview, "The second war ended in 1945 and by 1947 everybody was talking of the next one. By 1948 who could believe that any international organization would be able to work this thing out? So that thrust you back right on yourself. What you felt yourself, your eagerness for life, that was the important thing, and that meant jazz, liquor and fun." I might add that for many others it meant drugs too. A Greenwich Village friend who saw these types almost daily told me that by "fun" these devotees of Beat meant the free indulgence in sex.

Holmes' conclusion was exactly the same as the one I made in *The*

Spiritual Crisis of Man, that the world-crisis forced us to look to ourselves. But whereas he thought the next step was "jazz, liquor and fun," I thought it was to develop our inner spiritual resources.

Jack Kerouac's novels have been bestsellers and have done more to make known the ideas and conduct of the "beatniks," as he called them, than any other books. Neal Cassady, the hero of three of them and once his close friend, said, "Marijuana is the mystical shortcut to beatific vision, the highest vision you can get." He also said: "Everyone is trying to get out of their mind one way or another, and marijuana is the best, the easiest way to get to the Eternal Now."

It is true that Allen Ginsberg, the leading poet of the Beat Generation movement, spoke in the same interview of "beat" meaning "seeing the world in a visionary way, which is the old classical understanding of what happens in the dark night of the soul, in Saint John of the Cross' conception. . . . The primary fact of any beat writer of any interest is that each of them has individually had some kind of Kafkaian experience of what would ordinarily be called the supernatural. I had an illumination of eternity which lasted for a few seconds and returned three or four times. These were blissful experiences . . . I was loved by God." But this further statement merely shows the confusion and chaos which has mingled liquor and jazz with mysticism and Zen Buddhism. Need we be surprised to learn that Ginsberg was treated for three-quarters of a year in an insane asylum, or that he has experimented with several different kinds of drugs?

What is the real value of illuminations when the recipient is unbalanced to start with and becomes still more unbalanced after them? Is there not a clear case here for introducing the one thing these "Beat Generation" mystics reject—the discipline of the Long Path? They want the Overself's treasure but do not want to pay the price for it.

Even as I wrote these thoughts I was delighted to hear my old friend Dr. D.T. Suzuki, then the world's leading authority on Zen and Mahayana Buddhism, make a public protest in Boston against those Westerners who take shelter for their weaknesses under Zen's umbrella. "One has to be on guard," he said, "against the misunderstanding of the idea of freedom by many who study Zen. They seem to think it means the freedom to do what one likes, and especially the freedom to be licentious. Real freedom is very different from this and comes from a deeper level."

The fact is that these young people were not really looking for truth in its highest and purest sense. They were looking for thrills. They were mostly sensation-seekers just as much as the narcotic addicts are, although in a different way and through different means. The remainder were trying to get the supreme enlightenment free of cost, without giving up anything, without giving up the ego, without undertaking any discipline. They were caught in a coil of self-deception.

72

They boast they have no need of moral disciplines and mystical exercises, no use for the writings, records, and biographies of the great masters.

73

If it were possible to mount up to this summit in a single step, as these schools claim, and then stay there, never coming down again, then would not these schools have ousted all others in the competition of ideas and practices for existence?

74

The Short Path teacher, such as Krishnamurti, insists on explaining their own divinity to all people and rejects the assertion that there are many incapable of understanding it.

75

The belief that one can take a headlong dive into the Real and stay there permanently is rife.

76

The truth of Zen attitude—letting go of restraints, avoiding reflection, refraining from self-observation, acting spontaneously, and being natural—is that it is true only on the intuitive level. It is there the only proper and possible attitude. But how few have really attained this level! How many have merely taken their very ordinary impulses, their very human desires, their very animal lusts, for profound intuitions! Thus they merely continue to act as they would have acted anyway, for the same reasons and by the same motives. The results will continue to be the same too. They are as far from true enlightenment as everyone else but with this great difference: that whereas the others do not pretend to be superior or illumined, they do. It is a fantastic self-deception, a foolish egoism that if exaggerated could lead to lunacy. Only a master can hold such an attitude with perfect fitness and propriety, only such a one can afford to "let go" of all self-control without falling into the dangerous swirling waters which are always ready to engulf the man who behaves as he pleases, and gives himself up with complete abandon to what he wrongly imagines is "walking on." This is why the earlier Chinese Zen lectures and writings were often prefaced by the warning that they were intended for persons who were already properly instructed *and established* in "the virtues." Therefore the modern Western beginners should not let the temptation to exploit Zen for their own personal purposes lead them into a trap. The only "letting go" that they can safely indulge in is to let go of the ego, the only safe "walking on" is to walk away from their attachments.

77

This is an old debate. More than a thousand years ago several Indian Buddhist pundits met and argued with a Chinese Zen master whether enlightenment is gradual or sudden.

78

Why has Zen attracted artists and intellectuals? The answer usually given is that it has favoured expression through the arts and offered relief from the strain of logic. This is true for some adherents, but for others— the easy-going, work-shy "Bohemians"—the main attraction has been its indifference to discipline, to training. Many of them are painters who put blobs of formless colour on canvas and call it a work of art, musicians who throw together a cacophony of disjointed sound and call it a melody. They have evaded the harder way of learning the techniques of art already; it is a continuation of the same attitude to evade the harder way of learning the techniques of philosophical disciplined work on themselves. The Short Path teaching seems so simple, its practices attack the goal so directly, and the goal itself is set so near that no one need be surprised to observe the rapid growth of interest in Zen recently. Who wants to work patiently through the rigours of the Long Path, who wants to toil through preparatory stages when a swifter, perhaps even sudden, way is available? Moreover, the Zenists assert that they want to be "natural" and that moral discipline is artificial imitative discipline. So they throw overboard all disciplines, all work on themselves, and give lust, passion, impulse, and egoism a full and free rein.

79

Those who believe that they have the right to demand a full and immediate enlightenment without previously setting up the conditions favourable to its reception, will either become disappointed by their failure or hallucinated by their imagined success. "Nothing for nothing" is Nature's law. They must give if they want to get—give up some of the barriers to enlightenment which exist in their own ego and to which they cling.

80

Those who seek swift enlightenment, who want to pass from their present condition of obscurity with a speed that will be miraculous, ought to ask themselves whether they are entitled to receive something for nothing.

81

The Short Path enthusiast wants to catapult himself suddenly from the quest's beginning to its ending, without having to pass through all the usual intervening and successive stages.

82

He follows Zen or some other Short Path *cult*, imagining it will enable him to jump out of his skin, to change the entire polarity of his essential nature in the twinkling of an eye. And this too without any effort. Does he really succeed in doing it? Only in his talk.

83

It is not enough to repeat a few high-sounding phrases and expect to be immediately and totally illumined.

84

The hope of suddenly or swiftly getting established in the Overself by way of the Short Path naturally attracts the young and enthusiastic much more than the middle-aged and blasé. For the latter have seen every development in their consciousness come on a little at a time, and often brokenly.

85

It is true that enlightenment can remove our accumulated moral defects all at once in a sudden and single joyous experience. But it is also true that we are unlikely to get more than the first degree if we have not previously worked upon ourselves to prepare properly for it.

86

Old cults like Zen and new ones like "The Undivided Mind" offer freedom from moral restrictions and ascetic controls. This attracts those who are seeking an excuse to let loose their physical instincts and impulses. They do not see that such a doctrine of freedom is only for adepts, not aspirants.

87

There is a special temperament which scorns the process of gradual ripening, of natural growth. It belongs to the man who is unwilling to work patiently and irritated by laborious self-discipline. He is convinced that some secret may be found. Some method exists or some teacher is available to bring about an immediate and successful result just as a push-button does. All he has to do is to seek out and discover the Secret Method or teacher.

88

It is easy to see why the Short Path is so attractive to so many people. Why cultivate the virtues one by one, or the qualities one at a time? Why plod through them in all their varied details? Why engage in extreme effort and undergo patient discipline? Why weary yourself labouring after what is so hard to obtain on the Long Path, when here is a way whereby they will come of themselves, springing spontaneously and almost unbidden into existence, easily and naturally?

89

It is really a kind of spiritual arrogance which believes it has only to jump from its present standpoint to the divinest level, as so many ill-equipped Zen adherents believe. Spiritual humility will seek, and be satisfied with, a more modest result.

90

Today it is needful to describe plainly and simply what the Zen Buddhist writers hide in puzzles and riddles. This is better for the modern mentality.

91

If he is to satisfy his quest for higher joys, his craving for inner peace, his longing for a knowledge of truth and reality, he must pay a price. Such things are not free.

92

They look for an abrupt rebirth like Saint Paul's, for a sudden upthrust of spiritual power.

93

Those who would like to get the prize all at once, without work, sacrifice, or time, should not wrongly imagine that the Short Path is for them.

94

They expect to be caught up in a spiritual whirlwind and borne away after minutes into a spiritual ecstasy from which there would never again be any descent.

95

These schemes of spiritual redemption which claim to proceed by leaps and jumps, which abolish the climb up ladders and the crossing over of bridges, will appeal to the unbalanced enthusiast and the unpractical visionary.

96

Are they entitled to have all their defects swiftly cast out and their deficiencies automatically supplied just because they have given their assent to a particular cosmic maxim or their time to a particular meditational practice?

97

These "Sudden Enlightenment" votaries, the "Salvation by Saturday" brigade.

98

Nowhere in physical nature do we observe this leap across a chasm, but everywhere everything passes gradually and little by little from one condition to the next. Why should the transition from ego to Overself contradict this universal fact?

99

Those who are ill-qualified for the Short Path, who come to it in order to escape the tiresome disciplines of the Long Path, who want a sudden and swift enlightenment without having to pass through the gradations of slowly preparing themselves for it, usually find themselves thrown back in the end.

Limitations of the Long Path

100

What is the use of trying to improve oneself by Long Path methods? There will be no end to it. One can go on and on and on practising it. After all, although this will give one a better ego, it will not give one liberation from the ego itself. Furthermore, the idea of rebirth is tied in with the idea of such self-improvement through many lives. Both in turn are based on, and wholly enclosed in, the ego—hence illusory.

101

This constant preoccupation with the ego gives a subtle power and importance to it, and draws him away from his real being in the Overself. For it is what he takes into his consciousness which affects him in character and body, in thought and conduct.

102

It comes to this paradox—that the farther they travel on the path of ego-effort, the farther they move from their goal, and the less they try to approach their Source, the closer they come to it!

103

This constant looking at oneself, this endless and exaggerated self-consciousness, may not lead to purification from fault and humility if it breeds new faults and new prides.

104

If the Overself is timeless, unaffected by the clock's ticking, how could acts performed in time, exercises of the mind done by the clock, bring a man into the Overself's eternal consciousness?

105

The Long Path, despite its magnificent ideals of self-improvement and self-control, is still egoistic. For this determination to rise spiritually is directed by *willed* ambition—willed by the higher part of the ego.

106

Most of the work of the Long Path is, in the end, ego-grounded. Many aspirants either adore or else hate themselves.

107

The follower of the Long Path may become filled with anxiety about his future progress and guilt about his past or present history. Or, like the early Stoics and the medieval ascetics, he may be continually engaged in fighting himself. Struggle and war then become the miserable climate in which he lives. Real peace of mind is far from him. If we penetrate analytically to the base of this situation, we find that it exists because he depends primarily on his ego's strength, not on the Overself.

108

Saint Teresa perfectly understood the nature of, and difference between, the two paths, and described them well and briefly. She wrote: "It is a great grace of God to practise self-examination, but too much is as bad as too little, as they say: believe me, by God's help, we shall accomplish more by contemplating the Divinity than by keeping our eyes fixed on ourselves."

109

There are certain patterns of thought which reflect the idea that attainment of this goal is almost impossible, and that the needed preparation and purification could not be even half finished in a whole lifetime. If these patterns are held over a long period of years, they provide him with powerful suggestions of limitation. Thus the very instruction or teaching which is supposed to help his progress actually handicaps it and emotionally obstructs it. His belief that character must be improved, weaknesses must be corrected, and the ego must be fought looms so large in his outlook that it obliterates the equally necessary truth that Grace is ever at hand and that he should seek to invoke it by certain practices and attitudes.

110

The fact is he is depending too much upon himself and too little upon the Overself. After all, help cannot lift itself by its own bootstraps.

111

Is the perfecting of character a cause of enlightenment or is it an effect?

112

If they expect too little of themselves, they become lazy and indifferent; if too much, they undergo needless torment. Too much feverish tension or desire to make progress or get mystical experience has driven aspirants a little mad in the past, although these have never been and could never be philosophic aspirants but the religious or the occult-minded sort. Their zeal is admirable but their fanaticism needs to be firmly discouraged. They tie themselves in knots through wanting to create new virtues when it is more important to remove the old hindrances, so as to open themselves to the Overself and its grace. The belief that they alone, unaided, can attain complete enlightenment by their own personal efforts, places too heavy an obligation upon them, too large a burden, and it is not even a necessary one.

113

The Long Path seeker who solemnly inflicts self-denials and self-disciplines upon himself in hope of finding freedom will one day have to make the transition to the Short Path.

114

The Long Path keeps the mind continually *searching*, whether for increased holiness or increased truth. It is never quiet, content, at peace.

115

In looking back at the past, the more evolved men find certain things unpleasant to remember and unbearable to analyse. This is a helpful result for the Long Path: it weakens the lower elements of character by strengthening disgust with them. But it is negative and depressing. And in the end they must go on to the Short Path, where such preoccupation with the ego is abandoned, where a positive and cheerful identification with Overself is sought.

116

These contrary periods come to most seekers until the Short Path is discovered, entered, and travelled. A stable attitude will then be one of its natural effects; a steady calmness will be more easily maintained than before.

117

All attempts to liberate the self from the self by the self are obviously doomed from the start.

118

If self-hate becomes morbidly excessive it may lead to suicide. This is one danger of the Long Path's asceticism.

119

It is certainly better to remove faults and remedy weaknesses than to leave them as they are. But it is not enough to improve, refine, ennoble, and even spiritualize the ego. For all such activity takes place under the illusion that the ego possesses reality. This illusion needs to be eliminated, not merely changed for another one.

120

The Long Path creates a condition favourable to enlightenment, but since it is concerned with ego, it cannot directly yield enlightenment. For its work of purifying the ego, however necessary and noble, still keeps the aspirant's face turned egoward.

121

The principle of so improving or purifying or training or developing the ego that it will gain illumination is a fallacious one. For the ego is the false self, and nothing that is done to it can produce the true self. To believe otherwise is to go on clinging to an illusion.

122

A knowledge of the heavenly Overself cannot be had by studying, improving, or developing the benighted and fictitious ego. The only way in which it can be got is by direct experience of it. This axiom is the basis of the Short Path.

123

The Long Path exercises and disciplines are excellent but their results are inconclusive. They give the chance to progress but do not and cannot give final enlightenment and full self-mastery.

124

Everything that he accomplishes in the way of self-improvement, self-purification, or self-mastery is accomplished by the force of the ego. No higher power, no grace of the Overself, no faith that transcends materialism is needed for these things. Whatever it is, and however beneficial it be, reform of the ego's character will not lead directly to the destruction of the ego's rule. For although the ego is willing to improve or purify itself, it is not willing to kill itself.

125

The ego cannot produce an egoless result. This is why the Long Path is only preparatory and cannot be a sufficient means to a successful end.

126

The Long Path man makes his life into a problem and his quest into a prison. By his understanding what he has done, the problem will vanish. By his perceiving the situation as it really is, the walls of his prison will fall down.

127

He must free himself of this egoistic way of looking at his life, his character, his goal, which the spiritual life of the Long Path, as well as the unspiritual life before it was engaged upon, really possesses.

128

The Long Path of personal control and virtuous practice is necessary and must be followed. But it is still within and related to the world of darkness. It is useless as a means of entering the world of light.

129

Such is the fertile nature of the ego that openings for its improvement, reform, or amendment are endless. This is why the Long Path must be abandoned at some time if the ego itself is to be uprooted.

130

To carry the Long Path work to such excess that it fills you with powerful guilt complexes, that it makes you unrelaxedly harsh and grim with yourself—this is to destroy yourself.

131

These Long Pathers, these self-conscious strivers after near-perfection, are still striving within the ego and, in the end, however nobly, for the ego. For they are trying to improve it, not lose it. If the latter were their real goal they would be interested in neither its improvement nor its worsening since both activities are only aspects. Why should they deal with it at all? Why not try the opposite course, the Short Path, which silences the ego, not by striving to do so but by ignoring it through fastening attention upon the Overself?

132

The Short Path advocate may pertinently ask his Long Path friend, "Why not make the end into the beginning? Why not directly still the mind, empty it of thoughts, instead of attaching it to some idea and concentrating upon that in the earlier stages only to drop it in the later ones? Why let it go on what the Australians call 'a walkabout'?"

133

Then he comes to realize the magnitude of what he undertook in the first rush of enthusiasm, and the littleness of his qualification for it. Then only does he see that the Long Path leads to an inaccessible peak. He is overwhelmed and fails to see the great preparatory service it rendered him.

134

Spirituality needs time to develop: the spark needs fanning; but this need not be turned into an excuse for surrendering completely to the Long Path's limitations.

135

The narrow limited presentation of the path to enlightenment needs rebuttal. And this can be found in the cases of men who entered and remained in the light not by the persevering practice of yoga, or by personal guru-initiation, but by fastening interest, thought, feeling, devotion, faith on the light itself solely and exclusively.

136

The struggles against himself, the attempts and failures to live as if outer circumstances do not matter at all, lead the Long Path follower in the end, and by stages, from arrogant enthusiastic faith to humble anguished bewilderment, from acceptance to disagreement.

137

On the Long Path the aspirant is likely to probe some of his shortcomings too pessimistically, to condemn himself for them, but to be blind altogether to the most serious shortcoming of all—that of clinging to the personal ego in all circumstances.

138

If the Long Path's searching work on shortcomings is overbalanced, it increases his self-condemnation but strengthens his feelings of separation from the Divine Being that is his root.

139

Yang Chu described the Long Path travellers as searchers for a missing sheep who themselves got lost in the multitude of efforts involving a plenitude of details.

140

The Long Path has no property in itself which can turn darkness into light, the ordinary mentality into the illumined one.

141

Time continues itself, and the time-bound consciousness with it. The Long Path does not liberate a man from it but only improves him, at the best, prepares him. For what? For the Short Path, which alone offers freedom.

142

The root of all his efforts in self-improvement and self-purification is still the egoistic consciousness. Since that is the very consciousness which must be given up to let in the egoless Spirit, he must abandon these efforts and turn sooner or later to the Short Path.

143

It is as valid in logic as it is in practice that nothing that is done in time can produce the timeless, therefore no amount of study, purification, and meditation can make a man more divine than he is now. Then why have such ways been given out?

144

Why should a man strain himself to the point of having a nervous breakdown, or acquiring an ulcer, in trying to get the inner peace which is preventive of nervous breakdowns and renders him immune to ulcers?

145

To go on condemning oneself for past errors until it is a fixed attitude of mind is to push Long Path work to an extreme.

146

He has been seeking an unbroken perfection that no one has ever reached and no one can reach.

147

It is not enough to uncover his faults and confess his weaknesses, not even enough to correct the one and remedy the other. After all, these things concern only the stage of development he has already reached, and the ego only. He must also turn toward higher stages and to the egoless self.

148

The Long Pather can never be satisfied with the work he has done on himself or failed to do.

149

The labours of the Long Path are good and necessary. They weaken the ego and bring him part of the way toward the goal. But they will end in despair if he does not learn that they cannot bring him the rest of the way.

150

Moral disciplines have a definite place in life to make us better human beings but they do not lift us to the Overself's level. The Long Path, to which they belong, has a humanitarian value but not a magically transcendent one.

151

In *The Marble Faun*, Nathaniel Hawthorne writes: "We go all wrong, by too strenuous a resolution to go all right."

152

If he takes an excessive clinical interest in his own moral and spiritual state, continually observing his conduct and analysing his feelings to find the flaws in them, he loses his balance and becomes inwardly unhealthy. In putting too much emphasis upon his failings, he is giving too much attention to his own ego.

153

The idea that a man's own virtue can bring him to the goal belongs to the Long Path.

154

He may well ask himself at this point, as Yen Hui, the Chinese disciple of Confucius, asked, whether the Goal is not really an inaccessible peak, attracting climbers yet always defeating them in the end.

155

It is not any kind of activity of the ego which brings salvation. How could that happen? How can a man lift himself up by the hair upon his own head? Just the same he cannot touch the Overself spirit by his own virtue. It is only the activity of the Overself which will save him from the ego. But this he must provoke or invoke by taking to the Short Path.

156

The Long Path gives many benefits and bestows many virtues but it does not give the vision of truth, the realization of the Overself, nor does it bestow Grace. For these things we must turn to the Short Path.

3

THE DARK NIGHT OF THE SOUL

The upward flights of the aspirant's novitiate are bought at the cost of downward falls. It is as much a part of his experience of this quest to be deprived at times of all feeling that the divine exists and is real, as it is to have the sunny assurance of it.

At first the experience of reality comes only in flashes. Actually it is not the higher self which tantalizingly appears and disappears before the aspirant's gaze in this way, causing him alternating conditions of happy fruition and miserable sterility, but the higher self's loving *Grace*. Each time this is shed, the aspirant's first reaction is a strong sense of spiritual lack, dryness, darkness, and longing. This brings much unhappiness, self-discontent, and frustration. But it also brings both increased and intensified aspiration for the unearthly and distaste for the earthly. This phase passes away, however, and is followed by one as illuminative as the other was dark, as joyous as the other was unhappy, as productive as the other was barren, and as close to reality as the other seemed far from it. In that sacred presence a purifying process takes place. The old familiar and faulty self drops away like leaves from a tree in autumn. He makes the radiant discovery in his heart of its original goodness. But alas, when the presence departs, the lower self returns and resumes sovereignty. The period of illumination is often followed by a period of darkness. A spiritual advance which comes unexpectedly is usually succeeded by a period of recoil. Jubilation is followed by depression.

A greater trial still awaits him. The Overself demands a sacrifice upon its altar so utter, so complete that even the innocent natural longing for personal happiness must be offered up. As no novice and few intermediates could bear this dark night of the soul, and as even proficients cannot bear it without murmuring, it is reserved for the last group alone—which means that it happens at an advanced stage along the path, between a period of great illumination, and another of sublime union.

During this period the mystic will feel forsaken, emotionally fatigued and intellectually bored to such a degree that he may become a sick soul.

Meditation exercises will be impossible and fruitless, aspirations dead and uninviting. A sense of terrible loneliness will envelop him. Interest in the subject may fall away or the feeling that further progress is paralysed may become dominant. Yet in spite of contrary appearances, this is all part of his development, which has taken a turn that will round it out and make it fuller. Most often the student is plunged into new types of experience during the dark period. The Overself sends him forth to endure tests and achieve balance.

The most dangerous feature of the "dark night" is a weakening of the will occurring at the same time as a reappearance of old forgotten evil tendencies. This is the point where the aspirant is really being tested, and where a proportion of those who have reached this high grade fail in the test and fall for several years into a lower one.

Even Muhammed had to undergo this experience of the dark night of the soul. It lasted three years and not a single illumination or revelation came to brighten his depressed heart. Indeed he even considered the idea of killing himself to put an end to it; and yet his supreme realization and world-shaking task were still ahead of him.

He who has passed through this deepest and longest of the "dark nights" which precedes mature attainment can never again feel excessive emotional jubilation. The experience has been like a surgical operation in cutting him off from such enjoyments. Moreover, although his character will be serene always, it will be also a little touched by that melancholy which must come to one who not only has plumbed the depths of life's anguish himself, but also has been the constant recipient of other people's tales of sorrow.

The aspirant can rest in the passive self-absorbed state for a short time only, for a few hours at most. The relentless dictates of Nature compel him to return to his suppressed ordinary state of active life.

This intermittent swinging to and fro between rapt self-absorption and the return to ordinary consciousness will tantalize him until he realizes what is the final goal. It will end only when his egoism has ended. Up to now he has succeeded in overcoming it fully in the contemplative state only. He must now overcome it in his ordinary active state. But the ego will not leave him here unless the purpose of its own evolution has been fulfilled. Therefore he must complete its all-round development, bring it to poise and balance, and then renounce it utterly. With the ego's complete abnegation, perfect, unbroken, and permanent oneness with the Overself ensues.

2

After a deeply felt Glimpse or Rapture or Spirit in Development there may be a reaction. This takes the form of a temporary and minor Dark Night of the Soul. But this phenomenon is more certain to appear, and in its most dramatic form, after the second stage of meditation has been achieved but before the third (contemplation) is practised.

3

It is the dark night of the soul—that terrible and desolate period when the Divine seems as far away as the stars, when emotional listlessness and intellectual lassitude fall on a man, when he finds no help within himself and none outside himself. It is a melancholic experience undergone and lamented by Job and Jeremiah in ancient Israel, by John of Avila in seventeenth-century Spain, by Swami Ram Tirtha in modern India. "Oh, my dryness and my deadness!" is a typical cry of this period, found in Lancelot Andrewes' devotional diary, *Private Devotions*.

4

He who comes to the limit of his endurance is likely to utter his critical cry. The night is darkest just before dawn. He is almost ripe for that revelation which can open a new, hopeful cycle for him.

5

When "I am not," the Overself is. When the universe is, God is not. If the Overself did not hide itself, the ego could not come forth. If God were everywhere apparent, there would be no universe. In that deep underground mining operation which is the dark night of the soul, the saint's spirituality is utterly lost from sight, feeling, and consciousness. He is left for a while bereft of all that he has gained, while what remains of his ego is relentlessly crushed. Yet this is followed by a true and lasting enlightenment!

6

Even during the longest dark night of the soul, the Overself is not a whit less close to him than it was when it revealed its presence amid ecstasy and joy.

7

Dark Night of the Soul: The owl is blinded by light, which is therefore darkness to it.

8

When the dark night comes, its effect stuns him. His eager aspirations fade away into despondency and his spiritual exercises fall into disuse. Nothing that happens around him seems to matter, and everything seems so aimless, futile, or trivial. He has to force himself to go on living outwardly as usual. His will is listless and his emotion leaden. He feels inwardly dead, hardly aware of anything except his own state. The experiences and surroundings that each day brings him are passed through as in a dream.

9

We hear that William Blake was one of England's great mystics and we take it for granted that his mystical perception was easily put to work. Yet there was a time when Blake lamented that the light which was with him had gone out. How long this dark night of the soul lasted has not been recorded.

10

The inner nature becomes stiff, muscle-bound, unresponsive to the joyous evidences and serene intimations of the Overself. What is even worse, bringing a dark hopelessness with it, is the fear that this will become a permanent state. This is the famed Dark Night.

11

Both Spanish Saint John of the Cross and Hebrew Job of the Bible experienced and wrote of the darkness of the soul that falls on God's good earnest devotee.

12

When the fruits of the glimpse are seemingly withdrawn—and especially so when this happens if the glimpse has been brought on by the work of meditation—a deadness will seem to close in on the feeling and a dullness on the mind. If this condition goes deep enough, it becomes depressive and is more or less what the saints have called the Dark Night of the Soul. This is not permanent. The seeker should not despair, but his patience will be stretched and he must accept its happening. If he sees no cause for which he is to blame, then the acceptance becomes an act of faith and it will not be in vain.

13

So lofty is the goal to be reached but so low is his present position, that it would be unnatural for him not to feel at times shaken by despair or oppressed by futility. Such moods, when humanity's life seems pointless and his own purposeless, when labour becomes tedious and pleasure depressing, will come over him from time to time. These dry periods, when mystical life seems boring and unreal, dull and dreary, are to be expected. They are normal experiences in every aspirant's career and their remedy is in God's hands in His good time. He is being tantalized so as to make him prize the divine visitation all the more. Most of the seekers are tried in this way. Then it also shows how helpless he is. For the last word lies with divine Grace. Yet all this is no excuse for ceasing self-effort, and so he will have to go on with his meditations and prayers and studies. For it is their activity which induces the Grace to descend.

14

Henry Suso: "Hitherto thou hast been a squire; now God wills thee to be a knight. And thou shalt have fighting enough." Suso cried: "Alas, my God! What art thou about to do unto me? I thought that I had had enough by this time. Show me how much suffering I have before me." The Lord said, "It is better for thee not to know. Nevertheless I will tell thee of three things. Hitherto thou hast stricken thyself. Now I will strike thee, and thou shalt suffer publicly the loss of thy good name. Secondly, where thou shalt look for love and faithfulness, there shalt thou find treachery and suffering. Thirdly, hitherto thou hast floated in Divine sweetness, like a fish in the sea; this will I now withdraw from thee, and thou shalt starve and wither. Thou shalt be forsaken both by God and the world, and whatever thou shalt take in hand to comfort thee shall come to nought." The servitor threw himself on the ground, with arms outstretched to form a cross, and prayed in agony that this great misery might not fall upon him. Then a voice said to him, "Be of good cheer. I will be with thee and aid thee to overcome."

15

The dread phenomenon of the dark night of the soul makes its appearance in a mystic's life only a few times at most, sometimes only once. The devotions lose their fervour, the emotions become cold, and worship seems a futile exercise. There is no longer any pleasure to be got from the inner life, and experiences of mystical satisfaction are either rare or absent altogether. Meditation becomes dry, barren, and ineffective; often the very taste for it departs. Aspiration seems dead. Where there was once spiritual light in the mind and spiritual heat in the heart, there is now only darkness and ashes. A torpor of sheer fatalism settles over the will. Life becomes marked by emptiness, aimlessness, lack of inspiration, and drifts with the tide of events.

16

With the coming-in of the dark night there is a going-out of confidence in himself, an uncomfortable sense of failure, a pessimistic feeling that he will never again find peace, joy, or happiness.

17

The dark night of the soul has been known to last for several years. On the other hand, it has also been known to pass away in a single year. It is a trying time when the power to meditate, the desire to worship, the urge to pray, the hope of spiritual attainment, and even the feeling of God's benevolence desert the pilgrim.

18

He who suffers the dark night finds himself poised unhappily between the two worlds—the lower not wanted, the higher not wanting him.

19

When this drying up of all aspiration and devotion comes upon him without any traceable cause, the beauty and warmth of past intuitive feeling or mystical experience will seem unreal.

20

With the dark night there is a wish to withdraw from active life, from social responsibilities, and from personal duties. A feeling of their futility accompanies the wish, a vaguely pessimistic outlook surrounds it.

21

During the Dark Night he is neither spiritually alive nor spiritually dead. For though feeling deserts him, memory refuses to do so.

22

The Dark Night is not the result of any physical suffering or personal misfortune: it comes from a subtler cause. It induces a depression of enormous weight.

23

The sombre loneliness experienced during the Dark Night of the Soul is unique. No other kind of loneliness duplicates it either in nature or acuteness, although some may approach it. It creates the feeling of absolute rejection, of being an outcast.

24

A terrible inner numbness, an unbearable emptiness, is a prominent feature of the spiritual dark night.

25

The dark night is a tragic period. Hardly anyone emerges from it without bitter murmuring and rebellious complaint against the Divinity he earlier professed to adore. Wherever the man turns he can find no relief for his suffering. His conduct, under the suggestion of helplessness, becomes aimless and meaningless.

26

That paralysing emotional dryness and intellectual deadness is the Dark Night. He has lost the world and the flesh but he has not received heaven and the Spirit in return for them. Like a statue he wants nothing, expects nothing. He pretends to be alive but is really a mere spectator of a meaningless life.

27

With the dark night, a condition of mental dullness sets in. Real sustained thinking becomes a strain. This is because the mind loses its interest in things, being apathetic.

28

He is oppressed by the feeling of his own nothingness, by the realization that he is completely in God's hand.

29

His aspiration becomes tepid, his determination to find truth becomes lukewarm.

30

Hope withers in the heart and joy is put away during this dark night of the soul. The man once eager, passionate, and ardent in his aspiration, becomes dried and sapless.

31

He feels lost, becomes fearful, reproaches himself with sins fancied or real, and thinks that he is now permanently estranged from God as a punishment. Such is the "Dark Night."

32

He seems to walk absolutely alone in a condition of mental gloom and spiritual barrenness. No friend, no book, and no teacher can help because they have only words to offer and he wants to feel the divine, and not merely to hear words about it. It is, however, a phase which will adjust itself in the course of time. There is nothing he can do except to hold on to the sure faith that he will emerge from it at the time set by the wisdom of his higher Self. So he needs to be patient. It will not do him any harm but on the contrary will benefit him. It is certainly very unpleasant for the emotions. But it is necessary because the higher Self wants to train him to rise above them—even above religious emotions—and to live in intuitive calm. He is faced with the hard lesson of learning detachment from personal feelings but it is necessary to master it if he is ever to reach inner peace.

33

When the dark night of the soul falls he may find himself entering a desolate apathy, a loss of interest in things and matters for which before he had a keen appetite. Nought is the consolation to be found in surroundings and persons who formerly raised his enthusiasm.

34

During the Dark Night he lets go of the will in a fatalistic way, doing nothing to achieve any aim and expecting nothing to help him. He seems to have no freedom of choice, so remains forlorn.

35

The raptures, the aspirations, the devotions may be repeated many times, but in the end they are seen as part of the ever-changing picture which life itself is seen to be. Moreover in "the dark night of the Soul" they die off altogether.

36

Few are willing to make this change so Nature often forces it upon them by plunging them into "the dark night of the Soul."

37

The dark night is a prolonged stupor, a period of dull interminable waiting for some change to happen.

38

During these dark hours life seems to be lived for nothing, its desires a mockery, its figures a shadow, its events pointless, and the whole world illusory.

39

How real is his experience of the Overself, or how near he is to it, must not always be measured by his emotional feeling of it. The deep inward calm is a better scale to use. But even this vanishes in the "dark night."

40

When he enters the dark night of the soul, life becomes unreal and hollow. He is playing a role in a stage play, but it is all acting, it is not real. He has lost the basic interest in life and he performs what he has to do like a mechanical robot.

Its significance

41

To the informed quester, the dark night of the soul inside him is simply another phase of his growth. It is no more to be feared than the coming of dark night of the world outside him is to be feared.

42

It comes to this, that a man who is brought down by adverse events or by inward failure, who loses confidence in himself and hope for his future, who is stricken down by what John of the Cross called "the dark night of the soul"—such a man is unknowingly at a possible turning-point of his life. Let him surrender this poor crushed ego of his, this broken belief that he can successfully manage his life, and pray to the Overself to take it all over.

43

Accept the long night patiently, quietly, humbly, and resignedly as intended for your true good. It is not a punishment for sin committed but an instrument of annihilating egoism.

44

In this terrible experience of the dark night, the divine *seems* to have withdrawn itself and left him desolate, alone, bereft, and comfortless. Yet if he is to become more godlike he must become less attached and less desirous. The stage when he was intensely attached to the divine and ardently desirous of it belongs to the past. The time has come for him to come out of it. Just as he had to forsake the desire of earthly things in order to enter it, so he must now forsake even this last and noblest desire of all, even his godward aspiration. In doing this he will follow the Bible's injunction to "Be Still!" He will be himself and not yearn to be something other than what he is. He will be at peace.

45

They must even bring themselves to accept the Overself's apparent indifference and their own very real dryness with full submission.

46

If he is to be truly resigned to the divine will, he will fully accept the darkness and give his faithful consent to the hidden imperceptible work of the Overself in him.

47

The Dark Night is much less a dark night when he believes, understands, or possibly knows that it is a work of the Overself, a movement of Its grace.

48

(*On the Dark Night*) It is not generally known that a master not only can give illumination but also can remove the obstacles to it, that he may be used by the disciple's higher self for both these purposes. ——— was set free from a ten-year dark night of the soul by Eckhart. Nevertheless, no master is free to exercise this power with arbitrariness or with favouritism but only in obedience to the laws governing it.

49

It all seems so utterly futile, so bleak, so useless during the dark night of the soul. But wait—patience and more patience has positive results.

50

I have always preached the gospel of hope, because if it does nothing more, it encourages effort, gives a tonic to one's spirit, and helps one through the darkest moments. As the Comte de Saint Germain said: "Every tunnel has its end."

51

It was Miguel de Molinos who warned aspirants that the fulfilment of their aspiration could come only after the establishment of calm in their hearts. This held true, he further explained, even if the inner obstacles to such calm were of a spiritual kind, such as lack of enthusiasm for the quest, loss of interest in spiritual techniques, and depressed moods induced by failure, no less than for those of a worldly kind.

Modern aspirants should remember these words during the dark night when there is a loss of savour and interest in work, art, literature, self-improvement, and character-building.

The same thought may be put in a more poetic form, when the feelings are more likely to be touched and a stronger effect produced. To make use of some of the Latin poet Catullus' lines, written though they were in another connection: "My studies dead, my joy in everything is fled. Why speak, why call out? I am not heard."

52

He will need patience, for long dreary stretches of empty months will come to him.

53

He seems, in this desolate "night," to be up against a blank wall. But with patience he may find a way out. It is well to remember Abraham Lincoln's "This too will pass."

54

If the Overself did not lead him into and through the final dark night, where he becomes as helpless as an infant, as bereft of interior personal possessions as a destitute pauper, how else would he learn that it is not by his own powers and capacities that he can rise at last into enduring illumination?

55

Entry into the soul's dark night is an unpleasant affair, marked by a loss of the capacity to practise meditation upon spiritual themes, an inability to enter into the mood of spiritual ecstasy, and yet a repulsion toward giving his mind over to anything else. Although he does not know it, although he feels bereft and forlorn, this is actually a result of the Overself's working within the subconscious regions of his being. It is intended to carry his development to a further stage which can appear only when the dark night comes to an end. And although it may seem useless in his own view to impose such seemingly unprofitable suffering upon him, it is bringing him more and more out of the clutches of his ego. Quite often, he fears that this is some punishment fallen upon him for his own errors or omissions, but he is wrong.

56

During the "dark night of the soul," as it is called by Spanish mystics, the abrupt yet brief joy of the first awakening to existence of a diviner life is succeeded and thrown into vivid contrast by the long melancholy years of its loss. There will come to him terrible periods when the quest will seem to have been lost, when his personal shortcomings will magnify themselves formidably before his eyes, and when meditation will be dry sterile and even distasteful. Not only will it seem that the Divine is saddeningly remote, but also that it is impossible of access. Let him know this and be forewarned, know that even its seeming loss is actually a part of the quest's usual course. Hope must sustain him during such dark periods, and time will show it to be neither a groundless nor an unfulfilled feeling. Those years may be bitter indeed for the ego, may even seem wasted ones, but they have their meaning. First, they bring up to the surface and into kinetic activity all hidden faults, all potential weaknesses, all latent evil, so that they may be exposed for what they are and got rid of—often after their resultant sufferings.

All the aspirant's latent wickedness (as well as virtue) is actualized by degrees; all of his dormant tempting passions are aroused in turn; all of his animal propensities are brought into play against his worthier ideals; all his insincerities and greeds, untruthfulnesses and vanities sprout quickly from the seed stage into full-grown plants. The good qualities show themselves too at the same time, so that there is a terrible struggle within him, a struggle which the laws of the quest ordain he shall endure and complete alone. He becomes a dual personality. No master and no God may interfere with this momentous testing of a human soul at this critical stage of its evolution when the relation between the lower and higher selves is sought to be entirely changed. For it may not pass over into the new and higher life forever unless and until it is really ready for such life. All this happens through events and circumstances both ordinary and extraordinary by a natural law which governs all efforts to rend the mystic veil.

57

By freeing himself largely of attachments—and especially the subtlest yet largest of all, attachment to the ego—his heart is emptied. Into the void thus created, Grace can flow. Mystics who complain of the soul's dark night are led to know that it is a process whereby this space in the heart is being increased, a crushing of self into dust, to make room for Grace. If they are thus led to nothingness, let them remember that the Overself is no-thing.

58

Spiritual raptures, which are such a help and encouragement for the beginner, become a hindrance and stumbling block to the advanced disciple. The latter must learn to give them up without complaint, and to no longer expect or depend on them. The most effectual way to teach him that lesson is unfortunately for him also the most desolating. It is through the dark night of the soul. The absence of the higher self or God or grace in this condition is only a seeming one. Each is still there underneath the darkness. The situation is really paradoxical and beyond correct appraisal by the conscious mind, certainly by the suffering ego. He is being made to learn, by the severest experience, that the divine reality must not be confused with his conscious reactions to it, nor with his mental reactions to it, nor even with his emotional reactions to it, that it belongs to an unknown and unknowable realm that transcends human faculties and defies human perceptions.

59

The man who has seen reality during a temporary glimpse may later be subjected to its hidden operation without or within. In this way the higher power tests him, tries his faith, courage, patience, and, above all, sense of truth and capacity for discrimination. If the test reveals his weakness, then it is for him to provide the remedy: thus in the end he is strengthened. It is not enough to recognize the Real in its own homeland alone; he must be trained to recognize it under all conditions, even when it is hidden under thick illusion, even in the lowest ebb of the soul's dark night. These tests, which come both from within and without, help to give this training.

60

When he reaches this condition wherein his whole being seems emptied of hope and light, of certainty and reality, he learns the dread truth that nothing in himself can be relied on and that nobody outside himself can help him. This is the lesson of the "dark night of the soul."

61

If he is ever to learn and practise abnegation of the will, then this plumbing of the depths of the dark night is an essential experience. But it is essential only if he previously revelled emotionally in the ecstatic elation of the Glimpse.

62

He who has been through this "dark night" and absorbed its lessons thoroughly has lost all his pride.

63

When the aridity has half gone and the serenity has begun to come, life becomes a little more congenial, Nature a little more beautiful. It is time to bury the old negativities.

64

The "dark night" does more to detach a man from his ego, his interests, and his desires than the rapturous joys and emotional ecstasies. The awful feeling of being separated from or even lost forever to the higher power, works as a hidden training and secret discipline of all personal feelings.

65

He is forced into the seeming darkness by the processes of Nature. She wishes him to turn back and, on the one hand, to purify those parts of his character and, on the other hand, to develop those parts of his psyche which have remained undeveloped.

66

The dark nights which come to the inner man, when he feels deprived of peace and hope or especially when he feels utterly deserted by the Overself, are as necessary to educate him as the bright days when joy fills him because of the divine nearness.

67

Dark Night of the Soul: In passing through this, the greatest humiliation he has ever experienced, and passing through it resignedly, patiently, and without rebellion, he reduces the ego to a cipher, and destroys its power over him.

68

He has to regenerate his whole being—the intellect which thinks, the emotional nature which feels, and the practical will which acts. That is one meaning of the "dark night."

69

This second mystical crisis yields, as one of its fruits, a moral cleansing.

70

This is perhaps the greatest test of all, this phase of the aspirant's career which has been called "the dark night of the soul." Any one or all of several different causes may bring it on, any one or all of several different results may ensue. In that terrible darkness he will find himself absolutely alone, able to depend on nothing else than what he finds within his own innermost being. Without anyone to guide him and with none to companion him, he will have to learn an utter self-reliance if he is successfully to gain one of these results. It is useless to complain of the terror of this experience for, from the first moment that he gave his allegiance to this quest, he unconsciously invited its onset. It had to come even though the day of its coming was yet far off.

71

It is not only by the experience of feeling at times the presence of God that an aspirant may develop inwardly: it may also happen by the equivalent non-experience, by feeling quite deserted by God, quite left alone! This—the "dark night of the soul"—is just as essential.

72

The spiritual joys are intended to entice men—lethargic or reluctant as they are—onto the Quest, or to reward them when they have finished it. That is to say, they are for beginners and adepts. The spiritual drynesses are intended to purify the character, fortify the will, and detach men from the ego. That is to say, they are for sufficiently grown adults. It is the paradoxical irony of this situation that the joys of the beginner make him believe that he is very near to God whereas the desolations of the proficient make him despise himself.

73

(*Dark Night*:) When he realizes that even despair is egotistical, he will realize that it is not only the so-called evil passions that have to be curbed but also the depressive and melancholy emotions. He needs to remember that whenever he will again penetrate into the higher region of his being, any sadness, depression, or melancholy he may suffer from will diminish gradually and then, when he is stabilized in it, vanish entirely.

74

This period of crisis which may descend upon a Quester and which has been called the dark night of the soul is a period of spiritual stagnation, moral discouragement, and mental fatigue. Nothing and nobody seems able or even willing to help him and books themselves become useless, arid, and futile. Not only can he proceed no farther, but there seems no point in trying to do so. Yet, as I have often pointed out before, it is in this crisis when he seems most deserted that he is really being most guided, guided from a path, the Long Path, which has reached its end towards the Short Path, which he must now begin to travel.

4

THE CHANGEOVER TO THE SHORT PATH

The preparation on the Long Path

It would be wonderful if everyone, everywhere, could slip so easily into the kingdom of heaven, and just as easily stay there forever. But alas! the facts of human nature forbid it. People require teaching, training, purifying, disciplining, and preparing, before they can do so. And the course needed is a lifetime's, the work needed much and varied. That is why the Long Path is needed.

2

While giving all attention to the Overself, or to its remembrance, or to its various aspects, or to the idea of it, he forgets himself. This makes it possible to transcend the ego. And this is why the Short Path *must* be travelled if the preparatory work of the other Path is to be completed.

3

The Long Path serves to bring its votaries to the Short Path, on which alone they can complete their journey to the summit which they imagined was at its end.

4

Purification of the heart and calming of the mind are necessary prerequisites for penetrating into the Overself. They belong to the Long Path.

5

The Long Path calls on him to give up whatever is holding him in bondage, whatever is keeping him back, and, thus released, he will be free to go his way towards the specifically positive work of the Short Path.

6

The Long Path is taught to beginners and others in the earlier and middle stages of the quest. This is because they are ready for the idea of self-improvement and not for the higher one of the unreality of the self. So the latter is taught on the Short Path, where attention is turned away from the little self and from the idea of perfecting it, to the essence, the real being.(P)

7

It must never be forgotten that the work of the Short Path could only come into being on the basis of work of the Long one, and on the presupposition of its presence.

8

The struggles of the Long Path are absolutely necessary but they will not avail him of themselves; Grace must be added. For it brings extra power to him and enables him to do what otherwise he could not do.

9

Nature cannot be hastened. The bloom of a flower opens in its own proper time. If the Short Path yields immediate or quick results to some aspirants, it is only because they are persons of superior development. They have served their apprenticeship on the Long Path already, either in this life or previous lives.

10

The Long Path covers all the preparatory stages leading up to but not including the decisive attempts. It is concerned with the removal of obstructions to the coming of enlightenment, whereas these attempts, which belong to the Short Path, are concerned with the conclusive formulae of enlightenment.

11

If the Long Path equips him with the necessary strength, purity, and concentration, the Short Path makes use of this equipment to unite his consciousness directly with the Overself.

12

The long labours and arduous disciplines of the Long Path are valuable in their place and time. But there is no need to limit the Quest's lifetime engagement to it alone.

13

Yoga trains character, emotions, and especially mind's power of concentration. All this is not only a useful equipment for the Short Path practice but even a necessary one.

14

The move towards reality may, if too quickly made, bring on changes that the overwhelmed traveller cannot endure or cope with. The genius may, but most others have to withdraw and adjust to a slower, more suitable pace. This is why growing up, becoming prepared, is the first requisite, why the Long Path precedes the Short one.

15

Brother Lawrence may claim that his spiritual experiences are evidences of the result of the Grace of God, but others will claim that they are the result of his own efforts, of which the larger part is hidden behind the screen of time in former reincarnations. But the truth is not so limited as either of these views. It unites these two seemingly contradictory claims by putting them in their place and time.

16

Many fixations created in the past have to be removed before we can truly live in the present. This is Long Path work.

17

The attempt to liberate self by self must prove in the end to be a vicious circle, an experiment in futility. The Unconditioned cannot be brought by finite man into his grasp. It must come of Itself and bring *him* within Its Grace. Yet unless the attempt is made, unless the Long Path is travelled, the aspirant is little likely to be sufficiently equipped to succeed with the Short Path.

18

Miguel de Molinos: "It is useless to trust in the interior way of contemplation if the obstacles which hinder their progress and spiritual blight be not removed from the path of those souls that are called." In other words, the Long Path work must clear a way for the Short Path work.

19

The way to the goal does not lie through a cleansing of the ego alone: it lies also through a desertion of it. The first way is necessary only because it helps to make the second one possible.

20

He is to keep the thought of the goal itself continually before him, to give the mental consciousness as its principal occupation a meditation on the Overself. This is the basis of Short Path work and this is why, before he can hope to succeed, he must first have set himself the Long Path task of gaining some control over his thoughts.

21

If the Grace of the Overself is to take hold of the man, no part of his ego ought to offer resistance. This is why a preparation for the event is needed, a process of taking out of him those things which are certain to instigate such resistance. In other words, the activity of the Long Path is necessary to the successful treading of the Short Path.

22

The Long Path is an attempt to remove those things which obscure his inner vision and obstruct his spiritual inspiration. It is a training which unites impulse and goodness into a single fused thing.

23

The work of the Long Path is intended to set his wings free for the breathtaking flights and exalted experiences of the Short one. One by one he upheaves and throws aside the weaknesses which hold him down to the ground.

24

Ordinarily and properly, the Long Path is the first stage and roughly equivalent to the purifying of religious mystics. The Short Path is the second and more advanced stage, and equivalent to their growing or illuminating.

25

It seems pathetic to see these Long Path strugglers who want, and try so desperately, to find what, in the history of human effort, only a few have ever found. But it is not so pathetic after all if we remember that Nature will soon or late introduce them to the joyous discovery of the Short Path.

26

The "purification" which he is to seek through the Long Path is not the narrow limited and intolerant kind which too often is called by this name. It is not at all merely a harsh denial of the sexual instinct. It is a cleansing of consciousness, of his thought-life, his emotional life, and even of his bodily condition. Its aim is to prepare his consciousness so that it can receive the truth without deflecting or warping or blocking it. Inevitably the most important work and always the most difficult work along this line will be the elimination of the ego's tyranny.

27

The Long Path is needed because it leads to a measure of release from egoism and animalism. But it does not directly lead to the discovery of the Overself, its truth and reality. That is the Short Path's work.

28

All the exact instructions and precise techniques to be found in different parts of the world will be of no avail in the end to reach enlightenment, although they may well be useful to make him ready to receive enlightenment.

29

The Long Path is likely to come first in a man's spiritual career, with the bizarre result that he is required to become much more aware of what is going on within himself—his thoughts, feelings, and character—and then, with entry on the Short Path, to become much less aware of it, even to the point of ignoring it.

30

It needs some strength to deflect the onset of negative moods and to refuse to sit in darkness. It needs some patience to sit quietly waiting until one feels an entry into the presence of the Source of one's being. Only a few are born with these qualities ready-made. Others must attain them slowly by passing through stages of training and self-discipline.

31

The Long Path is the preliminary one, the Short Path is the ultimate one. Those who would skip the first because it is hard and unattractive and take only to the second because it seems quick and joyous invite failure—unless they possess rare genius.

32

Although the Short Path is quicker to travel than the Long one, the requisite personal equipment must be developed first on the Long Path, or the traveller will be bogged down by the ego which he vainly and delusively imagines away.

33

The attempt to ignore order of development in the Quest, to leap from the lowest to the highest stages, to miss all the intervening ones, is an attempt to get something for nothing. It cannot succeed. For the influx of Spirit needs a chalice clean enough to be fit for it, large enough to hold it. What would happen if the influx were poured into a dirty, cracked, tiny, and weak vessel?

34

If they approach Truth with a mind befogged by an active lower nature, how can they expect to arrive at its clear perception? This is why the work of the Long Path cannot be wholly substituted for by the work of the Short one.

35

Another reason for the need of the Long Path's preparatory work is that the mind, nerves, emotions, and body of the man shall be gradually made capable of sustaining the influx of the Solar Force, or Spirit-Energy.

36

Every negative thought and base desire is an obstacle to the attainment of the higher consciousness. This is why the Long Path's work is needed, for it is intended to remove all such obstacles. How can one invite that Consciousness to dwell in a body enslaved by lusts, or in a mind darkened by hates?

37

It is as needful to wait until the period of preparatory exertions is over as it is for life to germinate and put forth its green plant.

38

Until he enters the Short Path it cannot be said that Grace is more than partially possible. Until he has lifted himself by his own endeavours to some extent above the animality with which he struggles on the Long Path and into the calmness which is necessary to the practice of the Short one, he has hardly earned the reward of Grace in its fullness or frequency.

39

Mystical writers often quote the famous passage from Brother Lawrence about the noise and clutter of his work in the kitchen not disturbing his feeling of God's presence, but they rarely note that he worked hard for ten years at self-training before he was able to attain this blessed goal.

40

The way of the Long Path is an effort to abstract him from the bonds of physical appetite and passion which prevent his free thought and balanced feeling. It is an effort of disentanglement. But by its very nature this is only a negative attainment. It must be followed by a positive one. And the latter must enable the man to fulfil life's higher purpose in the midst of human worldly activity, while yet enabling him to keep the freedom he has won through self-discipline. Therein lies the superiority of the Short Path.

41

When he comes to recognize that the attractive promises of these Short Path cults cannot be realized by the dilettantes who eagerly pounce upon them, nor by those who lack strength and shirk discipline, he will be ready for this Path.

42

At first he learns that he is personally responsible for his thoughts and actions, for their results in himself and outside it in his destiny. Then if he accepts this truth and in the Long Path works upon it, he is led to the discovery of the Short Path and that he is God's responsibility.

43

It is true that he is conditioned in several ways and that the attempt to free himself from them by introducing other, and usually opposing, ways merely creates new bindings, new conditions. But to leave the statement there—as Krishnamurti does, and as Jean Klein tries to do—is misleading because it is a half-truth. These teachers regard yoga, for instance, as such a form of conditioning; yet Atmananda, who appears to be at least one source of Klein's inspiration, himself found that yoga was a *preparation* for Advaitic truth. In short, there *is* a progression among conditions; they are not developed in a circle but in a spiral.

44

Seekers do not come under the power of Grace until they have done, to a sufficient extent, what the Long Path requires from them. Then only are they likely to be ready for the Short Path, and to benefit by the Grace associated with it.

45

Entrance into the Short Path presupposes experience on the Long one. How can anyone go beyond the latter before he has travelled some distance along it? Are not the efforts he makes while on it merely preparing him for the effortless experiences of the Short Path?

46

What is the purpose of this Long Path inner work upon himself? It is to clear a way for the inflow of grace, even to the most hidden parts of his character.

47

When he finds that he is not getting either expected or promised results, he becomes disturbed. But his years have not really been wasted. They have prepared him for this next phase to come.

48

Although the Long Path does not directly lead to Enlightenment, it reduces obstacles, prepares the seeker, and opens his way for entry to the Short Path, which in turn can subsequently lead to enlightenment.

49

Not many are intuitive enough, developed enough, knowledgeable enough, and strong enough to take to the Short Path without previous preparation through the Long Path's disciplines.

50

The cleansing disciplines of the Long Path prepare and equip him to practise the blessing meditations of the Short one.

51

If he follows the Long Path, its goal will be reached little by little, slowly, and even then the transfer to the Short Path will have to be made. He will then be well-prepared, ready, and ably capable of meeting its demands to a measurable extent. The lightning-flash may come at any moment on this higher level.

Making the transition

52

He stands athwart the door and blocks it from opening to the gentle pressure of the very Grace which can bring him the help for which he calls out. Less preoccupation with his own ego and more with the Overself is what he really needs. This is the same as saying that the Long Path work now needs balancing with Short Path work.

53

If the end of the Long Path is spiritual stagnation, this is not to be taken to mean that the Long Path is not worth entering, nor that its efforts are valueless and so much time wasted. That would be an error. This so-called stagnation is really the "dark night of the soul," in Spanish Saint John of the Cross' phrase. It makes the man ready to receive grace.

54

His quest *for* God has reached its terminus but his quest *in* God will now start its course. Henceforth his life, experience, and consciousness are wrapped in mystery.

55

The transition from the Long to the Short Path is really a normal experience, even though to each person it seems like a major discovery.

56

The deliberately made efforts of the Long Path must in the end give place to letting the Overself-sun shine upon the whole being, blotting out dark negative places by its natural radiance. The first path gave needed preparation for the second one but cannot supplant it.

57

He must be willing to discard the familiar attitudes developed on the Long Path. There will be an inner struggle.

58

The changeover to the Short Path does not entirely cancel out his Long Path work but affects it in three ways. First, it reduces the labours and disciplines involved. Second, the reduced work is done without anxiety and without tension. Third, it frees him from the excessive sense of self-responsibility for his inner and outer life—that is, from excessive ego-depending.

59

He must call in a new power, and a higher power—Grace. He needs its help. For the ego will not willingly give up its sovereignty, however much it may become preoccupied with spiritual questions and even spiritual growth.

60

The secrets which the stillness has to tell him are not to be discovered through any activity of the fussy and pretentious personal ego. It cannot bring him even to one of them, so it had better stop all its activities for truth-getting on the Long Path and take to the Short Path.

61

The Ideal is there to help them, both to travel the Long Path and to make the transition in the Short one, where Grace will take over what they have started.

62

What were hitherto his virtues now become his vices.

63

The laborious, sometimes desperate self-discipline of the Long Path relaxes or even stops altogether. The effortless, sometimes ecstatic self-surrender to grace through faith, love, humility, and remembrance replaces it.

64

Whatever you do to work upon the ego, whether you remove this weakness or improve that faculty, it will always be ego and your consciousness will always remain within its tightly closed circle. In the time you give to such work you could be occupying yourself with thought of the non-ego, the Overself, and dwelling in this thought until the sunshine behind it bursts through and you bask in the glory.

65

If he is really done with worrying about the state of the ego, he will not visit it every day to keep a finger on its pulse.

66

He feels that a newer and other self is coming to birth.

67

To mourn over the past's supposed errors for too long a time, to indulge in self-pitying remorse for the remainder of one's life, is another trick of the ego and merely strengthens it. Better take to the Short Path!

68

The Long Path developed in him through yoga-meditation the capacity to find the inner Stillness. The Short Path added to it (1) the knowledge that the Stillness is himself, and (2) the practice of continuing remembrance to *be* the Stillness.

69

The Long-Pather who broods morbidly over his own vileness, who strains himself unnecessarily to achieve what the Overself does not ask him to achieve, needs to be instructed on the place and meaning of the Short Path.

70

The average spiritual aspirant is unduly self-centered. This is because he is so preoccupied with his own development, his own self-correction, and his own spiritual needs that he tends to forget a vitally important truth. This is that the last battle to be fought on the Quest—the battle which brings the ego finally and fully under the Overself's rule—is reflected to a lesser extent in the earlier battles of the Quest. This battle cannot possibly be won by the aspirant himself for the very good and sufficient reason that the ego is not willing to commit suicide, or to put it in another way, is unable to lift itself onto a plane of non-existence. Final victory can only come by the bestowal of Grace from the Overself, which alone can effect this seeming miracle. To attract this Grace the seeker needs to turn away from his self-centeredness to what is its utter opposite—preoccupation with the Overself. He is to think of the Divine alone, of the infinitude and eternity of the Higher Power, and to forget all about his personal growth for a while.

71

The emotional eagerness which marked his Long Path aspirations, the attempts to perfect himself, diminish gradually until he becomes almost indifferent to them.

72

If he keeps on fixing his attention upon fighting the wandering characteristic of his thoughts, he may find after many attempts that the task seems impossible. Why is this? It is because at the same time he is limiting himself to attention upon the ego. Let him move in the opposite direction and turn to the Short Path, let the thoughts fix themselves on the Overself, upon Its great stillness, Its serene impersonality. The ego will not and cannot remove itself by itself but by going outside to THAT which is its origin. The thoughts in the end are led into surrender to the power which transcends it and will master it.

73

If the Long Path ends in futility, confusion, and despair for many people, it does not necessarily do so for all people. Some make the transition from it to the Short Path without such suffering.

74

There are two different approaches to the task; both are legitimate, but one belongs to the Long Path and the other to the Short Path. The first is forcibly to control the undesirable feelings and thoughts. The second is to seek their source in the ego and, by understanding it at this deep level, lose interest in them and, turning away, stop continuing to feed them.

75

They are too self-conscious about their work and progress on this quest, their adoption of it and experiences in it. It is only when they leave this Long Path for the Short one that their attitude becomes spontaneous, unstudied, natural, their feelings released from ambition, affectation, and egocentricity. They begin to "grow as the flower grows," as Mabel Collins puts it.

76

If their Long Path ends in self-detestation, their Short Path begins in a deeper self-discovery, in a feeling of happy possibilities awaiting them if they could remain faithful to the new attitudes.

77

Let him rejoice at having found the Short Path with its freedoms and at having let go of the Long Path with its difficulties and tensions.

78

What a relief he feels when the strain and tension of the Long Path give place to the sweetness and detachment of the Short one!

79

It is not necessary to go through the struggles and toils of the Long Path after we have travelled it sufficiently far to develop some amount of the qualifications needed for the Short one. We can then desert it and, by Grace, go quickly through the change of outlook, standpoint, and consciousness necessary to travel the Short Path.

80

The same Grace which starts us off on the Quest carries us through to its end. The Short Path phase begins when we awaken to the presence of the Grace's source.

81

It rejects the striving to acquire afresh each individual virtue or quality and replaces it by the striving to effect the great transformation of all the character all at once by direct contact with the divine power.

82

Released from the hard disciplines of the Long Path, following the softer methods of the Short one, he smilingly enjoys the moments of Grace they bring him.

83

The ego with its Long Path efforts can carry the quest just so far. At that point, help from outside must be found. But this help is needed only to reveal the Short Path and open the entrance to it; otherwise attachment, desire, and dependence will again arise, even if on a higher level.

84

It is not easy to start a daring revolt against so much that we held for truth for so many years. To desert the Long Path even when dissatisfied with it calls for courage.

85

The Short Path of recognizing the divine existence here and now, whether or not the ego feels it, is the best path at a certain stage.

86

The sinful conscience, the feeling of guilt, belongs entirely to the Long Path. It vanishes with a few steps on the Short Path.

87

You cannot think two thoughts simultaneously. You cannot practise Advaitic identity with the Overself and with ego *together*. You must choose one or the other.

88

That same relentless determination which brought him so far along this path and gave him so much self-improvement, now becomes a formidable obstruction. It must be forsaken because the ego must surrender itself.

89

Although most seekers turn with relief to the ideas and practices of the Short Path when these are presented to them, others find it most difficult to do so. The thought of abandoning what has filled so many of their years and so much of their aspiration seems more than they can bring themselves to obey. But the old Chinese Ch'an Master Shu-chou reprimanded this attitude in sarcastic words: "There are only two diseases: one is riding an ass to search for an ass; the other is riding an ass and being unwilling to dismount." By this he meant that in the Long Path work the ego's search could only end in the ego itself, that the mind would only get another thought. "You yourself are the ass," he added. "Why do you ride on it? If you ride, you cannot cure your disease."

90

Where the Long Path ends and where the Short Path begins is not easily chalked out.

91

There are some aspirants of a morbid temperament who concentrate a morbid attention upon the idea that the eradication of detrimental faults will be a never-ending process, and they become unhappy and unbalanced in consequence. They need a corrective—indeed, two correctives. They will find these in the concept of Grace and the practice of the Short Path.

92

They would like the change to take place dramatically, in a moment of time. "The wind bloweth where it listeth," said Jesus, and Grace comes here or there at an unpredictable hour.

93

Not by his ego's own will can he take hold of this jewel, but only by the Grace substituting that other Consciousness for his ego's.

94

Although in the earlier stages and also in the middle stages of the quest it has to be consciously and deliberately followed, in the later, the more advanced stages where the Short Path comes into operation, the seeker must begin to forget himself and his efforts, must not come between the goal and its pursuits, must identify himself with the Overself by giving himself wholly to the idea of manifesting it in his inner and outer life. Therefore, he must be free of the kind of self-consciousness which makes him aware that he is a Quester. On the contrary, he has to make spirituality a natural thing, free from self-consciousness.

95

The man who seeks his soul or his God or his truth with such thirst, and for so long, could find it if he stops, waits patiently, looks deeply within, and lets it appear of its own accord. For he, the seeker, *is its concern.*

96

The Intermediate Path is a transition from the Long to the Short one. It consists in identifying oneself mentally with the higher self. This is immeasurably farther than identification with the ego but it is still tainted with a kind of self-centeredness. That is revealed when the pilgrim travels to the Short Path, where he seeks no identification of any sort whatsoever, bestows no more attention upon the "I," but thinks only of the higher self as it is in itself and not about its relationship with him.

97

Even if he has his moral and psychological successes on the Long Path they may, just because they are successes, inflate his ego with gratification and pride. Only when he changes his attitude and ascribes them to the Overself and regards them as defeats for himself can this not happen. He will then have transferred from the Long Path to the Short Path.

98

The very aspiration which followed attraction to the Overself may then change its colour by becoming an obstacle on his Way.

99

A time may come when his own personality is distasteful to him, when he begins to dislike his own traits of instinctive negative reaction and innate negative character. This is naturally understandable on the Long Path, but it may be minimized on the Short one.

100

To become their ruler you may fight desires. This is the harder way. Or you may forget them. This is the easier way. To follow it you must practise remembering the Overself *constantly*.

101

A great humility comes into him when at long last he steps aside from his ego sufficiently to allow the perception that it is not in his own power to enter the ultimate Enlightenment. Grace is the arbiter.

102

From the Long Path's merciless denigration of his own character he will swing to the Short Path's generous toleration of it.

103

The feeling of urgency in his spiritual yearnings has gone, the feeling of patient trustful acceptance has replaced it.

104

From now on he accepts himself as he is without tormenting himself because of what he is not.

105

The Short Path requires him to fall into amnesia about his spiritual past. The attempt to produce a perfect being and an impeccable character need not trouble him any farther.

106

This does not mean that the endeavours to nullify the bad should be totally abandoned, or abated. But they should be put in their place.

107

What a relief he experiences when he need no longer look at himself with the emotion of guilt. He feels set free.

108

But while philosophy includes both paths, the aspirant's individual need will indicate on which one the emphasis should be laid and when it should be transferred to the other path.

109

The Long Path strivings are lesser ones and must, at the due time, be absorbed in the Short Path's larger ones.

110

But even when the psychological requirements are fulfilled, the negative emotions cast out, and the positive thoughts cultivated, the inner self will not come to the surface of its own accord. A special kind of effort is still

needed. It will not be concerned with purgative measures but with trans-
mutative ones. It is at this point too that the help and grace of a Master is
likely to be of most value.

111

When he finds that the fight within, and against, himself is unending he
becomes either disheartened or illumined. That is to say, he abandons the
Long Path and the Quest together, under the delusion that the limit of the
one is also the limit of the other, or he abandons the Long Path and takes
to the Short Path.

112

The end of the Long Path is frustration. This may be an emotionally
disappointing blessing, since it forces the man to turn eventually to the
Short Path, whose end is fulfilment.

113

When this feeling of stagnation becomes chronic, it produces a sense of
frustrated helplessness. If any progress is to come, it must come through
an influence beyond the person himself, he thinks. This is an attempt to
throw responsibility elsewhere, to a deliverer or guru who will take over
and carry him to the goal. But there is another way open to him, and that
is to establish a totally new pattern from the one which he followed in the
past. This is the opportunity and call to enter the Short Path.

114

The average man is the victim of his own past, the slave of his personal
history. He is conditioned by its thinking, molded by its disciplines, and
dominated by its traditions. Its influence fades all too slowly. This is why
the transition from the Long to the Short Path is so often the consequence
of some unusual upheaval or some mesmeric contact.

115

It is not a question of choice between the two paths. The beginner can
hardly comprehend what the Short Path means, let alone practise it. So
perforce he must take to the Long one. But the intermediate, weary of its
toils and defeats, turns with relief to the other path, for which his studies
and experiences have now prepared him.

116

The end of the Long Path is signaled also by the sudden appeal which
the Short Path now makes to the aspirant. It tells him that he has quested
quite enough in the old way, which is the long way, the excessive way, so
that he has become obsessed by it. It tells him that he is now standing in
his own light, that he must get out of the way, and that this can be done
only by entering on the Short Path, which is preoccupied not with the

personal self and its advancement or purification or elevation, but with the Overself.

117

As he becomes aware of the slavery and illusion which ruled his past life, the struggle to escape from them leads to a psychic tension, ever increasing. This result may be unpleasant but it necessarily follows when an aggressive effort of the will is opposed to old habits of instinct, thought, and conduct. The proper time for starting the Short Path is indicated when these strains and tensions created by the Long one have been borne for so long a period that, unless they culminate in the relief offered by the Short Path, they can no longer be endured.

118

He comes in the end to recognize his ineffectiveness and incapacity, to admit that he cannot rightly hope to succeed on the quest by his own efforts or by his own qualities. This may make him unhappy but it also offers the opportunity to make himself truly humble.

119

The end of all his efforts on the Long Path will be the discovery that although the ego can be refined, thinned, and disciplined, it will still remain highly rarefied and extremely subtle. The disciplining of the self can go on and on and on. There will be no end to it. For the ego will always be able to find ways to keep the aspirant busy in self-improvement, thus blinding him to the fact that the self is still there behind all his improvements. For why should the ego kill itself? Yet the enlightenment which is the goal he strives to reach can never be obtained unless the ego ceases to bar the way to it. At this discovery he will have no alternative to, and will be quite ready for, the Short Path.

120

Most people believe such ideals are not realizable; but given enough time to develop they will be. That is, a fraction of seekers become ready for the Short Path when time, better understood, is less oppressive.

121

The Long Path man obstinately expects too much from himself until, late in the day, reality compels him to cease to do so.

122

"This is how I am." Once this acceptant attitude is reached, he is ready to turn to the Short Path.

123

Once he realizes that he cannot face two ways simultaneously, he will force himself to make a choice between them. The ego or the Overself?

124

Where is the aspirant who has the feeling that he is thinking what he should at all times or behaving well in all situations? On the contrary, even the sincere, wholehearted aspirant feels his unworthiness from time to time or becomes sad at his defects or discouraged by the seeming impossibility of attaining what the masters did, until he is inclined to abandon the Quest altogether. It is at such a moment that the appeal of one of the Short Paths may be experienced most strongly, as offering to put the goal within his reach at last.

125

Wearied of the long aspiration, the seemingly forlorn hope, they leave the Quest. Yet this is the very time to enter the Short Path.

126

Hopkins, the Jesuit priest-poet, abandoned meditation because of constantly recurring moods of self-disgust and hopelessness. This sounds exactly like the point where Long Path work should be brought to an end, being replaced by Short Path work.

127

This recognition that the Overself is constantly present with him heartens the proficient seeker but in the end frustrates the beginner. It is at this point that he is getting ready, quite unwittingly, to leave the Long Path.

128

Self-effort is not vain, not futile, yet there is a point where it must yield to grace, cease its labours, surrender its self-management.

129

If the Long Path disciplines increase his anxieties and frustrations to an insupportable point, it is probably an indication that he needs a shift to the Short Path—with its effort to shift identity into the Overself and establish him there.

130

Through humiliation and despair, failure and mistakes, the ego may be crushed to the ground. But the aftermath of this apparently hopeless situation may be the end of the Long Path, with the subsequent transfer to the Short Path, with its new hope, pardon, and peace.

131

The Long Path runs from the start of his quest to, possibly, an advanced stage, depending on the particular person's inner history. When he is getting ready for the Short Path, one sign may appear as a falling away from the Long Path. But here the possibility of error exists. The beginner may react from his early endeavours by getting tired of practice, discipline, or failures. He too may fall away, but for negative reasons.

132

He begins to see that in attempting to purify himself and to perfect himself he is attempting a tremendous task. The more he progresses, the more he sees how weak and sinful his character still is. The time comes when he can no longer receive in mute resigned patience the Oriental Master's teaching to practise patience equal to that required to empty an ocean with a spoon. It is at such a time that he may be ready to try the Short Path.

133

The Short Path depends on naturalness and spontaneity—quite the opposite of the Long Path's discipline and effort. The individual who turns aside from the latter at the right moment does so not because he spurns them or denies them or rejects them but because they do not serve him now.

134

The moment for departure from the Long Path is signaled by the full realization that all that he has really gained from practising its disciplines is only the practice itself, not the newer consciousness to which they were supposed to lead him.

135

The man on the Long Path reaches a point where he tends to overdo its requirements or to do them in an unbalanced way. He is then too self-conscious, too much ridden by guilt, oscillating between indulgence and remorse. Only when his efforts seem to be futile and his mind to be baffled, only when he gives up in exhaustion does he give up the tension which causes it. Then, relaxed, spontaneity released, the gate is at last open for grace to enter. In its light he may see that in one sense he had been running around in circles because he had been running around inside his own ego.

136

A point is reached on the Long Path when its regimens and disciplines, its exercises and vigilances, become irritating and depressing. They will then fail to accomplish their proper effects, will even be obstructive and may even be harmful. This is the time to turn away to the Short Path.

137

When a man gives up trying to make himself better because he feels that it is no use doing so, he has reached the right point to seek grace through the Short Path.

138

A man may take to the Short Path at any stage of his progress on the Long Path.

139

A man cannot go on constantly disapproving of himself without becoming morbid, sick, or defeatist. At some point, and at certain intervals, he must check this process of denigration by introducing an opposing one, by affirming his true identity, the Overself.

140

When he has reached this stage he will begin to understand that his further spiritual progress does not impose special acts such as disciplinary regimes and meditation exercises—excellent and necessary though these were in their place as preparatory work—but requires him simply to stand aside and be an observing witness of life, including his own life.

141

The positive value of setting up an ideal to work for is not without its limitations and perils. If the saving fact of a sane balance is not also present, or if the time is opportune for a turning away from the Long to the Short Path, then the distance between the ideal and the actual becomes filled with tensions and conflicts, with the anxieties and frustrations bred from them.

142

When his interest in himself becomes excessive and unhealthy, it is time to turn his back on himself. In the new liberty of the Short Path, no longer trembling between miserable awareness of his faults and overeager desire for spiritual flights, he can find peace, perhaps even joy.

143

To drop away from the Long Path at the proper time is not at all the same as relapse, if this is followed by entry on the Short Path. The more unrelaxingly and unremittingly he pursued it, the more will he react against it.

144

The processes and procedures of the Long Path require time. But the Overself is outside of time. To identify yourself with them is to shut yourself out from it. It is consequently needful when a certain point is reached—either in experience or in preparation or in understanding—to abandon the Long Path and take to the Short Path, with its emphasis on living in the Eternal Now.

145

When the inner call comes, as it will at the proper time, he need not have any hesitations about leaving the Long Path. No sentiment of loyalty need then be allowed to keep him captive to it. But changeover must not be effected too soon, or new weaknesses will develop, nor too late, or the chance for timely help will be missed.

146

When the likelihood of entering the superior consciousness seems no longer possible, when this hope which started and stayed them on the Long Path is finally thrown aside, then there is a natural reaction into feelings of resignation, frustration, cynicism, or despair, according to the personal disposition.

147

When he recognizes how abortive his aspirations now seem, how baffled his hopes, he reaches the critical point.

148

However tirelessly and relentlessly he pursues the Long Path, he may come one day to the tragic discovery that the ideal it proposes to him embodies a humanly impossible perfection. With that discovery he will fall into a numb inertness, a pathetic and hopeless state which could even bring his overwrought mind not far from a breakdown. He may feel alone and deserted. He may enter into the dark night of the soul, as some mystics name it. His ego will feel crushed. He will not know what to do, nor even have the strength of will to do anything more. At this point he must wait . . . out of bleakness and weakness there will presently come a guidance, bidding him respond affirmatively to a suggestion, a book, or a teacher directing him toward what is really his first step on the Short Path.

149

The advocates of the Short Path teach that with its entry, all necessity for the toils processes and disciplines of the Long one ceases. They are right. But they are rarely right when it comes to applying this statement to individual cases. For then it is nearly always applied prematurely. The results are then disastrous at most, disappointing at least.

150

When he has gone around the circle of his failings and wrong-doings a sufficient number of times, let him consider seriously whether the Short Path should not now be conjoined with, or replace altogether, the Long one.

151

When the Quest begins to mean so much to him that other things mean less, he is ready for its more advanced phase.

152

When it gets to the point that he regards his common faults as monstrous sins, it is time to turn to the Short Path. When he is so worried about the virtues he does not have that he forgets those which he does have, it is time to turn to the Short Path.

153

When too long a time is spent on the Long Path with too slow a progress, the urge arises to find another way. It is then that the Short Path becomes appropriate.

154

There is no doubt that many of those who attempt meditation at first find nothing for their labours even though at times they seem to be on the *verge* of finding something. It does not get realized. When after a sufficiently long period the seeming lack of success turns the effort into a bore, two things are indicated. A point has been reached where a greater patience is needed and the man must learn to go on waiting. Short periods without practice are then permissible if the strain is too much. The other indication is that the Short Path must be brought in or may even replace the work of meditation for the time being. But all this is subject to the qualification that the meditation is correctly conducted so that the method must be checked, the process must be understood and its purpose clarified.

155

If a point is reached when he becomes uneasy about his inner situation, its seeming lack of progress in the present and unfavourable prospects in the future, it may be a signal to stress the Short Path work.

156

The failure to recognize that there is a Short Path as the advanced sequel to the Long Path, as well as the necessary complement to it, is responsible for confusions, misunderstandings, and even errors.

157

When preoccupation with the disciplines and regimes, the restrictions and curbs prescribed on the Long Path becomes so excessive as to be morbid, or becomes too neglectful of the freedom, the satisfaction, and the happiness-bringing attitudes which truth should elicit, it is time to bring them to an end. They need to be replaced by the opposing practices of the Short Path—fears by faith, morbidity by joy, intolerances by indifference.

158

Even those who are satisfied to continue permanently the Long Path's preparatory disciplines will one day find an inner impulse rising spontaneously within themselves and leading them to the Short Path.

159

He reaches a point when he feels that he must rebel against the work demanded of him by the quest, and later—as a further consequence, and in some bitterness—against the very notion of the quest itself. This is simply a misunderstanding of his real position. All that he has to do is to turn around and enter the Short Path.

160

A time comes when he no longer feels the need for a technique but rather for freedom from all techniques.

161

When he reaches the stage of the Long Path where there is only stress upon his shortcomings, where negative traits are the only ones seen, there is needed a less ego-centered attitude. Too much obscures the higher goal he seeks.

162

When the Long Path work has been done to the point that it bores, depresses, or satiates him, admission must be made that he had better leave it for a while. Here is a turning point where the Short Path must be entered both for relief and for a fresh outlook.

163

All this willed striving for a condition of being which seems so far beyond, will reach its terminus at this point. From now on he admits the Overself into the game. He allows for its existence.

164

Another sign that the time may have come for a change to the Short Path is when meditation no longer yields satisfying results but becomes irksome and difficult.

165

When their Long Path has become a thing without cheer and without grace, it is time for them to turn toward the Short Path.

166

When a man has come to the end of his tether, dry of all hope for accomplishment of his aim by self-effort, he is ripe for the Grace-invoking effort of the Short Path.

167

The Long Pather who becomes overloaded with the seriousness with which he takes it, is preparing the inevitable reaction.

168

If the admission that he makes mistakes and has weaknesses may become a torment on the Long Path, the indifference to them may become one of the signs that he has moved to the Short Path.

169

If you are getting no result, no change in external situation, it is because you are not *practising*. You are dependent upon the feeble little ego. Cultivate the idea incessantly that the Overself *provides* and put yourself in dependence on its higher power. But do not attempt this before you have studied and appropriated the lessons of your existing circumstances.

5

BALANCING THE PATHS

Their contrast and comparison

The Long Path is devoted to clearing away the obstructions in man's nature and to attacking the errors in his character. The Short Path is devoted to affirmatives, to the God-power as essence and in manifestation. It is mystical. It shows how the individual can come into harmonious relation with the Overself and the World-Idea. The first path shows seekers how to think rightly; the second gives power to those thoughts.(P)

2

Most people who start the short path have usually had a glimpse of the Overself, because otherwise they find it too difficult to understand what the short path is about. The long path, through its studies and practices, is the period of preparation for the advanced quest. It is called the long path because there is much work to be done on it and much development of character and emotions to go through. After some measure of this preparation the aspirants enter the short path to complete this work. This takes a comparatively much shorter time and, as it has the possibility of yielding the full self-enlightenment at any moment, it ends suddenly. What they are trying to do on the long path continues by itself once they have entered fully on the short path. On the long path they are concerned with the personal ego and as a result give the negative thoughts their attention. On the short path they refuse to accept these negatives and instead look to the Overself. Thus the struggles will disappear. This change of attitude is called "voiding" them. The moment such negative ideas and feelings appear, then instead of using the long path method of concentrating on the opposite kind of thought, such as calmness instead of anger, the short path way simply drops the negative idea into the Void, the Nothingness, and forgets it. Now such a change can only be brought about by doing it quickly and firmly and turning to the Overself. Constant remembrance of the Overself has to be done all the way through the short path. The long path works on the ego; but the short path uses the result of that work, which prepared them to come into communion with the Overself and become receptive to its presence, which includes its grace. In order to understand the short path, it might be helpful to compare it to the long path which consists of a series of exercises and efforts which gradually develops concentration and character and knowledge. But the long path does not lead to the goal. On the long path you often measure your own progress. It is an endless path because there will always be new circumstances which bring new temptations and trials and confront the aspirant with new challenges. No matter how spiritual the ego becomes it does not enter the whitest light, but remains in the greyish light. On the long path you must deal with the urges of interference arising from the lower self and the negativity which enters from the surrounding environment. But the efforts on the long path will at last invoke the grace, which opens the perspective of the short path.

The short path is not an exercise but an inner standpoint to invoke, a state of consciousness where one comes closer or finds peace in the Overself. There are, however, two exercises which can be of help to lead to the short path, but they have quite a different character than the exercises on the long path. The short path takes less time because the aspirant turns around and faces the goal directly. The short path means that you begin to try to remember to live in the rarefied atmosphere of the Overself instead of worrying about the ego and measuring its spiritual development. You learn to trust more and more in the Higher Power. On the short path you ignore negativity and turn around 180 degrees, from the ego to the Overself. The visitations of the Overself are heralded through devotional feeling, but also through intuitive thought and action. Often the two paths can be treaded simultaneously, but not necessarily equally.

Often the aspirant is not ready to start these two exercises until after one or several glimpses of the Overself.

The "remembrance exercise" consists of trying to recall the glimpse of the Overself, not only during the set meditation periods but also in each moment during the whole working span of the day—in the same way as a mother who has lost her child can not let go of the thought of it no matter what she is doing outwardly, or as a lover who constantly holds the vivid image of the beloved in the back of his mind. In a similar way, you keep the memory of the Overself alive during this exercise and let it shine in the background while you go about your daily work. But the spirit of the exercise is not to be lost. It must not be mechanical and cold. The time may come later when the remembrance will cease as a consciously and deliberately willed exercise and pass by itself into a state which will be maintained without the help of the ego's will.

The remembrance is a necessary preparation for the second exercise, in which you try to obtain an immediate identification with the Overself. Just as an actor identifies with the role he plays on the stage, you act *think* and live during the daily life "as if" *you* were the Overself. This exercise is not merely intellectual but also includes feeling and intuitive action. It is an act of creative imagination in which by turning directly to playing the part of the Overself you make it possible for its grace to come more and more into your life.

3

The Long Path gives him the chance to destroy the mental and emotional effects of the ego's operation: the Short Path, to destroy the ego itself.

4

Whereas the aspirant on the Long Path believes that his nature is rooted in evil, the one on the Short Path believes that underneath the evil, his roots extend still deeper into goodness, God.

5

The demerits which the Long Path seeks to extirpate are small faults by contrast to the great sin of the ego which the Short Path seeks to cancel.

6

On the Long Path the man is preoccupied with techniques to be practised and disciplines to be undergone. On the Short Path he is preoccupied with the Overself, with the study of its meaning, the remembrance of its presence, and the reflection upon its nature and attributes.

7

The essential features of the Long Path are its concern with moral effort and its emphasis on character building; its injunctions to pray and meditate; its insistence on the constant striving for self-mastery through physical, emotional, and mental disciplines. The essential feature of the Short Path is its quest of the flash of enlightenment through intuitive feeling and metaphysical thinking. Some believe, and would be satisfied with, this flash to be brief. Others hope for its permanent abidance.

8

The Long Path is based on the beliefs of ordinary living, which start from the imagined reality of the person and therefore start with a fiction. The Short Path rejects this from the beginning and seeks to penetrate without delay to the unchanging and unchangeable Essence.

9

The difference in attitude and teaching between these two schools of thought is tremendous. One says that nothing else is needed than the finding of the real Self, for that will automatically wash out all faults and shortcomings. The other says that only by eliminating those faults and shortcomings can the real Self be found. Zen Buddhism and Ramana Maharshi belong to the first school, and Martinus to the second one.

10

Too much nonsense has been taught, written, and spoken in religious circles about the nature of man. One faction proclaims it to be originally sinful and unalterably evil. The only way to be "saved" from it is to accept the services of religion. Another faction, with a small following, asserts it to be originally divine and fixedly pure. Salvation is not needed, only recognition.

11

Saint Teresa seems to deny the possibility of reconciling the two ways of life when she writes, "To bring soul and body into agreement, walking according to justice and clinging to virtue, is the pace of a hen—it will never bring us freedom of the spirit."

12

The Long Path of earthly-animal man pursues and tries to deal with negative characteristics. The Short Path of higher developed man turns him towards a *repeated* confrontation with Overself; it deals with *positive* attributes and tries to identify with Overself.

13

The Long Path is concerned with relative matters, but the Short one is concerned with the Absolute alone.

14

The application of ethical teachings to the analytic study of experience is correct only for the Long Path. Since the Short Path teaches that there is no finite ego, there is no one to apply those teachings! Consequently there is no one to learn lessons from suffering and no one to commit the sins which create suffering.

15

The Short Path votaries ambitiously wish to soar too high; the Long Path adherents are content to advance little by little.

16

A contemporary guru told me that both sudden attainment and the long-time path theories are correct, but the former is rare in practice.

17

All rules for regulating social conduct and shaping moral character fulfil a proper purpose in making good men. But they do not directly lead to the discovery of the ego's unreality. Therefore they do not belong to the Short Path.

18

The Long Path is chiefly occupied with second stage work, with concentration and meditation, whereas the Short Path is chiefly occupied with contemplation.

19

If the Long Path seeks salvation chiefly through the building of character and the concentration of thought, the Short Path seeks it chiefly through worshipful meditation directly on the Overself.

20

Long Path = the ladder-climbing path. Short Path = the one-leap path.

21

In exaggerating the value of the ego's spiritual activity, the votary of the Long Path goes astray; but the votary of the Short Path who minimizes or denies that value altogether is also in error.

22

All that hatred of his sins and that struggle against his imperfections which teachers of the Long Path inculcate, is abandoned when he comes under the teachers of the Short Path.

23

Perhaps a good illustration of their actual relationship is the one given by a plowman's cutting up a field and his later sowing of the field. Plowing here corresponds to the Long Path, dropping the seed in furrows thus prepared to the Short Path.

24

The Long Path creates anxiety, because one wants to make progress and finds it difficult. The Short Path has to counterbalance it, because one then realizes that there is nothing to be attained, that one is already there.

25

The laborious effort and painful discipline of the Long Path bring him to a certain degree of spirituality but the easier, pleasanter, and quicker way of the Short Path brings him to a higher one.

26

To depend upon oneself for the truth may draw one nearer to it or push it farther away. Which result will happen depends upon which path—the Short or Long—we are travelling.

27

The Short Path refuses to give the ego any importance at all whereas the

Long one gives it too much importance. The first attitude looks at all life in the widest possible perspective whereas the second looks at its own life in a self-centered way, even though that self has been extended to include the ego's higher characteristics.

28

The Short Path does not deny anything taught on the Long one. It gives a greater truth.

29

On the Short Path he becomes aware of the fact of forgiveness. He leaves out the constant self-criticism and self-belittling, the painstaking self-improvement practices, of the other Path and begins to take full note of this saving fact.

30

If the immediate purpose of the Long Path is to train, discipline, and prepare the ego, the immediate purpose of the Short Path is to transcend it.

31

The basic idea is that the "lightning flash" simile belongs to the Long Path stage, hence its brevity and fitfulness, whereas "the leap over a deep narrow ravine" is the correct simile for the Short Path. If the seeker succeeds in reaching the other side of the ravine, he will be safely and permanently established in the truth. The ravine cannot be crossed by a series of gradual stages. If he does not succeed, then he merely stays in the darkness where he already was.

32

Although the two Paths are so sharply divided from one another in theory, they not seldom overlap in fact.

33

While the Long Path man is busy worrying about the evil in himself and in the world, the Short Path man is busy smiling at the good in the Overself and in the World-Idea.

34

The danger of becoming too self-centered exists on the Long Path but the danger of deifying the self exists on the Short one.

35

Moments which shame him into the miserable awareness of his shortcomings may appear plentifully on the Long Path but have no likelihood of existence on the Short one.

36

Confucius' injunction to acquire specific virtues is Long Path, whereas

Lao Tzu's counsel to let the mind become empty so that Tao may enter it is Short Path.

37

He can identify himself with ego or with Overself.

38

While he is on the Long Path, his efforts are given to improving the ego and purifying his nature, whereas on the Short one they are given to forgetting the ego and looking beyond his nature.

39

The Long Path meditates on the ego, the Short Path on the Overself. This is the basic difference between them.

40

The Long Path wants to purify and perfect the ego but the Short Path wants to find God. The Long Path deals with the little pieces of a design but the Short Path deals with the pattern itself. The Long Path takes one minor theme after another but the Short one takes up the main underlying theme alone. It is also the difference, as well as distance, between the immediate goal and the ultimate one.

41

The Quest contains two parts. In the first, or Long Path, the aspirant is made into a new person. In the second, or Short Path, he is made into an illumined one.

42

On the Long Path he fought the defects in himself every day and every step of the way. They were not to be tolerated. On the Short Path, he accepts himself because he accepts all life.

43

If the Long Path is occupied with getting rid of unwanted thoughts and feelings, the Short Path is the very opposite, for it occupies itself only with those wanted thoughts and feelings. Thus the move is a transition from negativity to positivity.

44

The Long Path devotee is more interested in his personal progress whereas the Short Path devotee is more interested in impersonal principles. The first identifies himself with a caged-in sect, a limited group, a set of wordy dogmas and authority, whereas the second identifies himself with spacious freedom of attitude and independence of thought. The first is an occultist, the second a mystic.

45

The metaphysical background of the Short Path is the very opposite of the Long Path's. The former finds only Good in the universe and only One Real Existence. The latter finds good and evil in constant conflict and millions of egos whose separateness is very real to him. The former regards the goal as being already and always present, whereas the latter regards it as lying at the end of a long journey over the Quest's route.

46

If on the Long Path he may sometimes despise himself for his weaknesses, on the Short Path he will glorify himself through the identity exercise.

47

The Long Path offers a negative process whose end result is to disidentify the man from his body. The Short Path offers a positive process whose result is to identify him with his Overself.

48

He may take up either of two positions. Both are difficult. The first is to look upon the successive births in a physical body, with their vicissitudes of experience, as wearisome, perhaps even unendurable. He must then cut the series by rooting out the desires beneath, the very craving for physical and personal existence. The second is on an utterly different plane. It is to turn his attention away from his own person altogether and to direct it towards That which is the only Real, the Supreme Source, the Ultimate Being.

49

All spiritual paths—except the Short Path—have elements of artificiality about them.

50

The Short Path rejects duality, acknowledges only identity with Perfect Being, and tries to achieve its aim by recognizing this identity. The Long Path accepts duality and tries to achieve the same aim by mastering the ego.

51

On the Long Path the aspirant is careful to observe the various rules of right behaviour prescribed for him; while on the Short Path he finds that, the Overself being the essence of the Spirit of righteousness, he can achieve all these noble purposes by the single act of uniting consciously with it.

52

The Long Path represents a looking of the eyes upon a horizontal plane, the Short Path represents a turning movement of them in an upward direction.

53

The Short Path looks to the Overself and away from the ego. Its thoughts are directed to knowing the infinite being, not to improving the human being.

54

The Long Path strives to attain a higher state whereas the Short Path establishes its present identity with that state. This it can do only by denying appearances.

55

Should a change of character be diligently pursued as a natural preparation of oneself for enlightenment, and as a special duty to make it possible? Should the enlightenment itself be directly pursued on the supposition that after its achievement there must inevitably follow a repudiation of the old faulty self and a repentance for its acts?

56

LONG PATH/SHORT PATH

You asked about the terms "Long Path" and "Short Path." I don't know who initiated them. They've existed since long ago and are paths to the attainment of spiritual realization. The Long Path means that it takes a long time and also that the path itself is difficult, and being difficult it takes a long time.

The term "Short Path" has the opposite meaning: it's short in time, and the amount of work is short. For example, in teachings like Zen they speak about sudden enlightenment. You can't get any shorter than that.

Of course, when people hear about sudden enlightenment, they want to join, to get enlightenment quickly. The Long Path is not very popular.

"Short Path" does not mean "sudden." It just means "shorter."

The Long Path is simply what is normally associated with yoga: the exercises to practise concentration, attention, relaxation of the body and the mind, ascetic self-discipline, self-control. These are taught in most of the schools; however, there is no set of rules that is studied. Basically it involves getting your thoughts under control and controlling your body, your thoughts, feelings, and will.

This is working on trying to improve yourself inside and your life outside also. The inner and the outer work is part of the Long Path. It's not so easy and may go on for a long time.

After years, people may get a bit tired and abandon the thing altogether, or withdraw and come back later.

Anyway, there comes a time to most—not to all—of those with special karma, those who have gone through the Long Path before, and they are plopped into realization. Examples are Ramana and Wei Wu Wei. They realize what is Truth, what is Real, what is the I. But these are exceptions.

The Long Path will be followed life after life with only some results, nothing dramatic.

But others get rather hopeless without results, and they reach a stage of pessimism or even despair over this impossible goal. This is where they abandon or turn against the quest. At this stage they are very ripe for a transition to the Short Path. (This is the method of the *Koan*, where the seeker is forced to reach a state of despair.) If he gives up in the proper way, he'll get a glimpse powerful enough to turn him around.

Others come to the Short Path in a very simple, natural way. They've done what they could on the Long Path, and they are brought into contact with the Short Path—either by a book, by a dream, or by their guru.

So the Short Path has begun. It makes life considerably pleasanter because you are supposed to make a 180 degree turn, putting your past behind you, looking first on the bright side, the sunny side, of your spiritual life. Very often a glimpse is given which starts you off on the Short Path, and you are shown what to do. You get new exercises, or no exercise at all. You see things which you missed before when you just saw the gloomy side. The exercises may be chosen by the seeker or by the guru. Each must find his own, but all are bright, cheerful, constructive.

But most important of all, now you are in the area of Grace. Now Grace is coming openly to work, and you can see it working, a power higher than your own, higher than your guru.

When you are in the area of Grace, anything can happen—anything—because you are not doing it. A higher power is doing it. It is really being done within you, in the heart, not in the head.

The heart is the centre. Here is the consummation, the union with God. It is here that you feel it most in the beginning. We have to end up in the heart, which means we have to meet Truth, Reality, in the heart with feeling. But it has to be understood in the head. There has to be discrimination between what appears and what is really there.

This Reality is what you are really seeking. What appears seems to be what you are seeking, but it is not.

You can't be a fool to understand the meaning of the world and of life. We must feel and think. The two together fuse in realization.

You both feel and know at the same time what you are, what God is, and what the world is.

Realization cannot be achieved on the Long Path. It cannot. It is a gift, and that means grace, the Short Path.

But you must work for it. There has to be the Long Path and the Short

Path, but you must not make the mistake of thinking you must mechanically stick to the Long Path. You may start with both, work the two together, and it becomes a sort of balance.

If you start the Short Path before you are ready for it, you may become unbalanced. But the Long Path may become dry.

There has to be life, feeling. The amount of Long Path and Short Path depends on the individual. If you don't know, you must ask your guru.

It seems complicated, and in a way it is. But in a way, it is very simple.

In the end you will reject both. There is no Long Path or Short Path. We have constructed them to conform to what we think. Buddha says in the *Dhammapada* that you yourself made up this picture you have of yourself, the picture you think is real. It is made by thought and can be undone by thought.

You could also say there is nothing to the whole thing: simply surrender yourself to God. This is true if you can do it.

We get over-educated, have to rationalize everything and spend time writing books and reading books which are not altogether worthwhile.

—January 1979

57

It is an error to believe that men can separate themselves permanently from normal human life, and themselves exist as if they were ghosts. They may succeed in doing so for a time, a period, sometimes even a lifetime, but in the end the bipolar forces which control development will draw them back. No such separation is desired or sought on the Short Path—as it often is on the Long one—and those who follow it can appreciate physical or cultural possessions and satisfactions. But because they are spiritually mature, there is always inner detachment behind this appreciation.

58

The Long Path is concerned with the human struggle to approach the divine, the Short Path with intuition of the divine presence in the human.

59

The Short Path is content with exercises done for their own sake, not for the sake of the results they bring. In this it is the opposite of the Long Path, which does them for results, and is attached to those results.

60

There is a harsh asceticism at one extreme, and an easy self-indulgence at the other. On the Long Path the seeker wars wearily between the two and lives in a state of unceasing tension. But on the Short Path, the tension ends as he rises above the plane of opposition upon which they exist.

61

The Long Path brings the self to a growing awareness of its own strength, whereas the Short Path brings it to a growing awareness of its own unreality. This higher stage leads inevitably to a turnaboutface, where the energies are directed toward identification with the One Infinite Mind. The more this is done, the more Grace flows by reaction into the Self.

62

Does truth come as a slow growth or as a sudden awakening? Does it take the ant's long path or the bird's swifter one, the second category or the twenty-third?

63

The Long Path follower, with his strenuous concern for self-improvement, his compelling anxiety for self-advancement to fulfil the inner purposes of life, may make life more difficult than it need be and himself become more humourless. The Short Path follower can afford to forget his past struggles, and begin to enjoy life.

64

The Long Path devotee is concerned with learning how to concentrate his thoughts in the practice of meditation, and later even with meditation itself, to some degree, so far as it is an activity among ideas and images. The Short Path devotee is not. He is concerned with direct union with the object of all these efforts, that is, with the Overself. So he substitutes contemplation for meditation, the picture-free, idea-free purity of the mind's original state for the image-and-thought-filled density of its ordinary state.(P)

65

The Long Path is more easily practised while engaged in the world, the Short Path while in retreat from it. The experiences which the vicissitudes of worldly life bring him also develop him, provided he is a Quester. But the lofty themes of his meditations on the Short Path require solitary places and unhurried leisurely periods.(P)

66

It might be said with some truth that the various Long Path processes are based upon the use of willpower whereas the Short Path ones are based upon auto-suggestion. The former employ the conscious mind in directed effort, whereas the latter implant ideas in the subconscious mind while it is in a relaxed state.(P)

67

The Short Path offers a swifter unfolding of the intuitional consciousness. It is not so bound to the limitation of time as the Long Path is. It seeks to identify the man *now* with his higher self.

68

The first path yields an iconoclastic self-*enlightenment* and one as swift as a bird's flight. The second yields a gradual self-*improvement* but one as slow as an ant's crawl.

69

Even the mere feeling of being alive brings content, satisfaction, and reconciliation. How far this is from later stages of the Long Path, with their exaggerated idea of his worthlessness.

70

The spiral path takes you out and round and upward—slowly. The paradox takes you straight to the top into pure truth and thus breaks with the crippling past. It is revolutionary, moving from one extreme (ignorance and illusion) to the other extreme (knowledge and reality, the very heart of the Overself).

71

Whereas the widely varied exercises in meditation of the Long Path evoke mental images and use the creative imagination in most cases, but empty consciousness of them only in some cases, the exercises of the Short Path evoke no images at all.

72

The Long Path votary works from systems, rules, plans, and techniques put down by its guides, but the Short Path votary has no path chalked out for him. He is forever "waiting on the Lord."

73

The Long way is also called the Earth Path. The Short way is also called the Sun Path. This is because the earth is subject to gloomy seasonal changes but the sun never varies in its radiance. If the Long Path is somewhat austere, the Short one is notably joyous.

74

The Long Path cuts a clearing in a night-dark forest whereas the Short one comes out into open noonday-lit space.

75

The Long Path doctrine teaches that man makes his destiny, forms his character, and attains his spiritual goal by his individual efforts. No God and no Grace can help him. Conscience is as prominent here as it is absent on the Short Path.

76

The memory of regrettable judgements, the self-reproach of hindsight have no place on the Short Path.

77

The man who is trying to find his way out of the cave's darkness by retreating backwards represents the Long Path. The man who reverses this attitude and walks straight towards the opening, where he sees a chink of light, represents the Short one.

78

On the Long Path we search for truth, reality, the Overself. That is, we use the ego's forces and faculties. On the Short one we keep still and let truth, reality, the Overself's Grace search for us instead. The ego is then no longer in the picture.

79

Pessimism can only appear on the Long Path, for it must disappear on the Short Path. Here the emphasis is on positive values; the declarations are affirmative ones. The Short Path inculcates joyousness and advocates contentment.

80

Whether the truth grows slowly in his mind or explodes suddenly in his feelings is less important than that it shall be the truth.

81

On the Long Path he identifies himself with the personal ego, even though it be the higher part of the ego, whereas on the Short Path he is only the observer of the ego. This shows up clearly in his attitudes. "What have I to do with my personal past?" he asks himself on the second path. "That belongs to a dead self, which is now rejected and with which I refuse to identify."

82

If the Long Path is too often, too largely an anguished one—because of the self-scrutiny to find the shortcomings in oneself which block the way—then the Short Path is a compensatory one, a joyful quest.

83

The man who enters the Long Path is too often seeking compensation for disappointment, whereas the man who enters the Short one usually is attracted to the joy of fulfilment in the Overself.

84

If the Long Path is based on belief in man's power to attain the Good, the Short Path is based on the contrary belief that all such efforts end in futility and failure. It is then that a higher power than his little ego must be called on. For although the ego is willing to do everything to spiritualize and improve itself, it is stubbornly unwilling to "lose its life" for God's sake.

85

Although it is quite correct to say that we grow through experience, that suffering has valuable lessons, and so on, we must also remember that these are only half-truths. The other half is that by Short Path identifications, we can so totally change our outlook that adverse experience becomes unnecessary.

86

There is no wish in the Short Path man to be better than he is, no desire to improve his character or purify his mind, no sense of being obliged to rectify the distortions brought about by the ego in both thought and feeling.

87

The work of the Long Path consists of the voluntary actions of human effort; but that of Grace, as manifested on the Short Path, has no direct connection with the self-conscious will.

88

The Long Path calls for a continued effort of the will, the Short one for a continued loving attention.

89

The Long Path sets up an attitude of yearning whereas the Short Path considers the Spirit an ever-present fact and consequently there is no need to yearn for it!

90

The Long Path practitioner looks upon illumination as something to be attained in the future when all requirements have been fully met, whereas the Short Path devotee looks upon it as attainable here and now.

91

How like a labyrinth is the seemingly endless, twisting Long Path! How straight and direct is the Short Path!

92

If the Long Path sets responsibility for a man's growth and salvation squarely on his own shoulders, the Short Path sets it on God.

93

On the Long Path his actions follow, or try—however badly—to follow, the rules. They are imitative actions. But on the Short Path he becomes an individual, living from the inside out.

94

The basic idea of the Long Path votary is that the goal must be reached in stages by constant striving through many lives to purify his character and perfect his wisdom. The basic idea of the Short Path is that it can be reached suddenly by constant meditation alone.

95

The outstanding characteristic of the Long Path is a feeling that he has to strive to be a quester. This feeling is absent on the Short Path.

96

It is only on the Long Path that a man seeks so desperately for truth and insight. All that feverish ambition fades away on the Short Path, where he learns to hold himself in peace and patience.

97

Whereas the Long Path brings its results by systematic advance, the Short Path brings them by chancing suddenly on them.

98

The Long Path is arranged in progressive stages, whereas the Short Path is not; it points to direct, immediate, and final enlightenment.

99

Whereas the Long Path man strives for growth, the Short Path man lets it come naturally without the interference of his egoic consciousness.

100

The Long Path is suited to those monks who live in community, in ashrams or monasteries. But the Short Path is suited to the individualist and to the layman-householder living in the world.

101

On the Long Path we analyse the past and study the present so as to learn the basic lessons of the ego's experience. On the Short Path we discard analysis and dispense with study; instead we contemplate the God in us. If the first path brings us unhappy reflections, the second one brings joyous intuitions.

102

The attempt to get rid of the faults and evils in oneself by using the powers of concentration and meditation belongs to the Long Path. But it is still occupied with the ego. For those who have turned to the Short Path, the object of meditation is entirely changed. It is no longer occupied with purifying, improving, or bettering the ego—it is occupied only with the transcendent self, and the thought of the ego, the remembrance of it, is left behind altogether.

103

If he begins with the Short Path he may feel that whatever is accomplished is self-accomplished and thus, subtly, insidiously, his ego will triumphantly reassert, or keep, its supremacy. But if he begins with the Long Path and, after all his efforts, reaches an inconclusive result, the consequent despair may crush his ego and point up his dependence on, and need of, Grace.

104

All the more elementary and religious and occult forms of meditation, including those used on the Long Path—all that lead to what the Hindu yogis call *savikalpa samadhi*—usually have to be passed through; but one ought not to remain with them. The pure philosophic meditation as ultimately sought and reached on the Short Path is to put the attention directly on the Overself and on nothing else.

105

The Long Path is an intermittent fight against the animal nature and the human ego. The Short Path is a continuous quest of the attention for the Overself.

106

The Long Path provides the aspirant with a task unfulfilled, waiting, and sometimes burdensome. The Short Path on the contrary is just something to be understood and lived; it is not a burden but a quiet, peaceful, ever pleasant and ever present consciousness.

107

The Long Path requires the aspirant to work on himself, make various reforms, practise certain exercises, and contribute his own personal efforts in various ways. But the Short Path is less concerned with what he does than with what is done to him. Why? Because it is the path of grace. He is to be passive, to receive.

108

Time, growth, and development, with their circles and spirals, belong to the Long Path. They must not be permitted to usurp the place of the Short Path, with its supremacy at the top of everything.

109

Whereas the Short Path is to be practised at all times and in all places, by continuous remembrance and constant self-recollectedness, the Long Path is to be practised at set times and in special places, by formal exercises.

110

The Long Path man is aware of many or most of his weaknesses and faults, and is tormented by this knowledge. The Short Path man blissfully ignores them or, if he fails to reach this formulated goal, is sure they will fade away and dissolve under the higher self's grace.

111

If the Long Path creates despair about oneself, about the frustration of one's spiritual hopes, the Short Path creates joy about one's close relationship with the Overself and the feeling of its acceptance of one.

112

The Long Path is based on the inevitability of gradualness, the Short Path on the inevitability of suddenness.

113

It is the personal ego which operates the will and tries to bring about the result. This is quite proper and pertinent on the Long Path practice. But when attention is turned away from it to the Short Path, it is no longer the will but the higher power which should be looked to for the result.

114

The work of the Long Path is to loathe and remove the ego's sins; that of the Short Path is to love and receive the Overself's grace.

115

If the Long Path followers tend to have little sense of humour in matters relating to the quest, the Short Path ones tend to have much of it.

116

The achievement by the Long Path method is a forced one, the result of doing some exercise, working on character, following some technique. But it is all an ego-fabricated thing.

The Short Path way leads to the opposite, to a new birth, a new transformed man, salvation itself. But this comes about quite naturally, without the ego's participation, for it comes about by the Overself's grace.

117

The pettiness of ashram favouritism and sectarian politics is no fit atmosphere for the Short Path votary.

118

The follower of the Long Path constantly or intermittently feels the urge to improve himself but the follower of the Short one rests untroubled. He has surrendered himself to the higher power, which necessarily means that he has abandoned or denied every kind of urge in himself too, including the self-improvement urge.

119

The key to holding the Glimpse has been given by Lao Tzu: "When the superior man hears of Tao he does his best to practise it. When the intermediate man hears of Tao, he sometimes keeps it, and sometimes loses it." This means that practising the Short Path is the way to permanent result, for it is the way to win grace.

120

What the Japanese Zenists call "The Sudden Path" and the Tibetan Sages "The Short Path" are closely similar in important points. Both prescribe that the work be done in a joyful attitude. Both teach that the goal *is* also the means. Both claim to offer a rocket flight to Reality.

121

Emerson is an excellent example of the Short Path man.

122

According to Mahayana there are three requirements for the aspirant: (1) moral discipline of greed, anger, and lust; (2) meditation; (3) wisdom—cultivation of intuition and discrimination. The first two constitute, in our division, the Long Path, and the last one is the Short Path.

123

The Rumanian mystic Emilio Carrer, who has a Krishnamurtian outlook and arrived at his own original thought and experience, summed up his views to me in the following words: "(a) In ideas and beliefs form no conclusions and allow no fixations. (b) We have to be conscious of consciousness. (c) In contacts with other persons have no intentions, as this will introduce the ego."

124

Monseigneur Zamet, a spiritual director of the Abbess Mère Angélique of Port Royal, wrote her: "I beseech you to occupy yourself less with virtue than you do, for you are too much attached to it, and more concerned with it than God asks you to be. It will never be by your cares or your attention to yourself that you will be virtuous. It is a gift from on high, for which more than your industry is needed." This wise man also wrote: "If her angers displease her, let her endure them in that they are very excellent for ruining her self-love." He also told her that it was madness to be so much obsessed with one's own unworthiness that one refused grace.

125

Buddha found his way to Enlightenment within six years and with no guru. This is to note that the depth of concentration he used was such that he would not let go until he kept his oath and reached Nirvana. This meant not only determination but also faith that there *was* such a truth as Nirvana.

126

Light on the Path: "It is useless for the disciple to strive by checking himself. The soul must be unfettered, the desires free. But until they are fixed on that state wherein there is neither reward nor punishment, good nor evil, it is in vain that he endeavours."

127

Can the Indian yoga systems be brought under this classification? The Way of Knowledge [*gnana*] culminates the Short Path; the Royal Way of Concentration [*raja*] culminates the Long Path. The Ways of Religious Devotion [*bhakti*] and Muttered Affirmation [*mantra*] belong, in their simple elementary forms, to the Long Path, but in their subtler advanced forms to the Short Path. The Way of Physical Control [*hatha*] is obviously a Long Path one.

128

Some mystical sects, like the Quietists of the seventeenth and eighteenth centuries in France and Spain, sought to achieve all through meditation alone but believed the achieving agent was Grace alone, or the Holy Ghost, as they called it. They were more than humble in this matter and thought that they were quite incapable of doing anything by themselves: spiritual growth had to be left entirely to the Spirit.

129

The Short Path position is supported by such Mahayana texts as the *Vajra-Samadhi Sutra*, where Buddha says: "Be it only as little as a single thought, the five components of ego are born at the same time. Let beings but repose their minds in a condition of calm. They will not have a single thought. This Absolute, this suchness, contains all the *dharmas*."

130

In theological language the Long Path stands for *repentance* from sin, the Short Path for *faith* in the Overself.

131

Swami Premananda: "I say to people, Don't give up anything: they will give you up. Do you have to give up darkness? No, you have only to bring in the light. So long as you are trying to resist something, you are having it constantly with you."

132

When Krishna says, "Relinquishing all individual (personal?—P.B.) efforts, take refuge in Me alone," he summarizes the Short Path in a few words.

133

Kabir: "I close not my eyes, nor torment my body. But every path I then traverse becomes a path of pilgrimage to the Divine."

134

Hindu script: "He alone grasps Him who does not grasp Him. Anyone who understands Him does not know Him."

135

HMS in *Theosophist*: "There is no true practice of Zen as long as it has an end in view, for then there is one eye on the practice and the other on the end, thus leading to lack of concentration and lack of sincerity."

136

Patanjali's *Yoga Sutras* tell us that reality may be sought along two paths: (a) discrimination, which would be an obstacle on the other path; but leading only to a limited relative insight tethering consciousness to a seed or "kernel of bondage"; (b) the other path on which, as A.J. Van Leeuwen says, "No-seed samadhi leads to perfect freedom." Van Leeuwen significantly adds: "Then the search is at an end, because the seer has discerned its uselessness. He comes to rest and finds nirvanic peace between the wings of the mystic swan Kalahamsa. When he brings his I-thought to rest by destroying his attachment to the I-ness (which is something else than ceasing to think as is tried to achieve in contemplation, and entirely different from petrifaction of the mind by concentration), then the opposites melt together. Be-ness has been attained, freewill has become the same as fate, freedom and law have become identical, drop and ocean enter each other, thesis and antithesis are cancelled out and sublimated into synthesis."

137

Yuan-chiao Ching—this book states that the Buddhist phrase "obscuration by Principle" means not knowing that the mind itself is principle, but seeking it in the mind, so that principle itself becomes an obstacle. (The reference here is to the Principle of Nature, Spirit.)

138

The whole course of Christian practice has been affected by misunderstanding the call to repentance issued by John the Baptist and later by Jesus himself as being only a call to ascetic penance. It included that but the emphasis was in no way there. Far more did it mean not only a change of mind, as Melanchton proved to Luther, but also to "experience a new consciousness." It looked forward to entry into a higher state, not backward to the past sinfulness.

139

Jesus put more emphasis on the Short Path than on the Long one, on the kingdom of heaven within man than on the animalistic urges and earthly shortcomings that afflict him.

140

Shen Tsan Zen school: ". . . radiant is the wondrous Light. Free it is from bondage of matter and senses. . . . Never defiled is Mind-nature. . . . By merely casting away your delusions the Suchness of Buddhahood is realized."

141

P.G. Bowen said that, following his master, "A.E.," he taught no special exercises in concentration or meditation. He wrote: "The outstanding error of learners, in whom it is excusable, and of many teachers, who teach without wisdom, is that they associate Occultism with practices rather than with PRACTICE. I teach the LIFE of concentration and meditation, a Way of Life wherein consciousness becomes concentrated."

142

The Patanjali Long-Path yoga school tells us we are weaklings, whereas the Vedanta Short-Path school tells us of our potential divine strength.

143

Kongo Kyo (Zen Buddhist): "Awaken the mind without fixing it anywhere."

144

When Jesus counselled, "Cast thy burden . . ." he was phrasing a perfect invitation to travel the Short Path.

145

The Master Dogen: "The path of Ignorance and the path of Enlightenment—we walk in dream!"

146

Eckhart: "I already possess all that is granted me in eternity."

147

Kabir on the Short Path:

O Sadhu! have done with your good and bad,
Yoga and counting the rosary, virtue and vice, these are nothing to Him.
One day your eyes shall suddenly be opened, and you shall see . . .

Kabir also says, "Dive into that Ocean of Sweetness; thus let all errors of life and death flee away."

148

This idea of the existence of a double path is not new although it is unfamiliar. Nor is it specifically Indian. As long ago as the fifth centuries the Buddhist monk Seng-Chao, a disciple of that Kumara Jiva who translated so many Indian texts for the Chinese, taught that all the effort and study and practice of exercises were not enough to attain enlightenment but were only a necessary preparation for it.

Their combination and transcendence

149

It is a matter that comes to the careful observer's attention that in groups or societies, in ashrams or institutions, where what is practised corresponds to the Short Path—however roughly and imperfectly—the results are very mixed and often saddening to the leaders. Where no attempt is made to bring in the Long Path's corrective work, where there is no striving for self-improvement, the end is a confused one—some satisfactions but more disappointments.

150

The Vedantins, Zen Buddhists, Christian Scientists, and even to a certain extent Ramana Maharshi and Sri Krishna Menon said that self-identification with the Reality, thinking of this identification constantly, would be enough to attain the spiritual goal. This is called the Short Path. The opposite schools of Patanjali's Yoga, the Roman Stoics, and the Southern Buddhists reject this claim and say that it is necessary to thin down the ego and purify the mind by degrees through disciplines, exercises, and practices. This is called the Long Path. The Philosophic Method is to combine both of these schools of thought synthetically, with the explanation that both are necessary to complete each through the other—and that it depends upon the stage where the aspirant is as to which school is necessary for him or her to emphasize personally. Beginners need to give more weight to the hard effort of the Yoga school; but advanced persons need to give it to the Vedanta viewpoint, because in their case much of the ego-thinning and mental-emotional cleansing has already been done.

151

It is quite true, as the extremist advocates of the Short Path, like Zen, say, that this is all that is really needed, that no meditation (in the ordinary sense), no discipline, no moral striving, and no study are required to gain enlightenment. We are now as divine as we ever shall be. There is nothing to be added to us; no evolution or development of our real self is possible. But what these advocates overlook is that, in the absence of the labours listed, the Short Path can succeed only if certain essential conditions are available. First, a teaching master must be found. It will not be enough to find an illumined man. We will feel peace and uplift in his presence, but these will fade away after leaving his presence. Such a man will be a phenomenon to admire and an inspiration to remember, not a guide to instruct, to warn, and to lead from step to step. Second, we must be able to live continuously with the teaching master until we have finished the course and reached the goal. Few aspirants have the freedom to fulfil the second condition, for circumstances are hard to control, and fewer still have the good fortune to fulfil the first one, for a competent, willing, and suitably circumstanced teaching master is a rarity. These are two of the reasons why philosophy asserts that a combination of both the Long and Short Paths is the only practical means for a modern Western aspirant to adopt. If, lured by the promise of sudden attainment or easy travelling, he neglects the Long Path, the passage of time will bring him to self-deception or frustration or disappointment or moral decline. For his negative characteristics will rise and overpower him, the lack of preparation and development will prevent him from realizing in experience the high-level teachings he is trying to make his own, while the impossibility of balancing himself under such circumstances will upset or rob him of whatever gains he may still make.(P)

152

The Long Path of the Yoga discipline is occupied with the cleansing and correction of his sins but the Short Path's affirmation brings their forgiveness. The first way is self-reproachful and sadly repentant. The second is self-relaxing and cheerfully untroubled. The philosophic student must learn to combine these two parts in his mental outlook and to use this double method in his practical approach.

153

The Long Path expresses a partial truth. The Short Path expresses another—although higher—partial truth. Bring the two parts together and the result will be that whole truth which man must have for the adequate guidance of his life.

154

The Long Path is needed to make a man or woman ripe for receiving truth, but only the Short Path can lead to it. This is the answer to the dilemma created by the claims of the Wu Wei school. Its practical application is: *act* as the Long Path requires by working on and improving the self, but *think* as the Short Path enjoins by holding the attitude "There is nothing to be attained. Realization is already here and now!"

155

When the Overself is present in a man's consciousness, It is present in all his thoughts and actions. They are then under Its rule, they proceed from It. The man does not have to *seek* for any particular virtues, for all can and will then come of themselves as needed. Only then is any virtue solidly established. But until this presence is permanently secured, it would be foolish to cease working upon oneself, correcting oneself, improving oneself. A merely intellectual and theoretical acquaintance with this doctrine is inadequate. It is necessary until then to practise a coexistence of Short and Long Paths.

156

The yogi—especially the yogi of the Southern Buddhist sect—who refuses to accept this Vedantic view, refuses unconsciously to accept the forgiveness of his karma. For if he were to practise identifying himself with the infinite being, the resultant inundation and dissolution of his ego would wash his sins away. The attitude of guilt and the feeling of being a miserable sinner, the mood of repentance and remorse, are useful and necessary at certain times and stages but are obstructive and harmful at the wrong time or the wrong stage. It is also sinful to reject forgiveness when it is available. The fact is that the Long Path is incomplete without the Short one.

157

There is no compulsive necessity, as most advocates of one or the other side seem to believe there is, to choose fully and finally between them, no real need to reject the one because the other is accepted. We may go along with the Vedantins and say that the One alone is real. But we may also go along with the dualists and say that the world around us and the human being are, in another sense, also real! It is quite fruitless to bring the two views into fanatical controversy with one another, far more useful to bring them into amicable relation. Why divide them when they serve us so well when reconciled?

Every time there is an attempt to communicate these truths by speech or in writing—let alone teach them to disciples—there is a falsification of the Vedantic tenet that there are no others! Then why do the Vedantists preach, teach, lecture, and write? Does this not show the utter impracticality of their position, true though it is as an ultimate metaphysical one?

The bliss that meditation practice at its deepest brings to a developed yogi does not annihilate the pain that the same yogi may feel when he resumes his ordinary active condition. Ramana Maharshi himself mentioned this quite a few times.

Iso Upanishad: "They enter the region of the dark who are occupied solely with the finite. But they fall into a region of still greater darkness who are occupied solely with the Infinite."

Nonduality in its extreme form is not to the taste of the masses. Instinctively they shy away from it. Let the two views accommodate each other. While these levels of reference ought not to be mixed together when theory and principles are concerned, there is one way in which there is considerable profit to be gained if the timeless eternal and universal atmosphere of Vedanta is kept at the back of the mind when the worldly problems have to be met. They can be met with this remembrance that one's true being is, and will be, safe and unaffected, and that whatever decision or action we are called to make, the first thing is to keep calm.

Each side—dualist and nondualist—is quite correct when they apply their teaching in its proper place, but quite wrong when they misapply. Thus, dualists who offer dualism as ultimate are wrong, but then nondualist Vedantists are also misconceiving the proper application of their tenets when they insist on applying their "no world exists, no ego exists" doctrine to human life generally.

158

The short path–long path, once understood, becomes a key to the solution of many problems and to the answer of many questions of Questers.

159

Those who depend solely on the Short Path without being totally ready for it take too much for granted and make too much of a demand. This is arrogance. Instead of opening the door, such an attitude can only close it tighter. Those who depend solely on the Long Path take too much on their shoulders and burden themselves with a purificatory work which not even an entire lifetime can bring to an end. This is futility. It causes them to evolve at a slower rate. The wiser and philosophic procedure is to couple together the work on both paths in a regularly alternating rhythm, so that during the course of a year two totally different kinds of results begin to appear in the character and the behaviour, in the consciousness and the understanding. After all, we see this cycle everywhere in Nature, and in every other activity she compels us to conform to it. We see the alternation of sleep with waking, work with rest, and day with night.(P)

160

The danger in both cases is in limiting one's efforts to the single path. It may invite disaster to give up trying to improve character just because one has taken to the Short Path. Yet it may invite frustration to limit one's efforts to such improvement. The wise balance which philosophy suggests is not to stop with either the Short or the Long Path but to use both together.(P)

161

This balanced objective which philosophy seeks calls for a balanced approach to it. The mind's dwelling on personal weaknesses and short-comings in the ego must be compensated by its remembrance of the strength and harmony in the Overself. It is as needful for the aspirant to practise disidentifying himself from the ego as it is to practise identifying himself with the Overself.

162

If the Short Path is not to end in fanaticism, extremism, self-delusion, or paranoia, the cultivation of balance is essential. This is why it is called the razor-edge path. The balance here required is to couple it sufficiently with the Long Path.

163

Such a double practice of the Short and Long Paths will not only lead to a fuller and better balanced progress but also to a quicker one. For these two opposite activities will work upon him in a reciprocal way. His faults will be ground to powder between them, as if they were millstones.

164

On the Long Path he has used various forms of practice. Now at the portals of the Short Path, he may intermittently and temporarily discard them and then just as intermittently and temporarily practise them. In this manner he can unite the two paths.

165

Although the Short Path offers quicker results to the seeker, he dare not withdraw from the Long one without suffering the penalty for his un-wisdom.

166

The advocates of the Long Path claim that the mind must be trained and the heart must be cleansed before enlightenment is possible. The advocates of the Short Path claim that it is sufficient to deny the ego and affirm the higher self. The philosopher studies the facts revealed by observation and research and concludes that the methods of both schools must be united if enlightenment is not only to be lastingly attained but also not to fall short of its perfect state.

167

Just as we have two viewpoints in philosophy—the immediate and the ultimate—so we have two paths to the philosophic goal—the Long and the Short. This double emphasis is not peculiar to philosophy for it may be found in Nature too.

168

It is true that the Long Path is only a preliminary one and that the Short Path is certainly a more advanced one. But it is also true that each is incomplete without the other. The best plan is to adopt as much of both paths as the aspirant can.

169

When one line of spiritual development is overemphasized, the need for the other line becomes existent but not often apparent.

170

The Long Path is splattered with discouragements. Only those who have sought to change themselves, to remold their characters, to deny their weaknesses, know what it is to weep in dissatisfaction over their failures. This is why the Short Path of God-remembrance is also needed. For with this second path to fulfil and complete the first one, Grace may enter into the battle at any moment and with it victory will suddenly end the struggles of many years, forgiveness will suddenly wipe out their mistakes.

171

Without this conquest of the lower nature no enlightenment can remain either a lasting or an unmixed one. And without suitable disciplines, no such conquest is possible. This is one reason why it is not enough to travel the Short Path.

172

People who think they have a number of faults may use that as an excuse to become passive and not try. But the combination is necessary. The danger of the Short Path is that he comes to think: "I am enlightened and have nothing more to do." It is another form of the ego. This happens often on the Short Path. So a balance between the Long and Short paths is most important.

173

The path of dealing with his shortcomings one by one is not only too long, too slow, but also incomplete and negative. It is concerned with what not to be and not to do. This is good, but it is not enough. It pertains to the little ego. He must add to it the path of remembering his higher all-self. This is a positive thing. More, it brings the Grace which finishes the work he has already started. It carries him from the ego's past into the Overself's Eternal New.

174

Wisdom counsels us to begin the Quest with the Long Path. When we have gone some distance on it, we may add the Short Path, changing the emphasis from one to the other by turns. This intermittent approach sets up a kind of reciprocal rhythm. The improvement of character opens the door of sensitivity a little wider to intuition, and the improved intuition helps to exalt character.

175

To all those who come to such a teacher for lessons in philosophy, he makes it plain that unless they are willing to discipline themselves on all three levels—physical, emotional, mental—he cannot teach them; that is, unless they are willing to follow the Long Path also.

176

The Long Path is paradoxically both a complement to the Short one and a preparation for it. It must first be practised alone. Only after some advance has been made can the time come for them to be practised conjointly.

177

A man cannot look in two directions at one and the same time. He may look at himself, his ego, or he may turn away and look above, at his Overself. In the latter case, if he has sufficiently thinned away the obstructions to it, grace may descend and lift his ego up to unite with his Overself. Then, and then alone, he will be able to live in both.

178

Both the austerity of the Long Path and the gaiety of the Short Path are needed: the first, if we are to endure life; the second, if we are to enjoy it.

179

The Long Path makes us look into ourselves and into our past for several of the sources of our present conditions. But in doing so, its revelations may discourage us, quenching hope and effort for self-improvement. Yet this would be to misuse them, so the Short Path corrects our attitude.

180

Let it be clear that the attempt to try the Short Path alone is not being decried. What is being said is that the likelihood of failure is great and that even if success is won, it will be a one-sided, ill-balanced, narrow thing.

181

The situation here is much the same as that which attends artistic creation. There are those who say that technique is everything and inspiration is illusory. There are others who say that inspiration is everything and technique is nothing. Is this not similar to the situation in spiritual circles, where the yoga school makes individual virtue and effort the price of enlightenment, and the opposing school makes waiting for inspiration and grace the price?

182

Whichever course he takes, let him not despise the other one. That is a mistake that only beginners make.

183

Ramana Maharshi was quite right. Pruning the ego of some faults will only be followed by the appearance and growth of new faults! Of what use is it so long as the ego remains alive? Hence the failure of mankind's moral history to show any real progress over the past three thousand years, despite the work of Buddha, Jesus, and other Messiahs. The correct course, which has always been valid for the individual, is just as valid for all mankind—get at the root, the source, the ego itself. But although Maharshi was right, his teaching gives only part of Truth's picture. Presented by itself, and without the other part, it is not only incomplete but may even become misleading. By itself it seems to indicate that there is no need to work on our specific weaknesses, that they can be left untouched while we concentrate on the essential thing—rooting out the ego. But where are the seekers who can straightaway and successfully root it out? For the very strength of purpose and power of concentration needed for this uprooting will be sapped by their faults.

184

There is a curious statement in *Tao Teh Ching* (49:1) that the Tao proceeds by contraries or by what it elsewhere calls rhythm. How does this affect the aspirant who is trying to attain harmony with it? The explanation is to be found in the need of including both the Long and Short paths, in the concentration upon opposites that the full and complete Quest requires.

185

There is this difference when the Long Path is entered alone and when it is entered with the accompaniment of the Short one, that in the second case there is added the light of guidance, the protection of peace, the acceleration of progress, and the harmony of equilibrium.

186

They are not really opposed to each other, but are in fact complementary. If the Long Path is a steep uphill climb, the Short Path is its sunny side.

187

He has to keep this inner stability and peace through times of public disaster or private distress. Long Path practices will help him attain it, but only intermittently. It is the Short Path which alone can establish it durably.

188
When concern with the ego-correcting requirements of the Long Path overrides concern with the ego-transcending requirements of the Short Path, it is time to take a fresh look at one's position.

189
The Middle Way is to synthesize the two teachings, to find a standpoint midway between them, to take from both what is needful for this attainment and what is appropriate to the circumstances.

190
Must he work through the Long Path's full cycle of study, discipline, self-betterment, and exercises before he tries the Short Path? No—not necessarily. It was the opinion of Govindananda Bharati, the sage who died in Nepal in 1963, that both could and should be followed simultaneously.

191
It is better, and brings life more into right balance, if both are followed simultaneously. But even so, in most cases it will be found necessary to emphasize the Long Path's practice of disciplines and cultivation of virtues.

192
There is a danger of becoming too preoccupied with concentration on self-improvement. A balance must be kept. To achieve this, he should also concentrate on the Self and the Non-Dual Impersonal Void-All. And he should do so joyously, happily. This is why the Short Path must balance the Long one.

193
The twofold way is indispensable: on the one hand the way of self-effort, working to overcome the ego, and on the other the way of Grace, through constantly seeking to remember your true identity in the Overself.

194
The Long and Short paths can no more be separated from one another than the two sides of a coin or the two poles of a magnet. Each would be meaningless without the other and therefore belongs to the other.

195
The two paths must not be kept separate in practice, whatever they are in theory. The beginner will naturally put his emphasis on the Long Path,

the proficient on the Short Path, but neither can afford to neglect one or the other path without perils and dangers or futilities and disappointments marking his way.

196

In theory the Long Path ought to precede the Short Path, but in actual practice such precedent endures for a limited time only, and then both paths are to be followed simultaneously.

197

If these two aspects of the Quest are followed properly and sufficiently, the Overself awareness will emerge in the very centre of his being quite naturally, if briefly, and with increasing repetition.

198

The question of conduct cannot arise where consideration is given to the ultimate nonduality alone; but on the practical plane, in the sphere of I and Thou, ethics must inevitably enter into consideration.

199

The self-power of the Long Path must be balanced by the other-power of the Short Path.

200

The following of both paths can be done either together, with the Long one subordinated to the Short one, or alternating in periods of a duration decided at the time according to the urge within himself.

201

It is neither wholly a self-salvational teaching nor a vicarious God-salvational one but a balanced union of both by *insight*.

202

"Be still and know that I am God" is the key to the enigma of truth, for it sums up the whole of the Short Path. Paradox is the final revelation. For this is "non-doing." Rather is it a "letting-be," a non-interference by your egoistic will, a silencing of all the mental agitation and effort.

203

If he begins by testing philosophy as a way of life, he must end by establishing it as such. But this settling down needs time, until he realizes that time itself is illusory. He may then assert the "Now-Here" attitude.

204

Once we become conscious of this truth the scales fall from our eyes. We give up our bondage to the erroneous belief in limitation. We refuse to entertain this false thought that there is some lofty condition to be attained in the far future. We are resolute that the Self shall recognize itself *now*. For what shall we wait? Let us stack all our thoughts upon the Reality, and hold them there as with a spike; it will not elude us, and the thoughts will dissolve and vanish into air, leaving us alone with the beauty and sublimity of the Self.

205

Just as a child has to learn the art of writing by slow degrees, so the student has to free his mind from erroneous views and to train his habitual thought to hold to the remembrance of the True and the Real little by little. But just as the single manipulation of an electric light switch instantly reveals *all* the objects in a room, so suddenly the maturation of insight reveals the here-and-now actuality of the True and the Real.

206

The limitation of the Long Path is that it is concerned only with thinning down, weakening, and reducing the ego's strength. It is not concerned with totally deflating the ego. Since this can be done only by studying the ego's nature metaphysically, seeing its falsity, and recognizing its illusoriness, which is not even done by the Short Path, then all the endeavours of the Short Path to practise self-identification with the Overself are merely using imagination and suggestion to create a new mental state that, while imitating the Overself's state, does not actually transcend the ego-mind but exists within it still. So a third phase becomes necessary, the phase of getting rid of the ego altogether; this can be done only by the final dissolving operation of Grace, which the man has to request and to which he has to give his consent. To summarize the entire process, the Long Path leads to the Short Path, and the Short Path leads to the Grace of an unbroken egoless consciousness.(P)

207

The sun's warmth and beauty brings out the flower's growth. It does not strive, struggle, or push. This is a good simile of the Short Path's final phase, taught also in the Chinese doctrine of *wu-wei* (inaction) and the Indian doctrine of *asparsa yoga* (without-effort method).

208

To live neither in the present nor in the future but in the eternal calls for a power of self-mastery that is extremely rare and for a perseverance in self-reform that is truly heroic.

209

The end of the quest is the end of the quester. No longer does he identify Being with the little routine self, awareness with the ordinary ego.

210

Lao Tzu teaches that Tao will do it all—so let be, let Tao act in its own way and its own time and without your fretting anxiously trying everything—it's not necessary.

211

He gives each moment the best that is in him, and so living from moment to moment becomes a glorious adventure.

212

Do not lament the difficulty of bringing about this basic change in thinking. The Overself is there. Believe in it.

213

The voice of the Overself is as clear as the voice of Jesus: "Go and sin no more, thy sins are forgiven thee." Do not weigh yourself down with perpetual self-reproach and recurring feelings of guilt.

214

Whereas the yogas of the East and the occultisms of the West were communicated according to the capability of the others to receive, or to their qualifications and development, these things do not enter the picture here. What is given out is given freely to all. Jesus is not a teacher assigning marks at an examination, he is a benevolent philanthropist! Salvation is taken out of the ego's hands altogether; the only requirement is "Do Nothing, for that will be ego-doing."

215

With the withdrawal from all outward-directed attachments, he becomes aware of his own inner self. With the awareness of his own real Self, all outgoing attachments drop away from him. Thus by whichever of these two paths he approaches the goal, it merges in the end with the other one.

216

The notion that the truth will be gained, that happiness will be achieved, that the Overself will be realized at the end of a long attempt must be seen as an illusory one. Truth, happiness, and the Overself must be seen in the Present, not the future, at the very beginning of his quest, not the end, here and now. It is not a matter of time. This is because time is a trick the mind plays on itself; because the past, the present, and the future are all rolled into one eternal NOW; because what is to happen has already happened.

217

The more he practises identifying himself with the timeless Now (not the passing "now"), the more he works for true freedom from besetting passions and dragging attachments. This is the Short Path, more heroic, perhaps, but in the end much pleasanter than the Long Path.

218

Why all this effort to be wiser than you are, little man? Why not savour the Oriental contentment of accepting what Nature has given you? Why disturb yourself with such strivings and broodings?

These are perilous questions to put to young ardent souls, eager to prepare themselves for the life that stretches ahead of them. But they are questions which the quester of many years must come to in the end.

219

It was said in Palestine that those who seek shall find. But it was also said in India that those who do *not* seek shall find.

220

He who finds that the Path has vanished, that he can say, "I am neither seeking truth, nor finding it," has reached the Short Path even though he does not know it.

221

Why wait for a realization always deferred to an ever-receding future? Bless the present hour, and thus every hour of your life!

222

Those who look for advancement by looking for inner experiences or for discoveries of new truth do well. But they need to understand that all this is still personal, still something that concerns the ego even if it be the highest and best part of the ego. Their greatest advance will be made when they cease holding the wish to make any advance at all, cease this continual looking at themselves, and instead come to a quiet rest in the simple fact that *God is*, until they live in this fact alone. That will transfer their attention from self to Overself and keep them seeing its presence in everyone's life and its action in every event. The more they succeed in holding to this insight, the less will they ever be troubled or afraid or perplexed again; the more they recognize and rest in the divine character, the less will they be feverishly concerned about their own spiritual future.

223

The real Short Path is really the discovery that there is no path at all: only a being still and thus letting the Overself do the work needed. This is the meaning of grace.

224

The sense of time's pressure which spurs the Long Path follower disappears from the Short Path follower. He becomes careless of time and squanders it shamelessly, as if he has INFINITE LEISURE.

225

He no longer feels any desire to reform the world or to improve himself. He accepts both just as they are.

226

The last phase of the Short Path has no special procedure, no specialized method. Life is its Way, or, as the Chinese sage said, "Usual life is very Tao."

227

Let even the Short Path go, at the proper moment, and sit loosely to life.

228

Wu Wei has a double meaning: first, letting Life, Mind, act through you by yourself, becoming still, thought-free, and empty of ego—you are then not doing anything, but being done to, being used; second, pursuing truth impersonally. The usual ways seek personal attainment, achievement, salvation. The aspirant thinks or speaks of "my mind" or "my purification" or "my progress"; hence such ways are self-enclosed, egoistic. Whatever repression of ego that there is occurs only on the surface and merely drives it down to hide in the subconscious, whence it will re-emerge later. These methods are Long Path ones, hence are destined to end in futility and despair. The deeper way of *Wu Wei* is to lose the ego by doing nothing to seek truth or to improve oneself; adopting no practice; following no path. The Short Path turns realization over to Overself so that it is not your concern any longer. This does not mean that you do not care whether you find truth or not, but that whereas ordinary care for it arises out of desire of the ego or anxiety of the ego or egoistic need of comfort, escape, or relief, Short Path care arises out of the stillness of mind, the serenity of faith, and the acceptance of the universe.

229

Chuang Tzu's assertion that the self must be shaped quite undeliberately "like Tao itself" is the Short Path's "naturalness" advocated here.

230

"The kingdom of God is within you." We may rightly take the simple meaning of this sentence, its pointer towards the place and the practice of meditation. But there is a second meaning, seldom understood, its pointer towards time and immediacy: the kingdom is here and now.

231

For the practitioner of the Short Path, *sahaja*, the quest is no longer for something remote from everyday life, nor for something wrapped around with mystery. When André Gide wrote, "People ought to talk about God only naturally," he, the non-mystical humanist, wrote more wisely than he knew.

232

Why create needless frustrations by an overeager attitude, by overdoing spiritual activity? You are in the Overself's hands even now and if the fundamental aspiration is present, your development will go on without your having to be anxious about it. Let the burden go. Do not become a victim of too much suggestion got from reading too much spiritual literature creating an artificial conception of enlightenment, just as too much reading of medical literature by a layman may make him the victim of hypochondriac tendencies. Do not be satisfied with the self-conscious spirituality which comes from forced growth and harsh unnatural asceticisms, or from egocentrically watching personal progress. That is a better and truer spirituality which is natural, as natural as waking from sleep; which is unforced, because not the result of following technique and practising exercises; which is unconscious, growing and blooming as the flower does; which is drawn by the Overself's beauty and warmth and peace.

233

It is an error, although a reasonable one, to believe that attainment comes only when the whole distance of this path has been travelled. This is to make it depend on measurement, calculation—that is, on the ego's own effort, management, and control. On the contrary, attainment depends on relinquishment of the ego, and hence of the idea of progress which accompanies it. It is then that a man can be still; then that he can, as the Bible promises, "know that I am God."

234

"Make tomorrow today"—this is the injunction of the Short Path teaching.

235

None of us can do more for our spiritual growth than to get out of its way! This business of trying to do something with the mind or practise some exercise with the body in order to come closer to the Overself is based on the Long Path belief that it is *we* who have the power to attain that desire and desirable state. But instead of trying to reach the Overself, why not *let* the Overself reach us? This can be done only if we will get out of its way.

236

Bodhidharma was asked, "How can one get into Tao?" The answer was: "Outwardly all activities cease, inwardly the mind stops its panting."

237

We need the spiritual assurance which looks for enlightenment not in some long-drawn-out future but today.

238

The world is carried in the mind and, ultimately, is the mind. But in trying to extend this knowledge of what the world is, to what the mind is, we make it into a second thing, an object apart, and fail to find it, for this it is not. So if looking for it cannot lead to awareness of it, ceasing to look for it is the first step. This is the same as taking to the Short Path.

239

It may properly be said that no man ever comes to the end of this Search. But that is because he one day comes to know that the seeking attitude is itself one of the last obstacles, and must be dropped.

6

ADVANCED MEDITATION

There are three progressive stages in this technique. First, the student proves to *himself,* by following the master's guidance, that the ego is fictitious and illusory. Second, he concentrates diligently on Short Path meditation techniques to dig beneath the ego and escape from it. Third, he proves to himself the fact of Nonduality, that there is only the One Mind's existence.

2

Ordinary meditation is still preoccupied with his own ego and therefore is still barred from ascending to the Himalayan peaks where alone God is to be felt and found. The meditator is still too wrapped up in his own development, his own problems, his own aspirations. Advanced nondual meditation forgets all that in order to remember and identify itself solely with God.

3

The student must therefore understand that the exercises which follow are special and advanced applications of the more elementary technique of meditation described in our earlier books.

4

If he is to succeed with the Short Path, he must practise its techniques continually, must revert to them so often that they become second nature and best pleasure.

5

"Give yourself to the Overself" is simple to say, but one must descend and ascend through a number of levels before its full majestic meaning is realized.

6

Four of the fundamental features which distinguish the philosophic meditation exercises from the others and which stamp them with marked superiority are (a) their metaphysical character, (b) their permanent results, (c) their impersonality, and (d) their universality.

7

Grace is of two kinds. The ordinary, better known, and inferior kind is that which is found on the Long Path. It flows from the Overself in automatic response to intense faith or devotion, expressed during a time of need. It is a reaction to seeking for help. The rarer and superior kind is found on the Short Path. It arises from self-identification with the Overself or constant recollection of it. There is no ego here to seek help or to call for a Grace which is necessarily ever present in the Overself.

8

These exercises are for those who are not mere beginners in yoga. Such are necessarily few. The different yogas are successive and do not oppose each other. The elementary systems prepare the student to practise the more advanced ones. Anybody who tries to jump all at once to the philo-sophic yoga without some preliminary ripening may succeed if he has the innate capacity to do so but is more likely to fail altogether through his very unfamiliarity with the subject. Hence these ultramystic exercises yield their full fruit only if the student has come prepared either with previous meditational experience or with mentalist, metaphysical understanding— or better still with both. Anyone who starts them, because of their appar-ent simplicity, without such preparation must not blame the exercises if he fails to obtain results. They are primarily intended for the use of advanced students of metaphysics on the one hand or of advanced practitioners of meditation on the other. This is because the first class will understand correctly the nature of the Mind-in-itself which they should strive to attain thereby, whilst the second class will have had sufficient self-training not to set up artificial barriers to the influx when it begins.(P)

9

Being based on the mentalist principles of the hidden teaching, they were traditionally regarded as being beyond yoga. Hence these exercises have been handed down by word of mouth only for thousands of years and, in their totality, have not, so far as our knowledge extends, been published before, whether in any ancient Oriental language like Sanskrit or in any modern language like English. They are not yoga exercises in the technical sense of that term and they cannot be practised by anyone who has never before practised yoga.(P)

10

Although the writer regards it as unnecessary and inadvisable to disclose in a work of popular instruction those further secrets of a more advanced practice which act as shortcuts to attainment for those who are ready to receive them, suffice to say that whoever will take up this path and go through the disciplinary practices here given faithfully and willingly until he is sufficiently advanced to profit by the further initiation of those secrets, may rest assured that at the right time he will be led to someone or else someone will be led to him and the requisite initiation will then be given him. Such is the wonderful working of the universal soul which broods over this earth of ours and over all mankind. No one is too insignificant to escape its notice, just as no one is deprived of the illumination which is his due; but everything in nature is graduated, so the hands of the planetary clock must go round and the right hour be struck ere the aspirant makes the personal contact which in nine cases out of ten is the preliminary to entry into a higher realization of these spiritual truths.(P)

11

Distant though it seems from all matters of a historical nature, all happenings in time, and all social experiences, the persistent affirmation of Mind's truth and reality will bear visible consequences. This is not less true of personal lives than of world events. But remember—only if harmony with the higher laws is obeyed.

12

Those who have gained glimpses, through long research or through hints in the classic texts, of what happened within the soul of candidates for the higher initiations of the Ancient Mysteries, whether of Greece Egypt Chaldea or Polynesia, will perceive that the exercises here revealed bear a certain resemblance to the exercises which were imposed upon these candidates during their period of training. And such indeed must be the case because the same pristine hidden teaching gave its inner nourishment to those remarkable institutions called the Mysteries, however externally different they necessarily were because of local needs and conditions.

13

These higher forms of yoga are not accessible to those who have insufficient leisure for reflection—that is, to most people.

14

If he begins his meditations as a coldly intellectual enquiring sceptic, without faith in the divine soul but willing to investigate experimentally if there be one, he will be brought to continue them at a certain stage of advancement as a warmly aspiring believer; and this will happen not by any desire of his own but by the Grace of the Overself. The gap between these two phases will be a dark night of the soul.

15

These are exercises in applied mentalism.

16

The privilege of these daily communions with the Overself is a blessed one.

17

The glimpse is to be welcomed as a relief from the unsatisfactory limitations of ordinary existence. But because it gives enlightenment only temporarily, it is not enough. It is necessary to seek out the way of getting a permanent result. Such a result is the best means to measure the value of any technique.

18

Books and discussions can, at best, serve only as guides for the individual inward search. This search for the True Self should be accompanied by efforts to impartially observe, improve, and develop that personal self which is ordinarily accepted as the be-all and end-all of existence. Constant attempts to cultivate and maintain awareness of the True Self—the Overself—together with making it the object of his deepest love and humble worship, are among the qualifications essential to progress.

19

He already knows the value of meditational practice for such things as self-improvement and inner peace. But there are higher values which are brought out by the integral philosophy of truth. To find these, he must carefully study *The Wisdom of the Overself* and experiment with any of the exercises given therein that appeal especially to him.

20

The grand illumination itself is sudden but the process of achieving it is a task so complex that it can be carried through only by successive stages. For the obstructions to be cleared on the way are heavy and numerous while the advances involve shifting from one tentative standpoint to another. The way to ultimate being cannot be travelled in a single leap; there must be a time-lag until the moment when it actually dawns. The interval naturally falls into elementary, intermediate, and advanced stages. Nothing once gained in yoga need be discarded; only we take it up into the wider gain which absorbs and preserves but also transcends it. The newer knowledge does not disqualify the results of earlier investigations. For the price of advanced yoga must be paid partly out of the profits got from elementary yoga. For want of a better term, we have sometimes designated the highly advanced meditation exercises here given as "ultramystic"—for a study of them will reveal that the common or popular forms of yoga do not exhaust the possibilities of man's quest of the Overself.

21

Successful results from these meditation exercises can be got much more quickly and much more easily if he begins their practice after he has thoroughly convinced himself of mentalism's truth and after having kept this conviction alive by constantly gravitating back to it during reflective moments.

22

Philosophic mysticism adopts the external form of ordinary mysticism for most of these exercises, but contains a superior innermost core. Whereas the ordinary mystic exercises in their lower phases aim at rendering the mind concentrated and undistracted and in their higher phases seek to know either the self or "God," the philosophic exercises are expanded into contemplations of the infinity of being and the universality of consciousness. Thus the latter are all-embracing whereas the former are limited. The ultimate result of the former is peace but of the latter, enlightenment as well as peace.

23

Only by a personal discovery of the soul, and consequently only by going "inside" himself to discover it, can a man know himself.

24

The yogi who sits on his bamboo mat, placed on an earthen floor under a grass-thatched roof, deaf to all noises around, blind to all scenes, his attention held firmly within, has turned back to the innermost and attained spiritual integrity.

25

It refreshes the heart and renews the will in the most extraordinary way if we sit with hands crossed in the lap or open on the knees and with mind surrendered, quiet, empty.

26

Do not let the mind occupy itself with any thoughts whenever there is no actual matter needing attention.

27

In the advanced practice of meditation it is not only required that the body shall be utterly relaxed but also that it shall be without the slightest movement from head to foot.

28

It is an error to think of the advanced contemplative practices as specially intended for sitting only. *In the end* they are just as much for walking and standing.

29

It is better not to fix a firm duration for this period but to let its terminal moment be dictated by the inner voice.

30

Exercise: The eyes look out at the far horizon, as if unconcerned with what is happening immediately around them.

31

In this matter of utilizing the body for the yogic practice, the eyes are first turned inward so that the outer surroundings are not considered. When this ability is sufficiently established, the next step is to turn them upward and hold them like that for stated periods.

32

It is a condition of success that the emotions be relaxed, the body still, the surroundings quiet.

33

A day that does not contain such a precious luminous period will be counted a day that is barren and lost.

34

The advanced form of meditation merges into contemplation. Here there is no special need to adopt any one posture or to sit in any one way. It is then a practice done in a more inwardly absorbed condition; the physical body and surroundings are less present or quite ignored.

35

The establishment of a regular evening ritual of mental quiet at the advanced level will be easy, pleasant, and successful. For the arduous struggles of a beginner are absent, the up-and-down moods or vacillations of an elementary level have vanished.

36

He is to sit as quietly and as unmovingly in body as he is to be still and attentive in mind.

37

When he has reached the stage of advancement the rules prescribed for beginners and intermediates do not necessarily apply to him. He can now meditate whether sitting upright, as the prescription usually counsels, or lying limp on his back. His mind is not now so bound by these external conditions.

38

Each day he should take time out of his other preoccupations to wrap himself in a certain high mood, an exalting reverie.

Specific exercises for practice

39

To stop abruptly activities, movements, thoughts and hold one's mind in a state of suspense, yet relaxed, is another exercise if the relaxation is passive enough. It leads into a meditative mood or a glimpse. Useful exercises are to concentrate consciousness on the point between the eyebrows or in the heart centre or in the centre behind the solar plexus. These are of course only yogic exercises, but useful as preparatory ones. More important is the attempt to put his own person into a new perspective, to transcend his own ego from the Overself plane.

40

The exercises of sinking oneself in enjoyment of an artistic production constitute another Short Path method, provided they are followed up and completed by further stages described in the seventh and eighth chapters of *The Quest of the Overself*. These exercises will be useful only if the music, literature, or painting is truly inspired.

41

He must eliminate from his inner life the imaginary pictures of possible happenings favouring his ego. He must cast out misleading expectations of future attainment. Only pure truths should be considered.

42

Another useful exercise is to meditate on the divine Cosmic Plan. As a focal point for practice, it constructively engages both the metaphysical and the physical intellect. As a theme it exalts the self and purifies the heart, instructs the mind and enlarges the point of view.

43

Eckhart: "Of God himself can no man think and therefore I will leave all that I can think upon, and choose to my love that thing that I cannot think. And why? Because He may well be loved, but not thought on. By love he may be gotten and holden but by thought never. . . ." Compare: "Go up towards that thick cloud of Unknowing with a sharp dart of longing love, and go not thence for anything that befall."

44

When Jesus invites men to "cast all burdens upon me" and when Krishna invites them to "cast off all works on me" both are suggesting that we should *imagine* all our troubles being borne and all our actions as being done by the higher self, if we have not yet found it, and should actually let it displace the personal ego in practical life, if we have.

45

This exercise requires him not only to remember and stay in the highest concept of Supreme Being as often as possible but also to counter it occasionally by remembering the transiency of his earthly ego, experiences, and life.

46

The Zen votary is entitled to use the *Koan* and can get results from it. He can get *Satori*. For it is a nonintellectual device—like those of other approaches—to transcend intellect.

47

The method of meditation appropriate to this class of seekers is to transfer self-identity to the Overself in, and by, constantly repeated declarations of the truth.

48

If contact with people becomes at any time or in any situation unpleasant and nothing worthwhile can be done by discussion, he can always withdraw into that mental void.

49

His dependence on self-effort must be balanced by his dependence on Grace. If he relies solely on his own endeavours to better his character and develop his intuition, he may find himself frustrated and unhappy with the result. Grace is to be invoked by making contact through prayer and meditation with his Overself. But the meditation should be of a special kind—what may be called the practice of nonduality. In it he should seek to identify himself with the universal and infinite power, to forget that he is an individual.

Yoga of the Liberating Smile

50

A valuable practice of the Short Path is to *see* himself already enjoying the realization of its goal, already partaking of its glorious rewards. This is a visualizing exercise in which his own face confronts him, a smiling triumphant face, a calm peaceful face. It is to be done as many times every day as he can remember to do it.

51

By combining deep breathing with gentle smiling, both acts being done quite slowly, and by keeping the mind solely attentive to the body's condition, a relaxed half-drowsy state will develop. No other thoughts should be allowed to enter; the whole of his being should lie completely reposed in the rhythmic breathing and happily hypnotized by the lazy smile. Everything should be light and effortless. This is the Yoga of the Liberating Smile.

52

The Yoga of the Liberating Smile is to be practised at two special times—when he is falling into sleep at night and when he is waking from sleep in the morning.

53

This truth insinuates itself into the mind in all its quiet sublimity. We alas! can receive only the mere flavour of it, such is the resistance of our ego, whereas a Buddha, with squatting body and dreaming face, can receive the full total force of it.

54

So there he squats on couch, seat, or rug, unaware of time, the slightest of smiles hovering over his face.

55

Because the Short Path is an attempt to withdraw from the ego's shade and to stand in the Overself's sunshine, it must be accompanied by the deliberate cultivation of a joyous attitude. And because it is so largely a withdrawal from the Long Path's disciplines, it must also be accompanied by a sense of freedom. Hence its proper physical facial expression is the radiant smile. Its votary should look for beauty and seek to come into harmony at all times—in Nature, in art, in the world, and in himself.

56

He can practise the yoga of the liberating smile. When it appears, tensions go, desires fade out. It is peace-bringing.

57

There is the egotistic smile of the salesman, a surface affair, put on, something added and, at times, in total contradiction to the state of his feelings. There is the smile of the philosopher-mystic, a sincere and genuine outer reflection of his inner being.

Intercessory meditation

58

The secret of successful altruistic intercession during meditation is, first, to enter the deepest part of his own being, and then—but only then—to enter the deepest part of the other man's. Here he will begin by praying for his spiritual improvement and end by visualizing the thing as done. To spend a few minutes each day in such intercessory service for others is to bless not only them but also himself. All his other virtues flower more radiantly in the sunny air of such benign love. Nevertheless, a practical warning is called for here.

Do not carry your own troubles or your temptations or other people's troubles and situations straight into your meditation. There is a proper time and place for their consideration under a mystical light or for their presentation to a mystical power. But that time and place is not at the *beginning* of the meditation period. It is rather towards the end. All meditations conducted on the philosophic ideal should end with the thoughts of others, with remembrance of their spiritual need, and with a sending-out of the light and grace received to bless individuals who need such help. At the beginning your aim should be to forget your lower self, to rise above it. Only after you have felt the divine visitation, only towards the end of your practice period should your aim be to bring the higher self to the help of the lower one, or your help and blessing to other embodied selves. If, however, you attempt this prematurely, if you are not willing to relinquish the personal life even for a few minutes, then you will get nothing but your own thought back for your pains.

59

The exercise of drawing down the Life Force as a white light should be accompanied by deep rhythmic breathing. It will be effective only after inspiration has been sought in meditation, and partially found. Hence it is best performed just before, or just after, the stillness is reached.

60

The practice of extending love towards all living creatures brings on ecstatic states of cosmic joy.(P)

61

In this intently concentrated state he has the power to send beneficent thoughts over land or sea to a distant person and let them penetrate his mind.

62

He will help others more by holding them mentally in this inner peace than by falling into a state of nervous anxiety about them.

63

Would you have your friend live a better life? Picture only that better life in your thoughts of him.

64

In the deepest state of contemplation he is not able to be concerned about himself. How then can he be concerned about other men? "At such times," said Bonaventura "one must not think of creatures."

65

One of the deeper ways to help others is to bring them into meditation, if the meditation has been successful in making contact with the Higher Power. For then he can let it act upon himself in all his thoughts about the different areas of his life and by merely invoking the image or name of any person let it act upon that person too.

66

There is no doubt that the practice of meditation leads to a sensitizing of the meditator's mind, if only because he has to make himself passive and receptive during the meditative period. After the first great battle of achieving concentration has been won there is then a possibility that the thoughts, feelings, and moods of other persons may enter his own consciousness if they are either present physically or connected with him mentally. If those impressions are of a lower character than his own character they may either disturb him and give him some trouble in dealing with them, or at the least divert him from his habitual attitude, however briefly, or he may make the mistake of identifying them as being his own, of his own creation. For these reasons it is better for those who are still under development not to attempt by mental treatment to elevate the minds of others directly, unless it is done at the peak period of a meditation, when they have been able to reach a high level of purpose, concentration, and purity. The method of trying to improve others by telepathy is only safely used by adepts, who are firmly established in the higher spiritual position.

67

Exercise I: To Relieve Tension and Cultivate Relaxation

(a) Sit upright on a chair of comfortable height, with the knees and legs together, if comfortable, or slightly apart if not. Lean slightly forward, keeping the spine straight, and allow both the arms to hang down full length and lifeless, like heavy weights, from the shoulders completely relaxed.

(b) Both hands are then lifted very slowly at the elbows, almost to shoulder height, then abruptly dropped, palms upright, on the upper thighs. Keep the feeling of limpness and heaviness in the arms, with the lower part of the body utterly relaxed.

(c) Picture an ethereal aura of pure, white, electrifying Light all around you. Then, imagine this magnificent Light is actually pulling you upright by the top of your head. Its compelling force should, as a result, automatically straighten the spine, and the back of your trunk, neck, and head form a perfectly erect line. Finally, imagine the Light is pervading inside the whole of your body.

This exercise should give a feeling of physical refreshment and complete physical relaxation. It is also useful when having to listen to lengthy talks, lectures, and so on, or when reluctantly trying to practise meditation after a fatiguing day.

Exercise II: To Promote Harmony

Repeat Exercise I, then add:

(a) Try to see and feel that the aura of Light has an actual substance and that It is becoming part of you, that you are melting into It, becoming one with It. Next, think of it as being the pure essence of Love, especially in the region of the heart.

(b) When this Love has been experienced as a sensation of heart-melting happiness, let it then extend outwards to embrace all the world.

This exercise should give a feeling of being in harmony with Nature, the universe, with all living beings, and with humanity as a part of Nature.

Exercise III: To Heal Sickness

Repeat Exercises I and II, then add:

(a) Think of the white Light as being Nature's intelligent and recuperative Life-Force.

(b) Let it pour in, through the top of your head, passing directly to the solar plexus centre, which is the region which must first be worked on and affected if the healing force is to become efficacious. Thence send it to any afflicted area, remaining there. Feel Its benevolent, restorative, and healing presence working upon it.

(c) *In order to be fully effective this exercise must be accompanied by intense faith in the recuperative powers of this Light.*

Astonishing proof of its effectiveness in relieving a troubled organ or curing a diseased part of the body, when persevered in for a sufficient period of weeks or months, has been clearly shown by results. In some cases, paralytics have regained full use of their disabled limbs by following the outline given here.

Exercise IV: To Establish Telepathic Harmony or Help

Repeat Exercise I, II, and III (a), then add:

(a) Let the White Light enter the region of the heart, remaining there.

(b) Form a mental image of the face of the individual you wish to contact, and reduce it in size until it is small enough to fit into the palm of your hand.

(c) Place this tiny image in the centre of the white Light permeating your heart.

(d) Endeavour actually to *see* the individual there in your heart. This exercise should be used to promote physical or mental help to a distant friend, to bring about goodwill from one who has expressed enmity, or to establish a deeper spiritual relationship. It is also useful in the student-teacher relationship, because it promotes better sympathy and affinity, as well as strengthening the telepathic link. *Note*: Where imagination is well developed the attempt to visualize light may be used, but where either the intellectual or the instinctive preponderates over it, the attempt need not be made—only the unseen power invoked and directed by faith.

Night meditations

68

As taught in *The Wisdom of the Overself*, use the last few minutes in the twilight state of consciousness before falling asleep at night for constructive self-improvement. The best form this can take during your present phase of development is to relax in bed, empty the mind of the day's cares, and make definite, concrete suggestions about the good qualities desired and imaginatively visualize yourself demonstrating these desired qualities. Furthermore, you should go even farther and visualize yourself in possession of the Higher Consciousness, attuned to the Higher Will and expressing the Higher Poise. All this will be like seeds planted in the inner being and growing during sleep.

69

Character can be bettered and weaknesses can be overcome through the regular use of constructive exercises in meditation either at any time during the day, or just before falling asleep. Whatever the fault weakness or vice may be, it should be firmly coupled in meditation with pictures of its dangerous consequences, and then with a mental attitude of its danger and their horror. Such an association of ideas will tend to produce itself automatically whenever the fault manifests itself.

70

Pre-sleep fourth state exercise: The secret of a successful passage into the transcendental state consists in insisting on retaining consciousness but not on retaining self-consciousness. For if, at the moment when you are about to slip into the fourth state, you suddenly become aware that you are doing so, then you will at once be hurled back into the ordinary condition. The ego-sense has therefore to subside completely before the pass-over can be effected. So long as the ego knows what is happening to it, so long does the cross-over remain impossible. It must not be allowed to intrude itself at the fateful moment, yet neither must consciousness itself be allowed to lapse.

71

If, in the act of falling asleep, he invites the higher self through aspiration, he may one day find that in the act of waking up an inner voice begins to speak to him of high and holy things. And with the voice comes the inspiration, the strength, and the desire to live up to them.

72

It is a valuable exercise to review at night the events of the past day or to review in the morning those which can be expected in the coming day.

73

For qualified persons, and not many are, there is a form of meditational exercise which leads to a certain power over one's dreams and enables the practiser to get into and get out of those dreams. With further knowledge and practice he can even bring a dream under his own control. But not only are certain qualifications of a moral and mental character required of him, he has also to take certain risks which attend this enterprise.

74

All these pictorial suggestions and creative anticipations will take effect and retain their hold upon his mind after the meditation itself is nothing but a memory or after the sleep itself has been long forgotten. Time does not dispel but only confirms them. He will execute the suggested ideas even while unaware at the moment how or when he got them.

75

There is a verse of the *Koran* which says: "Arise in the midst of the night and commune with thy God. Thy ego will be crushed and things will be revealed to thee thou didst not know before and thy path in life will be made smooth."

76

When his ability to practise ultramystic meditation becomes well-developed, the student may frequently find himself suddenly waking up during the night at an hour earlier than that to which he is accustomed. His mind will be alert and attentive and he will not be able to fall asleep again. This is a signal to him to begin his meditation practice. If he heeds this mysterious and silent injunction, the ultimate inward effectiveness and ultimate outward results of such meditation will be far above the ordinary.

77

In those delicious moments where sleep trembles into waking, there is some sort of a beginning Glimpse but alas, it vanishes without fulfilling its promise as soon as the world of objects comes more fully into the circle of attention. And this is precisely where the value of such a state lies, both for the ordinary man and for the would-be yogi. *It has no objects.* It is "I" without a world. It is awareness-in-itself. True, it is fleeting and does not last, but a man can learn to practise holding himself to it.

78

In those first moments when awakening from the nightly sleep we may enter a heavenly thought-free state. Or, if we cannot reach so high, we may receive thoughts which give guidance, tell us what to do, warn us against wrong decisions, or foretell the future.

79

On awakening from the night's sleep, take the inspired book, which you are to keep on a bedside table for the purposes of this exercise, and open it at random. The higher self may lead you to open it at a certain page. Read the paragraph or page on which your glance first rests and then put the book aside. Meditate intently on the words, taking them as a special message to you for that particular day. In the course of your activities you may later find this to be so, and the message itself a helpfully connected one.

80

The point where one can pass from wakefulness to pure consciousness is naturally most difficult to find. Everyone misses it because habit-patterns compel him to do so. Much patience is needed for these exercises. This is indeed a task for one's whole lifetime. But there are easier objectives and more accessible goals which are quite excellent for most people of the present day.

81

There are certain intervals of consciousness between two thoughts—such as those between waking and sleep and those between sleep and waking—which normally pass unobserved because of the rapidity and brevity associated with them. Between one moment and another there is the timeless consciousness; between one thought and another there is a thought-free consciousness. It is upon this fact that a certain exercise was included in *The Wisdom of the Overself* which had not previously been published in any Western book. But it is not a modern discovery. It was known to the ancient Egyptians, it was known to the Tibetan occultists, and in modern times it was probably known to Krishnamurti. The Egyptians, preoccupied as they were with the subject of death and the next world, based their celebrated *Book of the Dead* upon it. *The Tibetan Book of the Dead* contained the same theme. Between the passing out of the invisible vital-forces body at the end of each incarnation and its entry into that state of consciousness which is death, the same interval reappears. If the dying man can lift himself up to it, seize upon it, and not let it escape him, he will then enter into heaven—the true heaven. And it was to remind him of this fact and to help him achieve this feat that the ancient priests attended his last moments and chanted the pertinent passages from these books. This mysterious interval makes its appearance throughout life and even at death, and yet men notice it not and miss an opportunity. It happens not only at the entry into death but also in between two breaths. It is possible to go even further and say that the interval reappears for a longer period between two incarnations for there is then the blocking out of all impressions of the past prior to taking on a new body. Plato must have known it.

Witness exercise

82

To play the role of an observer of life, his own life, is to assist the process of inwardly detaching himself from it. And the field of observation must include the mental events, the thought-happenings, also. For mentalism shows that they are really one world. In the end everything belonging to experience belongs to mental experience.

83

The student has to stand aside from the thought-forms, which means that he must stand aside from the person and look at it as something external to himself. If and when he succeeds in getting behind it, he automatically adopts the standpoint of the Overself. He must make the person an object and the Overself its observer. Now this element of pure awareness is something constant and unbroken; hence it is not ordinary consciousness, which is a discontinuous thing made of totalized thoughts, but transcendental consciousness.

84

The position of the impersonal observer is only a tentative one, assumed because it is a practical help perhaps midway toward the goal. For when it is well-established in understanding, outlook, and practice, something happens by itself: the observer and the observed ego with its body and world become swallowed up in the undivided Mind.

85

It is an experience wherein he finds himself aware of the ego from within itself and also, at the same time, aware of it as an observer. This is not to be confused with an experience wherein he finds himself standing behind his *body*, not identifying with it but observing it: yet he still remains in ego.

86

Scott in his search for the South Pole amid ice-bound Antarctic wastes and Smythe in his quest for the summit of Mount Everest amid terrible avalanches of stone and snow, reported in their written accounts the sense of not being alone, of being companioned by a mystic unseen presence which bestowed a strange calm. Scott's venture ended in heroic death whereas Smythe survived to enjoy the warmth and safety of his home. Both however knew what it was to be uncommonly blessed at the time, for Scott passed to his fated death with an utter serenity and an inward trust in its aftermath which took all the horror out of it for him. This noble passage to another stage of existence was not the miserable calamity which it was for many other men. What was the mystic presence which walked beside these men? Each may have had his own belief about it, may have constructed in imagination what his previous knowledge experience tendencies and outlook may have naturally persuaded him to construct. Each therefore may have had different ideas about it, but this would not affect the actual power which inspired and animated him at the time. For that power was nothing less than the Grace of the Overself, and if we understand the psychological secret of what happened to Scott and Smythe we may then understand that it is not only far-wandering explorers and high-climbing mountaineers who may call up the Overself by their brave trust. The same dangerous experience which has brought fear, horror, and despair to other men brought them dignified confidence and mystical enlargement of consciousness which made them aware for the time of the hidden observer. They had indeed suddenly but partially stepped into the transcendental state. Whoever successfully practises the Hidden Observer meditation will experience precisely the same sense of not being alone, of being companioned by a mystic presence which brings with it a benign sense of assurance and security. He will, however, experience much more than that.

87

Can he look at himself as if he were a total stranger, as if he were meeting for the first time an alien from a distant land? Can he treat his own speech and actions as if those of somebody else?

88

Although the aspirant has now awakened to his witness-self, found his "soul," and thus lifted himself far above the mass of mankind, he has not yet accomplished the full task set him by life. A further effort still awaits his hand. He has yet to realize that the witness-self is only a *part* of the All-self. So his next task is to discover that he is not merely the witness of the rest of existence but essentially of one stuff with it. He has, in short, by further meditations to realize his oneness with the entire universe in its real being. He must now meditate on his witness-self as being in its essence the infinite All. Thus the ultramystic exercises are graded into two stages, the second being more advanced than the first. The banishment of thoughts reveals the inner self whereas the reinstatement of thoughts without losing the newly gained consciousness reveals the All-inclusive universal self. The second feat is the harder.(P)

89

He must keep this part of himself firmly held back, must guard it against getting entangled with the world, must make it a silent observer and mere looker-on only.

90

He begins with self-watching, with immobilizing and stilling a part of attention to observe the mental and physical self. This requires frequent remembrance—not an easy task—and refusal to identify with what is thus brought into awareness—which is even less easy.

91

When a man has practised this exercise for some time and to some competency, he will become repeatedly aware of a curious experience. For a few minutes at most and often only for a few moments, he will seem to have stepped outside his body and to be confronting himself, looking at his own face as though it were someone else's. Or he will seem to be standing behind his own body and seeing his face from a side angle. This is an important and significant experience.

92

To become the Witness-self does not mean to contemplate one's gestures and listen to the sound of one's voice.

93

He feels that he is gazing down at himself from a height, seeing his personal ego for the trivial thing that it is.

94

If he were standing there, looking at someone else undergoing this experience, it could not be more objective, more impersonal, than now.

95

One special exercise of the Short Path is easily done by some persons and gives them excellent results, although it is hard to do by others. It consists in refusing to let remain any particular mental registration of the surrounding place or people, or of any physical experience being undergone. Instead the mental image is to be firmly dismissed with the thought, "This too is like a dream," and then immediately forgotten. The exercise may be kept up for fifteen to twenty minutes at a time. The practical benefit it yields is to give improved self-control; the metaphysical benefit is to weaken the sway of illusion; the mystical benefit is to enable him to take the stand of the Witness-attitude more easily; and the personal benefit is to make him a freer and happier man.

96

He has to learn a new art—that of remaining relaxed and at ease, almost an impassive observer, while his body or his intellect does its work in the world, performs in the role set for it.

97

His role is to play witness of what he is, how he behaves, the thoughts he admits, just as if he were witnessing someone else. This move-over from the actively-engaged person to the watcher who is impersonal and disengaged even in the midst of action, is one from drift to control. He must begin by putting the ego, his own ego, forward as an *object* of observation. He will not succeed fully in doing so, because he is involved on both sides—as subject and object—but the direction can be fixed and the work can be started. With time and practice, study and reflection, help and sincerity, some sort of impersonality and neutrality can be established. When inner stillness is fully reached, the work becomes much easier until it is completed by the grace of the higher Self, Overself. Of course, outside of meditation, he is conscious of his commonplace body; but he is also conscious of his awe-inspiring Overself. He sees the first as part of a passing show, himself as an uninvolved observer, and behind both the eternal Overself.

98

The first important need is to separate himself in thought and outlook from the animal side of his nature—not for any moral reasons but for metaphysical ones—and part of the inner work which this calls for is to take up the observer role. He is to look at the body (and its actions, desires, and passions) as if it were apart from himself—in short, to gain a detached view. This practice is fruitful because one idea can be used to counter or displace a second idea: both cannot be held in attention simultaneously. When this has been carried on for a long enough time to show its benefits, it may be used on a higher and more elusive level: he can adopt the impersonal observer attitude towards the ego itself, of which the body is of course a part.

99

He participates in every action not only as the performer doing it but also as the audience seeing it.

100

Let him play the part of a witness to his own ego, through all its experiences and vicissitudes. In that way he will be emulating by effort those enlightened men to whom the part comes easily and naturally by their own development.

101

Mindfulness is a Buddhist exercise, but practising the Witness attitude is a Hindu one. Pythagoras too gave an exercise which is in some ways similar.

102

His role in everyday life is a double one: that of being both the world's actor and a spectator.

103

The attitude of detached and impartial observer helps to protect him, to diminish his animality, and to correct his egoism even while he takes part in some of the chief concerns of human activity. As for the others, if he chooses to withdraw from them because he considers them unworthy of a philosopher, we should be grateful that someone has had the moral courage to do so.

104

As meditation is practised, further indrawing takes place and the apparatus for thinking is repudiated in turn. "I am not this mind." The process continues further; as the self ever draws inward he casts off, one by one, all that he once held to be himself.

105

Thus whatever he is experiencing physically, he trains himself to replace the unillumined thought "I am eating, hungry, walking" by the thought "*My body* is eating, hungry, walking." He recognizes that the bundle of sensations which makes up such experiences is not the true self, which it represents itself to be, but is only connected with it.

106

The question "Who am I?" is asked somewhere in that monumental ancient book *The Yoga Vasistha*. It was often included centuries later by Saint Francis in his prayers. But Sri Ramana Maharshi gave it central importance in his advice to spiritual seekers and meditators.

107

Not only all other men's bodies but also his own must be regarded as objects to Consciousness, as the not-self which is seen by the Self.

108

What is the practical use of enquiring, "To whom is this experience happening? To whom this pain, this joy, this distress, or this good fortune?" First, it makes him remember the quest upon which he is embarked by reminding him that it is the ego which is feeling these changes and that he is not to identify himself with it and thus limit his possibilities if he really seeks the higher self behind it. Second, it suggests that he look for the root of his ego and with it his hidden "I" instead of merely being swept away by what is happening within the ego itself.

"As-If" exercise

109

On this Short Path he searches into the meaning of Being, of being himself and of being-in-itself, until he finds its finality. Until this search is completed, he accepts the truth, passed down to him by the Enlightened Ones, that in his inmost essence he is Reality. This leads to the logical consequence that he should disregard personal feelings which continue from past tendencies, habits, attitudes, and think and act as if he were himself an enlightened one! For now he knows by evidence, study, and reflection that the Overself is behind, and is the very source of, his ego, just as he knows by the experience of feeling during his brief Glimpses. Bringing this strong conviction into thought and act and attitude is the "Heavenly Way" [or "As If"] exercise, a principal one on the Short Path.

He pretends to be what he aims to become: thinks, speaks, acts, behaves as a master of emotion, desire, ego because he would be one. But he should play this game for, and to, himself alone, not to enlarge himself in others' eyes, lest he sow the seed of a great vanity.(P)

110

It is objected, why search at all if one really is the Overself? Yes, there comes a time when the deliberate purposeful search for the Overself has to be abandoned for this reason. Paradoxically, it is given up many times, whenever he has a Glimpse, for at such moments he knows that he always was, is, and will be the Real, that there is nothing new to be gained or searched for. Who should search for what? But the fact remains that past tendencies of thought rise up after every Glimpse and overpower the mind, causing it to lose this insight and putting it back on the quest again. While this happens he must continue the search, with this difference, that he no longer searches blindly, as in earlier days, believing that he is an ego trying to transform itself into the Overself, trying to reach a new attainment in time by evolutionary stages. No! through the understanding of the Short Path he searches knowingly, not wanting another experience since both wanting and experiencing put him out of the essential Self. He thinks and acts as if he is that Self, which puts him back into It. It is a liberation from time-bound thinking, a realization of timeless fact.(P)

111

Practice of the "As If" exercise is like being spiritually reborn and finding a new way of life. It gives courage to those who feel grievously inadequate, hope to those who feel hooked by their past failures.

112

Exercise: In this pictorial meditation, he is to put himself in a tableau of achieved result. He is to see himself doing successfully what he seeks to do, and the sight is to be accompanied by intense faith and firm conviction. The desirable qualities of character are to be thought of as already existing and possessed, already expressing themselves in action and living. Furthermore they are to be pictured vividly and clearly; they must be understood without any uncertainty, dimness, or hesitation.

113

The "As If" exercise is not merely pretense or make-believe. It requires penetrative study and sufficient understanding of the high character and spiritual consciousness in the part to be played, the role to be enacted, the auto-suggestion to be realized.(P)

114

When the assaults of man's animal nature, the instincts of his body, have to be dealt with, a swift assumption of the AS IF attitude is necessary.

115

A part of the practical technique for attaining the inner awareness of this timeless reality is the practice of the AS IF exercise. With some variations it has already been published in *The Wisdom of the Overself*, and an unpublished variant has been included in descriptions of the Short Path as "identification with the Overself." The practitioner regards himself no longer from the standpoint of the quester, but from that of the Realized

Man. He assumes, in thought and action, that he has nothing to attain because he bases himself on the Vedantic truth that Reality, of which he is a part, is here and now—is not reached in Time, being timeless—and that therefore he is as divine as he ever will be. He rejects the *appearance* of things, which identifies man only with his ego, and insists on the higher identification with Overself also.

116

The self-identification with the Overself should be as perfect as he can make it. He is to *be* it, and not merely the student meditating on it.

117

He must sink himself in the imagined character of the ideal with intense feeling until he *becomes* the image itself.

118

This practice in the Short Path of self-identification with the Overself is to be done both casually at odd moments and deliberately at daily contacts in meditation. It is through them—whenever the identification is effectual—that Grace gets some of its chance to work its transformation upon him.

119

It is a useful elementary and preparatory exercise in learning detachment from one's own ego, to try to project it into someone else's from time to time. By imaginatively sharing in another's life and mind, situations and surroundings, so far as one can, by putting oneself into the point of evolution where the other stands, one gains more facility in extracting oneself from the inveterate self-centeredness of the ordinary man. It is a kind of mental histrionics, a play-acting which substitutes one kind of egoism for another and in the process loosens the replaced kind. For such a special exercise, it would be still more profitable to select somebody with whom one is normally unsympathetic, perhaps even an opponent or enemy. Other valuable qualities will then receive a stimulus. There is of course a danger in such a masquerade, the danger of becoming neurotically unstable to which so many actors and actresses are exposed. It can be avoided by practising the complementary and finishing exercise taken from the Short Path series of banishing both personalities in reverent self-identification with the Overself.

120

Whatever name be given to this exercise, whether "As If" or another, its essence is to consider the goal as already reached, to convert the end of the quest into the beginning. Is this too audacious an assumption? This elicits counter-questions. Why remain within the circle of the probable as if the circle of the possible did not also exist? Where did the saying "Adventures are for the adventurous" come from if not from human experience?

121

Even if he has no spiritual experience at all but only complete faith in it, even if he cannot live the role of the illumined fulfilled man, then let him act it. This is an exercise to be practised. Let him try to think and behave as if his quest is successful, let him copy the fulfilled philosopher.

122

The "Heavenly Identity" exercise is to be used without exaggerating its possibilities. It should not lead anyone into the belief that it can confer sudden enlightenment. The ego should not be allowed to set up a pseudo self-realization. Yet it remains a useful practice to offset the others which work differently.

123

This practice of picturing oneself as one ought to be, of visualizing the man free from negative qualities and radiant with positive ones that are part of the Quest's ideal, has near-magical results.

124

It is as if the Overself were hypnotizing him out of his lower nature.

125

Let him picture his own self as if it were at the end of its quest. Let him see it enthroned on the summit of power and engaged in tranquil meditation for his own joy and for mankind's welfare.

126

Stilling the mind stills also the thoughts and feelings which when active appear as obstacles. Questers are to take the Ideal for suggestion or the Exemplar for imitation, not to torment themselves with the continual thought of the impossibility of success, not to try in hopelessness and despair to create a perfect human being, but because this exercise has the practical value of lifting them, however little, from their present condition.

127

The practice aims at saturating the mind with this idea of true Identity.

128

He learns that he may set his own limits, that so long as he thinks all day that he is only this person, doing and speaking in the ordinary way what men usually do, then he is certainly nothing more. But if he starts the day on a higher level, thinking that he is divine in his inmost being, and keeps on that level as the hours pass, then he will feel closer to it. This is a practical procedure, one which has its effect on consciousness, on character, and on events.

129

The method of the Short Path is to affirm that in the heavenly consciousness of the Overself there is no evil, no wrong-doing, no sinfulness, and no faultiness; and that because the true being of man is there the aspirant should identify himself with it in faith, thought, and vision. In that threefold way he sees himself dwelling and acting in the Overself, and therefore without his specific sins and faults. He regards them as nonexistent and drops anxiety or concern about them. He does this as much as he can from morning to night and this fulfils Jesus' injunction to "pray without ceasing" in a deeper and philosophical sense.

130

Although these methods of picturing your possession of qualities of the Overself as you suppose them to be is helpful, they will not solve your final problem, will not dispose of the parasitic, clinging, personal ego for you.

131

Identity Exercise: He will not have to struggle as on the Long Path. There will no more be irksome effort. The mind will be glad to rest in this positive state, if he holds from the very beginning the faith that it already is accomplished, that the aspiration toward it is being fulfilled *now*, not at some unknown distant time. Such an attitude engenders something more than pleasant feelings of hope and optimism: it engenders subconscious power.

132

It is *now* and not in some future time of achievement that he should, in this exercise, regard only his best self as his Identity.

133

The old trouble-bringing attitudes and self-frustrating ways are the ego's. At the appearance of irritating circumstances, go into reverse by practising the "As If" exercise and thus lift up consciousness here and now.

134

If a man has acting talent, let him try it on this visualization exercise: let him copy the characteristics of illumination. It will be immensely more profitable to him than copying those of some worldly role on a stage. The latter may gain him a livelihood; the former will gain him LIFE.

135

The sage Asvaghosha suggested a practical method of realization which he called "following skilfully" and which was much like the "As If" method. It was more specialized, seeking to combat the habitual dualistic attitudes of thought and speech.

136

Chuang Tzu uses the term "heavenly identity" to express the sudden enlightenment that appearance and reality are basically one.

137

It is a part which he must act for himself, a character which he must take on again and again until it seems as natural to him as it ought to be convincing to others—until what was said about the great Garrick, "You wouldn't know he was acting," becomes just as applicable to him.

138

To practise the "As If" Short Path exercise successfully, it is necessary to let go and forget all past techniques and begin afresh; they are attachments and, to that extent, distractions. They may cause self-consciousness, anxiety for success, and impatience. The divinity is there, within you; have faith that it *is* so and entrust yourself to it.

139

Balance the "As if I am enlightened" exercise: Counter by "As if the Divine Mothers were present" whenever I speak to others, whatever I do, alone or in society. It notes and judges my speed and action. In the first example I am alone always; but in the second I am not, there is the other. The idea is not so much that it notes and judges our actions as that we are in a holy presence.

140

The "As If" exercise uses the kind of imaginative experience which has some affinity with the aspirant, with his temperament. It cannot be the same for everyone. Each will put into it some pictures created from his own ideal, but for all aspirants there will be certain elements shared in common.

141

He cannot be a philosopher part of the time and an unawakened unenlightened person the remainder (or most) of the time: but he can, for the sake of this exercise, imaginatively think that he *is* one. In the light of his antecedent personal history, the attempt may be an audacious one; but if his present longing, determination, and self-discipline are large enough, it may become a magical transforming one.

142

The "Identity" exercise is a changeover from humbly aspiring to a higher level to creatively imagining oneself as being there already. The dangers here are conceit, deceit, and complacency.

143

It is a vision of himself as he could be but transferred from future possibility to present actualization. This "Identity" exercise rightly belongs to the Short Path, for in the case of a beginner, whose knowledge is small, efforts limited, and character unpurified, its practice could be self-deceptive.

144
He shapes himself into another person in imagination, in faith, and in will. For a while he creates the illusion of a new destiny accompanying this new person. Is this not a veritable rebirth? Does he not get away from the old everyday person and forget him utterly through this miraculous transformation? He lives so completely in this visualized ideal self that there is no space left for the old faults, the old weaknesses to creep in.

145
See yourself as you ought to be. Try to act accordingly.

146
The aspirant seeks to feel in his own life the same inner state which illuminated men have described as being in theirs.

147
Even if it only be a pose that is cultivated, it still remains a valuable discipline and exercise which gives good results. For it has much suggestive power, this "As If" method, and is an essential part of the Short Path.

148
The "As If" attitude pays well, provided it is maintained rigidly after having been assumed.

Remembrance exercise

149
Why should the Short Path be a better means of getting Grace than the Long one? There is not only the reason that it is not occupied with the ego but also that it continually keeps up remembrance of the Overself. It does this with a heart that gives, and is open to receive, love. It thinks of the Overself throughout the day. Thus, it not only comes closer to the source from which Grace is being perpetually radiated, but it also is repeatedly inviting Grace with each loving remembrance.(P)

150
Any action must be properly timed if it is to give its best return, but this is the only kind which can be done at any time—*now*—and in any place—*here*. This simple movement of the mind in remembrance is easy enough for anyone at any stage of evolution to perform yet important enough for the wisest of us.

151

To acknowledge this Presence and this Power within him as continually or as often as he can, is a practice whose results are larger than its simplicity suggests.

152

The basis of this exercise is that the remembering of the Overself leads in time to the forgetting of the ego. To let the mind dwell constantly on the thought of the Overself, tranquillizes it. To bring the figure of the spiritual guide into it, strengthens it.

153

To keep the Overself constantly in our thoughts is one of the easiest ways to become worthy of its grace.

154

The student must place this seed-thought in his mind and hold to it throughout the day. He need not fear that he will lose anything material thereby. Let him remember the definite promise of the Overself speaking through Krishna in the *Bhagavad Gita*: "I look after the interests and safety of those who are perpetually engaged on My service, and whose thoughts are always about Me and Me alone." He will learn by direct experience the literal meaning of the term Providence—"that which provides."(P)

155

How long should a man practise this remembrance of the Overself? He will need to practise it so long as he needs to struggle with his ego.

156

No amount of exaggerated homage to a guru can take the place of remembering the Real.

157

Emerson knew this practice. "By His remembrance, life becomes pervaded with nectarine bliss," he said.

158

If the past is unredeemable, and the future unpredictable, what more practical course is open than to safeguard the present by constant remembrance of the divine?

159

The practice of recollection was, and still is, used by the Sufis, Muhammedan mystics, to draw the feelings more and more away from the earthly things to the divine.

160

The Overself, like a woman, wants to be loved ardently and exclusively.

The door upon which you may have been knocking a long time in vain will open to your frequent loving remembrances.

161

He may not mention such a thing as spiritual being but it is thought at the back, in the middle, and even in the front of his head. It is irremovable and irreplaceable.

162

The *Vedas* tell us that the constant remembrance and thinking of oneself as pure Spirit makes one overcome delusion and obtain Truth.

163

Constant remembrance of the Overself's presence becomes a way to counter the much more evident presence of the body and the world—that is, the illusion of matter.

164

His awareness is still only a babe; it needs to grow and growth calls for nourishment. This he is to give by the simple act of remembering and attending to it.

165

Fix the attention undividedly upon the Overself which is anchored in your heart-centre. Then everything you do during the day will naturally be divinely inspired action and true service. The Overself is your true source of power: turn towards it and receive its constructive guidance for your task of daily living.

166

By reorienting thought toward Overself, forgetfulness sets in for the little self: the measure of one is the measure of the other.

167

It is needful to reserve a part of one's being, consciousness, or thought, for this unique remembrance, which is of a value set apart from all others.

168

To remember the Overself's presence amid the bustle of everyday living is more cheerful than to remember Death's presence amid the fullness of everyday activity. But whereas the one is always desirable the other is only occasionally desirable. And whereas the thought of dying repels, disgusts, or frightens most men, the thought of the Overself exhilarates them.

169

By keeping close to the Overself he can gain its protective guiding or helpful influence. No day should pass without its remembrance, no enterprise should be begun without its invocation.

170

Forget "me" in the remembrance of "Thee."

171

Shams Tabriz: "Keep God in remembrance until the self is forgotten." Here is a whole yoga path in one short, simple sentence.

172

The best way to honour this immense truth of the ever-present reality of the Overself is to *remember* it—as often, as continuously, and as determinedly as possible. It is not only the best way but also the most rewarding one. For then its saving grace may bestow great blessing.

173

He will not even approach the hour of his daily exercise without feeling quieted and inspired. For he remembers that it was during such a period that the Overself gave him his most joyous experience, his most heartening moments.

174

To put oneself regularly into the practice of this remembrance is to come within the cheering warmth of these higher truths.

175

Better than any long-drawn yoga discipline is the effort to rivet one's hold on the here-and-now of one's divinity.

176

THE OVERSELF REMEMBRANCE EXERCISE

Name: It is so simple that it is called an exercise only for name's sake. In the beginning it requires effort just like any other practice.

How to:

1) To be practised at all times, in all places and under all bodily conditions. It consists of the constant loving recall to mind of the existence of, and his inner identity with, the Overself.

2) It involves the repeated and devoted recollection that there is this other and greater self, a warm, felt, living thing, overshadowing and watching over him.

3) It should be continued until he is able to keep the thought of the Overself as a kind of setting for all his other thoughts.

Glimpse: If he has ever had a glimpse of a supersensuous higher existence which profoundly impressed him and perhaps led him to take to the quest, it is *most important* that he should also insert the remembrance of this experience into his exercise. He should try to bring as vividly as possible to his mind the sense of peace and exaltation which he then felt.

Warning: One danger of this remembrance exercise is that it can become automatic too soon and thus merely mechanical and hollow. The remembrance must be a warm, felt, living thing if the spirit of the exercise is to be retained and not lost.

When to:

1) The inward concentration should persist behind and despite outward activity.

2) The Overself remembrance should be held in the back of the mind, even though he may appear to be properly attentive to external matters.

3) He should keep the exercise always or as often as possible in the mind's background while paying attention to duties in the foreground.

4) Though the foreground of his consciousness is busy attending to the affairs of daily living, its background abides in a kind of sacred emptiness wherein no other thought may intrude than this thought of the Overself.

5) The remembrance should become the unmoved pivot upon which the pendulum of external activity swings perpetually to and fro.

Free time: When he has free time, it should come to the fore. Every time there is relaxation from duties, he should let attention fly eagerly and more fully back to it.

How long: He should train himself in this exercise:

1) until it becomes quite easy and effortless;

2) until this inward concentration has been set in habitual motion;

3) until the remembrance continues of its own accord;

4) until its practice has become firmly and successfully established as ceaseless flow;

5) until the loving recall to mind of the existence of, and his inner identity with, the Overself becomes constant;

6) until the practice is absorbed in perfect and perpetual performance;

7) until he experiences the Overself unceasingly as the unannounced and impersonal centre of his personal gravity.

Potency: This method has a peculiar potency of its own despite its informal and unprogrammed character. Its unexpected effectiveness is therefore not to be measured by its obvious simplicity.

Grace: When the remembrance becomes ceaseless flow, the Overself will bring him a remarkable fruitage of grace. When he turns habitually inwards toward the Overself, grace can operate more readily in all matters.

When the grace starts working, this is likely to remove a number of internal and external obstacles in his path—sometimes in a seemingly miraculous manner—and eventually bring him to a truer self-awareness.

177

Constant Remembrance Exercises: The Overself is a term of which past experience may furnish no meaning. But perhaps you have had strangely beautiful moments when everything seemed to be still, when an ethereal world of being seemed very near to you. Well, in those moments you were lifted up to the Overself. The task you should set yourself is to recapture that blessed presence and feel once again that beautiful interlude of un-earthly stillness. If, however, you cannot recall such moments or if, recall-ing them, you cannot regain afresh their vividness and reality, then there is an alternative path. Make it your business to recall the picture and pres-ence of some man whom you believe is awake to his Overself-conscious-ness. Take him as your guru and therefore as an outstretched hand which you can mentally grasp and by which you can gradually lift yourself. Thus if the Overself is a vague abstraction to you, he, as a living person whom you have met, is not. He can easily be for you a definite focus of concentra-tion, a positive point in the infinite to which you can direct your inward glance.

178

Seize the odd moments for Remembrance practice, escaping from the web of self-thoughts into the Void of Being.

179

His practice of constantly bringing the Overself to mind is a valuable part of the aspirant's equipment. Each remembrance has a twofold value: first, as a mystical exercise to cultivate concentration, and second, as a recurrent turning-away from worldly thoughts to spiritual ones.

180

There are leisure moments or unoccupied minutes during the day which could profitably be used for this exercise.

181

If he can lovingly recall those moments when thought became incandes-cently bright and feeling was lifted high above its ordinary self, meditation upon them will be especially fruitful and profitable.

182

At odd moments in the very midst of worldly activity he is to recall what his mental and emotional state was like when he reached peak heights during formal meditation in seclusion. And for the brief space of those moments he is to try by creative imagination to feel that he is back on those heights.

183

In this meditation he reproduces the conditions which surrounded him at the time the Glimpse came. He fills in every tiny detail of the picture— the furnishings of a room perhaps, the faces and voices of other persons who were present, and especially how he became aware of the first onset of the Glimpse.

184

It could well be said that the essence of the Short Path is remembering who he is, what he is, and then attending to this memory as often as possible.(P)

185

Concentrate on reliving in intense memorized detail former moments of egoless illumination.(P)

186

In remembrance, he should once again love the beauty and revere the solemnity of this experience. If the effort to remember the Overself is kept up again and again, it attenuates the materialistic mental tendencies inherited from former lives and arrests the natural restlessness of attention. It eventually achieves a mystical concentration of thoughts akin in character to that reached during set periods of meditation, but with the added advantage of not stopping the transaction of worldly activity.

Moments of utter inward stillness may come to him. The ordinary familiar ego will then desert him with a lightning-like suddenness and with hardly less brevity. Let him fix these moments firmly in his memory. They are to be used in the ensuing years as themes for meditation and goals for striving.

187

A useful method is to stop whatever he is doing, remain still, and let his mind fly back to the thought of the Overself. He is to make this break several times a day, the more often the better, but he may find it easier to begin with only two or three times a day and gradually to extend the number over a few months.

188

Those moments when the feeling of something beyond his present existence comes to him are precious indeed. They must be eagerly welcomed and constantly nourished by dwelling upon them again and again, both in remembrance and in meditation. The loving recollection of those beautiful inspired moments and the intense concentration upon them is in itself a mystical exercise of special importance. This exercise is designed to help the learner transcend his attachment to externality, his tendency to live in the senses as though they alone reported reality.

189

It is not only needful to practise this remembrance as often as convenient or even possible, but also for as long as convenient or possible.

190

The earnest seeker is always busy, for whenever there is a slackness of time he has business to transact with the true self.

191

There is one method whereby the treasures found in meditation may be brought, little by little, into the active state. This is to try to recollect, at odd times during the day, the peace, bliss, strength, or truth, or any messages gleaned during the best moments of the preceding meditation. The more often this is done, the sooner will the gap between meditation and activity be bridged.

192

What Confucius called "the Superior Man" will constantly keep his mind on superior topics and not waste its energy on trivialities. And the best of all these topics is the Overself—the glimpses of its nature, the remembrance of its being his essential selfhood.

193

Hatim Hashim, a dervish of Khorassan, said: "Remember whatever you do, eat, enjoy, it is being seen by God who is looking at you. During the silence hour, meditate on God as the All-Seer." He also said, "He who looks up to God in the daily trials of life, and whose only hope is God and none but God . . ."

194

If he is to reconstruct this brief yet beautiful experience, he must work systematically every day to create within himself a condition of mental quiet for a few minutes at least.

195

He has to learn by practice the art of retreating at any moment into the mystic citadel within the heart.

196

Let him immerse himself in that feeling and little by little a powerful sense of well-being will penetrate his heart.

197

Concentrate on the remembered delight, the lovely silence, of some past Glimpse. Try to bring it into sharp vivid focus.

198

The effort at this higher stage (Short Path) is not to follow fixed schedules for mental quiet but constantly to remember Overself. If, however, he feels drawn to practise at any time, he does so.

199

If he practises this exercise in remembrance frequently throughout the day then every act not only becomes a necessary or a useful one but helps to carry him forward on his quest of higher being.

200

Although when feeling a descent of the stillness the aspirant is told to drop whatever he is doing and to hold himself in the stillness as long as he can or as long as it is there, he may also practise a useful exercise entirely on his own initiative at any time of the day involving a similar mental and physical posture. For this purpose he holds whatever he is doing whenever he wishes and as often as he wishes and keeps himself suspended, as it were, not moving, not thinking of anything else except the passive remembrance of the Overself. This special exercise of remembrance may be done for a single minute or for a few, just as he wishes.

201

He should try to remember the inner and outer conditions under which the glimpse came to him and, temporarily, try to make them again part of himself and his surroundings. He is to do so as if he were an actor appearing in this part on a stage. For the time being, he must think, feel, and live as if the experience is really happening, the glimpse really recurring. For the time being he must enter the world of imagination and copy the remembered details, the treasured impressions, as specifically as he can. The image which his past supplies is to be transferred to his present, brought to life again and reincarnated afresh. If he is unable to achieve such similarity at the first trial, this need not deter him from making a third, a seventh, and a twentieth trial on later days.

202

Recall the glimpse as vividly as possible. Select the highest experience that stands out in memory and recast it.

203

In this matter the words of the *Koran* must be taken literally: "Believers hasten to the remembrance of Allah and leave off all business."

204

When this stage is attained, the work he has to do in reorienting attention toward the Overself-thought is not any more for the particular sessions of meditation practice alone, but also to be kept up during the day's activities. Attention will have to be returned again and again to this simple but primary requirement.

205

There is no moment when this work of inner remembrance may stop. It ought to start at the time of rising from bed in the morning and continue to the time of retiring to bed at night.

206

It is possible that he may fall into the mistaken belief that because he has relieved himself of the duties and toils of the Long Path, he has little else to do than give himself up to idle dreaming and lazy optimism. No—he has taken on himself fresh duties and other toils, even though they are of a different kind. He has to learn the true meaning of "pray without ceasing" as well as to practise it. He has to meditate twenty times a day, even though each session will not be longer than a minute or two. He has to recollect himself, his essential divinity, a hundred times a day. All this calls for incessant work and determined effort, for the exercise of energy and zeal.

207

The next goal is to keep himself in the Consciousness, whether he lives with others in community or alone with himself in solitude.

208

This work of constant remembrance is one of self-training. The mind is accustomed by habit and nature to stay in the ego. It has to be pulled out and placed in the thought of the higher self, and kept there.

209

You should imaginatively recapture it as if its benign presence comes over you, its goodwill pervades you, its guidance helps you, and its peace enfolds you.

210

Continuous remembrance of the Stillness, accompanied by automatic entry into it, is the sum and substance of the Short Path, the key practice to success. At all times, under all circumstances, this is to be done. That is to say, it really belongs to and is part of the daily and ordinary routine existence. Consequently, whenever it is forgotten, the practitioner must note his failure and make instant correction. The inner work is kept up until it goes on by itself.(P)

211

The essence of the matter is that he should be constantly attentive to the intuitive feeling in the heart and not let himself be diverted from it by selfishness, emotion, cunning, or passion.(P)

212

One of the most valuable forms of yoga is the yoga of constant remembrance. Its subject may be a mystical experience, intuition, or idea. In essence it is really an endeavour to insert the transcendental atmosphere into the mundane life.(P)

213

The method of this exercise is to maintain uninterruptedly and unbrokenly the remembrance of the soul's nearness, the soul's reality, the soul's transcendence. The goal of this exercise is to become wholly possessed by the soul itself.(P)

214

This constant remembrance of the higher self becomes in time like a kind of holy communion.(P)

215

The first goal is to become absorbed in this recollection of the Overself and anchored in this affirmation of it.

216

Stick to the remembrance of the Overself with dogged persistence wherever you are and whatever you are doing. This is one of the easiest, the simplest, and the safest of all yoga paths to reach the goal effectively. Anyone, be he the most intellectual of metaphysicians or the most unintellectual of illiterates, may use this path and use it with success.

217

He must think as often and as intently of the Overself as an infatuated girl thinks of the next appointed meeting with her lover. His whole heart must be held captive, as it were, by this aspiration. This is to be practised not only at set formal times but also constantly throughout the day as an exercise in recollection. This yoga, done at all times and in all places, becomes a permanent life and not merely a transient exercise. This practice of constant remembrance of the Overself purifies the mind and gradually renders it naturally introverted, concentrates and eventually illumines it.

218

Take it with you wherever you go—first, in remembrance as Idea, then, as you develop, in actuality as Presence.

219

It is a long way from the custom which satisfies religious need by attendance at church for an hour or two once a week, to the recollection which thirsts and hungers every moment anew.

220

Whether he is leisurely at ease or actively at work, the practice of Remembrance can go on—the only difference between the two states being a difference of its intensity and vividness.

221

The practice of Remembrance begins with an act of choice, since it throws out of the mind all that it conveniently can without interfering with the work or matter in hand.

222

He is to keep the mind concentrated inwardly on the real self every wakeful moment until it will stay by itself in the real self. The aim is not to entertain a passing idea but to surrender to a habit which remains.

223

The woman far advanced in pregnancy may be attending to household duties—may cook, sew, or wash most of the day—yet not at any moment will her mind be completely carried away from the infant she is bearing inside.

224

With his mind constantly reverting to the Overself (like a silent *mantram*) as the Reality to which he aspires, the inner work goes on.

225

It comes with time and practice, this ability to move at will from activity to meditation, from working or walking to stillness or worship.

226

How can he adjust his vision of eternity to living prosaically in the here and now? It is hard and, like many others, he will fail. But repeated effort, undaunted practice, comprehension of the Short Path may enable him to do so at last.

227

"Be with IT" is the best advice for those who can understand it.

228

Once you have caught this inner note in your experience of your own self-existence, try to adhere firmly to the listening attitude which catches it.

229

Whether his body finds itself among thieves or his mind finds itself among theories, the aspirant's duty of being *aware* ever remains paramount. He may work in the home, the office, or the field, and this activity should be quite compatible with holding on to the higher consciousness, through practice of this Recollection Exercise. The latter need not get in the way of his ordinary faculties or perceptions.

230

The teaching of "the practice of the presence of God" by Brother Lawrence seems very simple to follow and very easy to do. After all, did he not succeed in it for upwards of forty years? But let us remember that he combined it with merely mechanical kitchen work. It did not and could not distract him from carrying out his tasks. But to combine it with intellectual desk work is quite another matter. Obviously this is far more difficult than combining it with simple manual labour.

231

The mind's faculties are all brought together in an intense projection out of himself into the unpicturable but inwardly sensed Presence, the Overself.

232

Reminiscence—recollection by the mind of its own identity—is itself equal to a meditation.

233

Let it be constant meditation on or remembrance of (and return to) the Ultimately True, the Supremely Important, the Absolute Real.

234

Every time he departs from the stillness there is needed a warning awareness. This does not easily or normally come by itself but by self-training, self-observation—"mindfulness," the Buddha called it. The feeling for it has to be persistently nurtured; first brought into being, then preserved at all hours of the day and in whatever surroundings he finds himself.

235

The Short Path not only requires him to turn his attention in the Overself's direction but also to maintain it there.

236

Be present at your thinking and breathing and feeling and doing. This is what the Buddha called "mindfulness." But the highest possible form of mindfulness is to be present with the Overself for, after all, the other four are concerned with the ego, even though they are attempts to free yourself from it; but here it concerns that which completely transcends the ego.

237

The loving, adoring recollection of the Overself, the constant return to memory of it amid the world's distractions, the reiteration of this divine thought as a permanent background to all other thinking, is itself a yoga path. Indeed it is the same as that taught by Saint Paul when he wrote, "Pray without ceasing" and "Bring every thought into captivity to Jesus Christ."

238

The immediate task is to become increasingly aware of the Overself's presence, or, if you are working under a master, of the master's presence in your own heart.

239

This seemingly simple exercise is of universal availability, for it can be done wherever he wishes and whenever he wishes. There is no moment which does not offer a chance to practise it, no situation in which it is not opportune. All that he has to do is to remember that he is a Quester, that he is also a divine being as well as an animal being, that he must act from his whole manhood and not merely from a fragment of it. But this remembrance is not to be struggled for; it is to be established as a natural habit and a relaxing one, whatever the tensions around him. The more he practises the more he can consolidate this way of life, this unique combination of acting in the world as if he knew nothing more than worldly demands and being within himself quite detached from the world.

240

When the naturalness of living fully in the Divine Presence while working in the world becomes a daily experience, the man will be living and existing at one and the same time on different levels.

241

"As a bird may go to roam in the sky and still think of its young one; as a mother may be engaged in household duties and yet think of her child; as a she-monkey may leap from tree to tree and yet clasp its young one to her bosom; even so we should constantly think of the Lord of the three worlds," sang the Indian poet Janabai.

242

The successful philosopher is no dreamer: he keeps his practicality, his interest in world affairs, his willingness to accept responsibility, thus remaining an effective servant of mankind. But all this is done *within* the Remembrance.

243

When activity of any kind, in work or in leisure, takes place in this atmosphere of remembrance, it becomes sacramental even though the ordinary observer may not know it.

244

To keep up this remembrance all the time, in all circumstances, requires practice and perseverance to an extent that seems beyond the ordinary. But they are actually within everyone's untapped resources and untouched reserves.

245

The double awareness practised by women who knit a woollen garment at the same time that they talk with one another is one familiar example of the mind's power in this direction. It makes plausible the double awareness practised by the sage, whose movement and activity in ordinary worldly life is concurrent with his rest in the background of transcendental spirit.

246

In this way, and by this regular observance, he sets up gradually a new rhythm in his mental and emotional worlds, imposes little by little a new pattern on his behaviour.

247

The young man who longs to see his sweetheart once again, the professional man who nurtures the ambition to get a higher position, and the businessman eager to secure a contract—each revolves in his mind the same intrusive thought again and again. It is in fact the background of all other thoughts all the time.

248

The continuous remembrance of the Overself as the unseen background upon which the personal panorama unfolds itself enables us to keep a proper perspective upon events and affords us the final cure of troublesome ills.

249

Meditation should so develop that it becomes a constant attitude of recollectedness. The set exercises in concentration for short periods belong to the earlier stages and are intended simply to obtain mental control.

250

The practice of this remembrance exercise may be pushed so far that it comes to haunt the man to a surprising degree.

251

The goal is to remember the Overself without interruption and at all times.

252

He must work unwearyingly at this task of self-recollection, for it is important that he shall not show spiritual-mindedness out merely because he has let business-mindedness in.

253

He has a mirror in his hand all the time.

254

He learns to look away from the ego and turn to the Overself. He keeps his thoughts as often as possible on the remembrance of the latter's infinite ever-presence. He keeps his heart occupied with the feelings of peace, faith, harmony, and freedom that this remembrance generates.

255

This act of recollection requires no effort, no exercise of the power of will. It is an act of turning in, through and by the power of love, toward the source of being. Love redirects the attention and love keeps it concentrated, sustained, obedient.

256

He is wrong to object that you can't hold two different thoughts at the same time and that hence you can't remember God and attend to worldly details simultaneously. You can. God is *not* a thought, but an awareness on a higher level. Mind does not hold God. Certainly, mind can't have two objects of thought, for they are in duality, but they can be held by God's presence. Only here is the union of subject and object possible. All other thoughts are in duality.(P)

CONTEMPLATIVE STILLNESS

No picture of a beautiful landscape can ever be a substitute for the landscape itself. All ideas of the higher consciousness are at best pictures in thought, and can never be a satisfactory substitute for the consciousness itself. If he wants to pass to the reality pictured by them he will have to pass out of the second stage into contemplation, the third stage.

2

If he progresses with these ego-crushing efforts and with these ever-deepening meditations on the Divine, he will come nearer and nearer to the true core of his being.

3

The ultramystic exercises *follow after* and *are the sequel to* ripe reasoned thinking. They banish thoughts only after thoughts have done their utmost work, whereas ordinary yoga banishes thoughts prematurely.

4

At this exalted stage, mind abides immersed in itself, not in its productions and functions.

5

This condition of concentrated quietness is what the Master Lu Tze quaintly describes as "the condition in which you sit like a withered tree before a cliff."

6

When the ego contemplates the Overself with perfect attention, there is dismay in hell but joy in heaven.

7

Meditation often leads to fatigue but contemplation never. The one takes strength from him, the other gives it to him.

8

If meditation may have unfortunate results when its concentrative power is applied negatively or selfishly, contemplation—its higher phase—may have similar results when its passive condition is entered without previous purification or preparation. Miguel de Molinos knew this well and therefore put a warning in the preface of his book *The Spiritual Guide* which treats with the authority of an expert the subject of contemplation. "The doctrine of this book," he announced, "instructs not all sorts of persons, but those only who keep the senses and passions well mortified, who have already advanced and made progress in Prayer."(P)

9

There is a single basic principle which runs like a thread through all these higher contemplation exercises. It is this: if we can desert the thoughts of particular things, the images of particular objects raised by the senses in the field of consciousness, and if we can do this with complete and intelligent understanding of what we are doing and why we are doing it, then such desertion will be followed by the appearance of its own accord of the element of pure undifferentiated Thought itself; the latter will be identified as our innermost self.(P)

10

Now an extraordinary and helpful fact is that by making Mind the object of our attention, not only does the serenity which is its nature begin to well up of its own accord but its steady unchanging character itself helps spontaneously to repel all disturbing thoughts.(P)

11

There is, in this third stage, a condition that never fails to arouse the greatest wonder when initiation into it begins. In certain ways it corresponds to, and mentally parallels, the condition of the embryo in a mother's womb. Therefore, it is called by mystics who have experienced it "the second birth." The mind is drawn so deeply into itself and becomes so engrossed in itself that the outer world vanishes utterly. The sensation of being enclosed all round by a greater presence, at once protective and benevolent, is strong. There is a feeling of being completely at rest in this soothing presence. The breathing becomes very quiet and hardly perceptible. One is aware also that nourishment is being mysteriously and rhythmically drawn from the universal Life-force. Of course, there is no intellectual activity, no thinking, and no need of it. Instead, there is a k-n-o-w-i-n-g. There are no desires, no wishes, no wants. A happy peacefulness, almost verging on bliss, as human love might be without its passions and pettinesses, holds one in magical thrall. In its freedom from mental working and perturbation, from passional movement and emotional agitation, the condition bears something of infantile innocence. Hence Jesus' saying: "Except ye become as little children ye shall in no wise enter the Kingdom of Heaven." But essentially it is a return to a spiritual womb, to being born again into a new world of being where at the beginning he is personally as helpless, as weak, and as dependent as the physical embryo itself.(P)

12

In the third stage, contemplation, the mind ceases to think and simply, without words, worships loves and adores the Divine.(P)

13

When a hushed silence falls on a man or on a whole group and is properly received, that is, welcomed and sustained, there is then one of those uncommon opportunities to let mystical peace reveal itself. The happening may originate in the man's or the group's poignant aspiration for a higher kind of life, or at the close of listening to great religious music, or on entry into a grand or ancient forest landscape. This is the moment to touch its healing pervasive depth, ordinarily so elusive.

14

To think about thinking leads the understanding towards the verge of its own source. To contemplate contemplation leads it directly into that source itself.

15

It is a condition where every intervention of thinking—however rational, however plausible—is a sacrilege.

16

"Contemplation for an hour is better than formal worship for sixty years."—Muhammed

17

"It is immaterial whether, for this purpose (meditation), an external object, an idea, a concept or nothingness, is focussed. It is a question of practising pure quiescence. The mere accumulation of force which absolute stillness brings with it creates an increase in one's power of concentration. It is unbelievable how important for our inner growth is a few minutes of conscious abstraction every morning."—Count Keyserling

18

In the profoundest state of contemplation, the thinking faculty may be entirely suspended. But awareness will not be suspended. Instead of being aware of the unending procession of varied images and emotions, there will be a single joyous serene and exalted consciousness of the true thought-transcending self.

19

He will find himself in the mind's deep silence, the heart's gentle stillness, reached after forsaking the ego's activity.

20

"While in the opinion of society contemplation is the gravest thing of which any citizen can be guilty, in my opinion of the highest culture it is the proper occupation of man."— Oscar Wilde

21

He is a sailor, taking spiritual soundings in the deeper water of his own being.

22

In this stage of contemplation, the externalizing faculty of his mind ceases to operate. This means that he can no longer see hear feel smell or taste any physical objects. But it does not mean that he can no longer form corresponding ideas of those objects. To arrive at such a situation is indeed the work of the following stage. Therein even the possibility of imagining every kind of external experience completely disappears.

23

Silence often falls upon a group only to embarrass them, to fill their minds with discomfort, and to oppress their hearts with disquiet. Yet it could be made, through contemplation, to bring exquisite felicity.

24

To sit in the stainless silence, watchful yet passive, is the proper art of contemplation.

25

The mind then becomes so serene and immobile that there is not even the thought of a thought.

26

During such meditations the place around may seem to be filled to overflowing with a sense of the divine presence.

27

What he finds so deeply within himself is neither a thought nor an emotion. It is a fused knowing-feeling.

28

There is a state of mental silence, when no analytic thinking, logical deliberation, or argumentative discussion is possible. The mind is so stilled that all its discursive operations stop completely. By its very nature this state cannot last. It is temporary—from a few minutes to a few days.

29

In this condition, with mind shifted away from sensory experience into a fixed self-absorption and stilled to the utmost degree, the meditator may be said to have mastered contemplation.

30

The mind becomes as still as if he were in the deepest largest cave penetrating a mountainside.

31

When the requisite preparatory instruction has been passed through, and when the mind lets thoughts go, lets objects go, lets the ego go, it comes to know itself, to perceive itself, to discover itself as Overself.

32

In that stillness, far from the physical activities, emotional excitations, and mental changes of everyday life, "the awareness of awareness" becomes possible, the Mind itself is isolated. The real being of a man is at last discovered and exhibited.

33

The Japanese system of defense called karate has been demonstrated on the James Bond secret agent films before millions of cinema and television viewers. Despite this, there are still only a few experts in Europe who have passed the tests necessary to admit them into the higher grades called Black Belt. Discussion with one of these adepts brought out some common ground between the practice of karate and the practice of contemplation. One of the principal feats necessary to achieve the Black Belt grade is to cut through one or even two bricks with a single blow of the outside edge of the hand. If the karate pupil concentrates on the brick itself, he will never succeed in breaking through it. He must instead concentrate on the ground beneath the brick, thus admitting no thought of doubt, fear, or hesitation as to whether or not he can cut the brick. In fact, during the moment before striking the brick, he must suspend all thinking. And if any such negative thoughts do enter his mind, he must then abandon the attempt altogether for that period. The emphasis is laid on immediacy, on direct penetration unobstructed by thoughts of any kind. The meditator whose mind is centered on his own working of the meditation technique is like the karate pupil who fixes his mind on the brick. This is a mistake. But the meditator who fixes his mind on the Overself is like the pupil who concentrates his thought on the ground below the brick itself, and this is what leads to success. Obviously, such advice is not suited to the early or elementary stages of meditation where concentration is required. On the contrary, it belongs to the more advanced stage where success comes not from trying but from letting go, relaxing.

34

The mere absence of thoughts is not necessarily presence of Reality-Consciousness.

35

Thinking lies still as if it were a dead faculty, the mind void of movement, emptied of thoughts.

36

There are plenty of misconceptions about the nature of mystical contemplation. They range from the utterly absurd to the perfectly reasonable. A serious one is that the aim of such contemplation is to lose consciousness. Anyone who has been hit over the head can do that!

37

In that deep state the mind is at perfect equilibrium. The forces which ordinarily drive it into conflict or passion are thoroughly restrained.

38

His consciousness, freed of thoughts, is then *in itself*, unmixed and unprojected.

39

Those who know this method and can practise it successfully, know also the extraordinary change which comes over their whole being when the mind is stilled.

40

When his thoughts are brought into a stilled condition and his awareness fully introverted, a state resembling sleep will supervene but, unlike sleep, it will be illumined by consciousness.

41

In this state of "conscious sleep" there is no awareness of the physical body and no movement of thoughts succeeding one another. The Stillness alone reigns.

42

This state is indescribable. He is neither asleep nor awake.

43

The resultant condition is no negative state. Those who imagine that the apparent blankness which ensues is similar to the blankness of the spiritualistic medium do not understand the process. The true mystic and the hapless medium are poles apart. The first is supremely positive; the second is supinely negative. Into the stilled consciousness of the first ultimately steps the glorious divinity that is our True Self, the world-embracing shining One; into the blanked-out consciousness of the second steps some insignificant person, as stupid or as sensible as he was on earth, but barely more; or worse, there comes one of those dark and malignant entities who prey upon human souls, who will drag the unfortunate medium into depths of falsehood and vice, or obsess her to the point of suicide.(P)

44

It is not a dreamy or drowsy state. He is more lucidly and vitally conscious than ever before.(P)

45

It is not just ceasing to think, although it prerequires that, but something more: it is also a positive alertness to the Divine Presence.(P)

46

This last stage, contemplation, is neither deep reflective thinking nor self-hypnotic trance. It is intense awareness, without the intrusion of the little ego or the large world.(P)

47

It is something far deeper than mere restful quietness, something dynamic and intense.

48

In this strange experience he seems to be doing nothing at all, to be mentally quite inactive, all his forces having reached a full stop. Yet the Overself is intensely active.

49

When he is settled down in this final stage, his mind takes on a diamond-like quality—hard and unchangeable in its identification with its deepest layer, bright and positive in its radiation.

50

The stillness is not a cold one: it is living, radiant.

51

The ever-shifting intellect has at last been established in the eternal stillness of the soul that now dominates it; the leaping mercury has been solidified and the alchemical instrument prepared wherewith human base metal can be turned into spiritual gold, immune to the corrosive acids of earthly experience.

52

There are definite stages which mark his progress. First he forgets the larger world, then his immediate surroundings, then his body, and finally his ego.

53

The differences between the first and second stages [concentration and meditation, respectively—ed.] are: (a) in the first there is no effort to understand the subject or object upon which attention rests, whereas in the second there is; (b) concentration may be directed to any physical thing or mental idea, whereas meditation must be directed to thinking about a spiritual theme either logically or imaginatively.

In the third stage [contemplation—ed.] this theme pervades the mind so completely that the thinking activity ceases, the thoughts and fancies vanish. The meditator and his theme are then united; it is no longer separate from him. Both merge into a single consciousness. To shut off all perceptions of the outer world, all physical sense-activities of seeing hearing and touching, is the goal and end of the first stage. It is achieved when concentration on one subject or object is fully achieved. To shut off all movements of the inner world, all mental activities of thinking, reasoning, and imagining, is the goal and end of the second stage. It is achieved when the subject or object pervades awareness so completely that the meditator forgets himself and thus forgets even to think about it: he is it. To shut off all thoughts and things, even all sense of a separate personal existence, and rest in contemplation of the One Infinite Life-Power out of which he has emerged, is the goal and end of the third stage.

54

In these first two stages, the will must be used, for the attention must not only be driven along one line and kept there but must also penetrate deeper and deeper. It is only when the frontier of the third stage is reached that all this work ceases and that there is an abandonment of the use of the will, a total surrender of it, and effortless passive yielding to the Overself is alone needed.

55

In the second stage he is to banish some thoughts and keep the others. In the third stage he is to banish all thoughts and keep none. This is the most difficult.

56

The second and third stages may have five stations from start to finish, although this is not the experience of all aspirants. In the first, the body becomes numb and its weight vanishes. In the second, a fiery burning force uplifts the emotions and energizes the will. In the third, a sensation of being surrounded by light is felt. In the fourth, the man is alone in a dark void. In the fifth he seems to dissolve until there is nothing but the infinite formless being of God.

57

This withdrawal of attention from the immediate environment which occurs when deeply immersed in thought, looking at the distant part of a landscape, or raptly listening to inspired music, is the "I" coming closer to its innermost nature. At the deepest level of this experience, the ego-thought vanishes and "I-myself" becomes merged in the impersonal Consciousness.

58

The third stage is successfully reached when he forgets the world outside, when he neither sees nor touches it, neither hears nor smells it with his body, when memory and personality dissolve in a vacuum as the attention is wholly and utterly absorbed in the thought of, and identity with, the Overself.

59

The body sits, squats, or lies like a motionless statue; the senses are lulled and lethargic, but the mind is quite conscious of where the meditator is and what is happening around him. Only in the next and deeper stage does this consciousness pass away, does the physical self, involved in place and time as it is, lose both: only then is the body robbed of its capacity to move and act.

60

Explanation of diagram: The deeper he looks into his own nature—a procedure which cannot be done without practising meditation—the nearer he will come to the truth about it.

	First Hour	Second Hour	Third Hour
(a) conscious individual mind	(a) attention plunging down		
(b) unconscious individual mind		(b) attention plunging deeper	
(c) impersonal and universal infinite Mind			(c) attention at its deepest level

In the first stage of penetration, his external surroundings, and the whole world with them, vanish. In the second and deeper stage, the feeling "I am rooted in God" alone remains. In the third stage the "I" thought also goes. In the final stage even the idea "God" disappears. There remains then no idea of any kind—only peace beyond telling, consciousness in its pure ever-still state.

If he stops at levels A or B, he is still unable to fulfil his purpose. It is just as if a composer of a piece of music were to stop halfway during its composition. Only by penetrating still farther into the depths of his being until he reaches level C will he be able to undergo that tremendous, profound, and radical change which may be called the first degree of illumination. So sudden and so startling a change could not have come unless he had had the perseverance to make so prolonged a plunge.

Few mystics pass the first degree. The rapture of it detains them.

Experiencing the passage into contemplation

61

As he enters this immobile state, not only do his eyes close to the scenes of this world but his mind closes to the thought of it. The reflected change appears on his face, which is transfigured, mysterious, and serene.

62

The lines of the face become somewhat rigid, the eyes mostly or wholly closed, as he retires into himself and into abstraction from this world. That which draws him magnetically through noisy thoughts to the state of silent thoughtlessness is none other than the soul itself.

63

The world recedes and the last fringes of it in awareness seem a long, long way off. The sensation is exquisitely comforting.

64

He is beginning to succeed when his absorption is so deep that the world outside seems a thousand miles away.

65

At this point he may lose touch with the outer world and no longer see or sense it in any way. The consciousness sinks away from place and form, the passing of time and the solidity of matter, into its own being.

66

The world is more and more shut off as his concentrated attention moves inward until it vanishes altogether. It is then that he may become aware of his unknown "soul" and its peace.

67

In this state the feeling of the passage of time and the perception of forms in space may or may not vanish, according to its depth.

68

The deepest meditation takes the meditator to a completely different level of consciousness. It causes him to drop all thoughts about the world and especially about himself.

69

One cannot experience the outside world in exactly the same way as he is experiencing the inside self. In both ways he is experiencing God, but there is a difference. At the deepest possible point of meditation one reaches the stillness; there is no world-experience any more. Beyond it one cannot go: even the "he" is lost.

70

This feeling of extreme lightness, of entire independence from the body, may grow to such an extreme point of intensity that the idea of being actually levitated into the air may take hold of his mind. He is in such a state that inner reality is confused with physical reality.

71

He feels that his hands become heavy, hard to move. This is because he is half-separated from his body. Soon he feels quite free of them, light as air. The mental change accompanying this liberation is quite extraordinary. He feels that he would smile gravely and tranquilly, if only he could, but he feels only on the verge of doing so, not being quite able to finish it.

72

In that deeper state when the body is held still with concentration, the mind paradoxically feels most liberated.

73

In this deep state the body, while one's consciousness of it remains, assumes a fixed position of its own accord. A powerful force surges through it, straightening the spine, lifting the head, and stretching the feet.

74

There is a strange dislocation of consciousness' seat, pushing it out of his body slightly, up above his head and somewhat behind his torso.

75

There will be no sensation of weight in his physical body and a light airy feeling will replace it. It will also seem as though a heavy inner body has fallen away from him, leaving an ethereal detachment, a delightful liberation, as a result.

76

When he has climbed to this mystical altitude of being where concentration becomes finished and perfect, he will possess the power of entering at will into the inwardly pleasant though outwardly strange condition of rapt absorption. The body will rest rigid and immovable, the eyes will be tight shut, half-closed, or wide open but staring emptily straight before him into space, the face paler than usual, the pulse-beat lower than normal, the breath-cycle slower quieter and shallower, but the mind fully alive.

77

If the consciousness has not previously been prepared, by competent instruction or intuitive understanding, to receive this experience, then the passage out of the body will begin with a delightful sense of dawning liberation but end with a frightful sense of dangerous catastrophe. Both knowledge and courage are needed here, otherwise there will be resistance to the process followed by an abrupt breaking away from it altogether.(P)

78

Consciousness is withdrawn from the senses and nervous system, even life itself is largely withdrawn from the heart and lungs, until the man himself is centered in the higher self.

79

He feels that he is losing command of his senses and that he is lapsing from the safe real normal consciousness of his everyday self.

80

There are stories of Socrates in the Grecian wars and of a nameless yogi in the Indian mutiny, absorbed in such deep contemplation that neither the noise and tumult nor the violence and strife of battle were enough to break it. Each remained bodily still and mentally serene for hours.

81

Saint Teresa writes about what she terms "the trance of union": "As to the body, if the rapture comes on when it is standing or kneeling, it remains so." If, when starting the meditation period, you are suddenly transfixed with the stillness or if it occurs during non-meditation times, remain in the place and attitude as you are. Do not move—or you break the spell. It is then irrecoverable. Never resist this "possession." Obviously this is possible only if alone.

82

In this deep level of meditation, he will scarcely be aware of the body. What awareness there is will objectify it as something he uses or wears, certainly not as himself. He will feel that to be a purely mental being.

83

His power of abstract concentration, of withdrawing into a thought or a series of thoughts, or of having no thoughts at all, shows in the eyes, in their long-sustained stillness, their brilliance and "not-seeing" physically because focused on nothing in particular.

84

The body stilled as if by an outside force, its limbs unwilling to move and its breathing diminished to gentleness—this is the best condition for the higher Consciousness.

85

Noises and sights may be still present in the background of consciousness but the pull and fascination of the inner being will be strong enough to hold him and they will not be able to move his attention away from it. This, of course, is an advanced state; but once mastered and familiar, it must yield to the next one. Here, as if passing from this waking world to a dream one, there is a slip-over into universal space, incredibly vast and totally empty. Consciousness is there but, as he discovers later, this too is only a phase through which it passes. Where, and when, will it all end? When Consciousness is led—by Grace—to itself, beyond its states, phases, and conditions where man, at last, is fit to meet God.

86

There is a mood of deep abstraction when, although the eyes are open, he appears to be looking beyond the immediate surroundings with no precise focus but with apparent wonder.

87

It will feel as if his scalp had been painlessly lifted off his head and as if the mind had been indescribably liberated in the process. It is now released in its own native element—intensely alert, immensely clear and utterly concentrated, gloriously beautiful and serenely percipient.

88

You will experience the sensation of rising, of hovering over your body.

89

The body seems far away, but *I* seem closer than ever. For I feel that now I am in my mind and no longer the body's captive. There is a sense of release. I am as free as Space itself.

90

In this third phase, contemplation, there is a feeling of being surrounded by the immensity of infinite space with one's own being somehow connected with it.

91

He will feel that he has become an air-being, bodiless and weightless.

92

The stage of contemplation has its own definite signs. Prominent among them are its thought-free emptiness, its utter tranquillity, its absence of personal selfishness.

93

He enters the third stage, contemplation, when the thought or thing on which he fixed his mind alone remains there whereas the consciousness that he is meditating vanishes. He finishes this stage when this residue is none other than the Overself, thus transcending his personal self and losing it in the Overself.

94

When this third stage is reached, there is a feeling, sometimes gradual but sometimes abrupt, that his thought activities have been cancelled out by a superior force.

95

The third stage of practice, contemplation, is definitely a joyous one. There is a subtle feeling of great comfort, sublime ease, at times even expanding into a rich and refined blissfulness.

96

We enter into paradise when, in contemplation, we enter into awareness of the Overself.

97

Those who have their first experience of the delightful peace which may be briefly felt in contemplation may become emotionally excited and mentally thrilled by it. These experiences are useful and helpful, especially for the encouragement they give; but it must be remembered that they are not in themselves the main object of meditation, for they still deal with the person, the personality, even though on its highest and best levels. Only when contemplation leads to a forgetfulness of the personality and a total immersion in the Higher Being is this purpose achieved.

98

When consciousness is stripped of its contents and stands in naked simplicity so that it can be seen as it really is, a tremendous quietude falls upon us. All strivings cease of their own accord.

99

A sudden mysterious tranquillity descends upon him, a feeling as if he were not there at all.

100

His efforts at this stage will be saturated with the hope and expectancy with which one watches a slow sunrise.

101

There is a great calm in this state: not a great rapture, but a patient attentive repose in the higher power.

102

Bring to these intervals your suffering and disappointments, your weariness and burdens, and let them slide into the Mystery that suffuses some of these moments.

103
Once he has been able to establish himself in this inward self-isolation and to adjust himself to its entirely different level of being, he will experience delight and feel peace.

104
All thoughts are submerged in the stillness. The overheated brain is cooled. The emotions are reined in. The profoundest peace reigns in the whole being.

105
He stands on the verge of a great and enigmatic stillness. All Nature seems arrested, all her processes within himself come to a halt.

106
The beginner's ecstatic rapture will grow by degrees into the proficient's impassive serenity.

107
Ecstatic moods, trances, or swoons are not sought by the philosopher, as they are by the saint; but if they do happen to come, as they might, through his meditations he takes care that they will find their proper place and leave his inner equilibrium undisturbed.

108
As he enters this fourth dimension of the Soul, infinite well-being pervades him.

109
The peace of contemplation, when achieved, falls upon us like eventide's hush. The brain's busy travail stops, the world's frantic pressure upon the nerves ends.

110
When there is no consciousness of the world, yet Consciousness-in-itself remains, ecstasy follows.

111
He is submerged in the peace as though it were a great wave.

112
In this state the thought-making activity comes to an end, the intellect itself is absorbed in the still centre of being, and a luminous peace enfolds the man.

113
In this state the world is not presented to consciousness. Consequently none of the problems associated with it is present. No ego is active with personal emotions and particular thoughts. No inner conflicts disturb the still centre of being.

114

He feels that he is upon the very edge of a great revelation, one that will open a new world of beauty and truth for him.

115

His mind is so concentrated that his body makes no movement at all. His thought is so intensified that no one else's thoughts and feelings can come into the focus of attention and sometimes not even their physical presence.

116

While the higher mystic experiences are mostly the same universally, the personal beliefs and teachings of the mystics differ, and usually take some or all of the form of the religious tradition into which they were born.

117

All his fears melt in this triumphant tranquillity as though they had never been.

118

When the flowing stream of thoughts is brought to an end at last, there is indescribable satisfaction.

119

Here is a condition where the only world is the world of pure blissful being itself.

120

The beauty of those calm moments when the tumult of the mind has been stilled, is supreme.

121

When the mind falls into stillness, when time stretches the moment out into a limitless life, man stands on the inner edge of his true soul.

122

The Overself should not be reached merely in trance; it must be known in full waking consciousness. Trance is merely the deepest phase of meditation, which in turn is instrumental in helping prepare the mind to discover truth. Yoga does not yield truth directly. Trance does not do more than concentrate the mind perfectly and render it completely calm. Realization can come after the mind is in that state and after it has begun to inquire, with such an improved instrument, into truth.

123

If he lets *all* his mental energy be absorbed in contemplation of the Real, a state in between waking and sleeping must follow. If he stays in this state too long, a further condition may ensue which is comparable to trance.

124

Saint Catherine of Siena passed often into deep trances, during which she lay bodily rigid and mentally rapt in ecstasy. On some of these occasions her entire physique became so hot that her face was flushed red with blood and covered with drops of perspiration. This is Spirit-Energy.

125

There are physical symptoms of the dawning of the semi-trance state. They are a feeling of tightness around the scalp and of pressure between the temples.

126

The deepest trance state involves the slowing down of all bodily activities to an almost imperceptible level. Even the working of the cells comes nearly, but not quite, to an end. The state, therefore, is a kind of death and, indeed, if prolonged too far, may sometimes result in death.

127

When the practiser is really proficient he may encounter a very profound state of "yoga sleep." This is difficult to describe. It is mysterious and enigmatic. He will not even be quite sure whether or not it happened, but will probably deduce its factuality from the length of time that must have been spent in it. He will not remember anything about it since he is very vaguely aware that total unconsciousness did not occur, that it was not ordinary dreamless sleep, that some kind of spiritual experience was present of which he can form no conception and obtain no understanding. The end result after emerging will be satisfying and pleasant, calming and detaching.

128

With the feeling of the ego's displacement, all feelings of devotional worship or mystical communion also come to an end. For they presuppose duality, a relation which vanishes where there is only the consciousness of a single entity—the Overself.

129

Contemplation, in its fullest measure, is a rehearsal for death. For in letting all thoughts go, we let the world go, we let possessions go, and lastly we let the body go!

130

For the meaning and use of the term "transparency" in describing mystic experience, note (a) Mabel Collins' book on Patanjali uses the title "The Transparent Jewel," (b) the Chinese painter Pata Shan-Jen, seventeenth century: "When the mind is transparent and pure as if reflected on the mirrorlike surface of water; when it is serene. . . ." (c) a Chinese modern writer on art, Juo Chang Chung-yuan: "There is a calmness . . . the atmosphere is of rare transparency . . . his innermost being tranquil."

131

The mind slides into a blankness, where time is not, the movement of hours unmarked by ticking watch, and where the pleasurableness of non-being takes over.

132

At first strange transformations may take place in his space-time sense. Space is grotesquely narrowed while time is grotesquely slowed down. A far-off tree may seem within hand's reach while the movement of a hand itself may seem an hour's work. The concentration of attention becomes so extreme that the whole world narrows down to the preoccupation of the moment. This stage passes away.

133

In this complete stillness, the mental waves come to rest and with them the sense of time is thrown out of function or else so strangely changed that a few minutes become a whole hour.

134

Time itself is erased by the mysterious Power of the Stillness.

135

In that deep state of contemplation the ego becomes a mere potential, the consciousness is unwrinkled by thoughts, the body is completely immobile.

136

By a penetrating to the profound stillness within and a letting go of the world with its turmoil, the higher power itself is found and met: its message is then able to penetrate his consciousness. Such stillness provides the correct condition for letting the man become absorbed into it. For the period in which this happens, his ego thought-simplex vanishes; be it only a few seconds, the pause is most valuable.

137

When the student attains to this stage of meditation, all sensations of an external world sink away but the idea of his own abstract existence still remains. His next effort must therefore be to suppress this idea and if he succeeds then this is followed by a sense of infinity.

138

In those moments when he has gone as deep as seems possible, when he is himself not there and the ego is obliterated, there is real freedom, and most especially freedom from desires, attachments, bonds, dependencies.

139

This is an experience—one of the unforgettable meditations—where the ego dwindles down to a mere point in consciousness.

140

In that passionless calm, where the littlenesses of the ego melt and dissolve, and its agitations sink and lose themselves, he may touch a few moments when he loses the sense of his own identity. The tremendous wonder of it, this delicious liberation from the confines of his own person!

141

All thoughts, and most important the world-thought and the ego-thought, melt little by little into the stillness.

142

How can one forget the first day when one sat in deep contemplation, feeling a mesmeric influence coming over him and drawing him deeper and deeper within, while the sensation of light surrounded him? Deeper and deeper one went until one forgot almost who one was and where one was. How reluctant was the slow return after having played truant to this world and to the ego!

143

That out of which it arises and to which it returns is a sublime stillness, a holy calm.

144

When the senses are completely lulled and the thoughts completely rested, consciousness loses the feeling of movement and with it the feeling of time. The state into which it then passes is an indication of what timelessness means.

145

The ego dissolves into that infinity of relaxed being which is unforgettable and therapeutic. All strains fade out, all pressures vanish with the gentle influx of this peace-filled mood.

146

In that sublime condition his reasoning capacity is powerless, for the thinking function ceases to act, the image-making imagination becomes dormant.

147

In the deepest phase of contemplation all power of speech will temporarily desert him, so rapt inwardly will he become.

148

He remains blissfully without thoughts, without even the thought that he has no thoughts.

149

If we search into the innermost part of our self, we come in the end to an utter void where nothing from the outside world can reflect itself, to a divine stillness where no image and no form can be active. This is the essence of our being. This is the true Spirit.

Still the mind

150

When the emptying of the mind is made the goal of the mind, then it is not really emptied even if this seems to occur. The unexpressed goal is also present, even though unthought during the time of the void. In short it is not a genuine, authentic emptiness. Yet this is the sort of thing that happens in most yogic circles. Only a philosophically informed mind can reach the real void.

151

This experience of self-annihilation (*fana*, the Sufis call it) teaches several valuable truths, but the one which needs mention here is that whether you feel the Reality in an overwhelming mystic experience or not, what matters is that you should carry the unfaltering faith that it is always there, always present with you and within you.

152

The mind is called pure not only when passions and desires have ceased surging through it, but also when thoughts and pictures have ceased to arise, especially the personal self-thought.

153

This exercise in emptying the mind of its thoughts begins as a negative one but must end as a positive one. For when all thoughts are gone, it will then be possible to affirm the pure principle of Thought itself.

154

That which IS, by its very nature, is out of time—while thinking involves a series of points in time. Thinking is finite and limits awareness to finite objects. Therefore, to contact the *infinite* we must go beyond thought. Because human intellect is too finite, it follows that our thoughts cannot encompass it. Since that which IS cannot be taken hold of by thinking of any kind, a part of the essential requirement for contact with it is the non-acting of the thinking function. The mind must be emptied of all its contents in order that its true nature—awareness—should be revealed. At present, it is always entangled with some thought so that awareness by itself is lost in that thought. Self disappears in the ego-thought, and the "I" mistakes the object for the subject—whether the object be the world outside it, or thoughts inside it.

155

When the mind enters into this imageless and thoughtless state, there is nothing in it to resist the union with divine consciousness.

156

If one remembers that speech is a form of communication with other men because it uses words, then he must conclude that thinking is a form of communication with himself since it also uses words. But that means he remains apart separate and distant from himself. This is why the art of meditation, which is the art of finding oneself, involves the practice of mental silence—cutting off words, and that which they express, thoughts.

157

If a state of vacant mind be deliberately and successfully induced, one of the chief conditions requisite to temporary awareness of the soul will then exist.

158

All that he has hitherto known as himself, all those thoughts and feelings, actions and experiences which make up the ego's ordinary life, have now to be temporarily deserted if he would know the universal element hidden behind the ego itself.

159

When the mind is able to remain utterly still in itself, it is able to see and recognize the soul.

160

Says the *Mukti Upanishad*: "There is only one means to control one's mind, that is to destroy thoughts as soon as they arise. That is the great dawn."

161

In the Tibetan work *Buddha Doctrine Among the Birds*, there is a single line which contains an entire technique in its few words. "Put your inmost mind into a state of non-action," it runs.

162

If he wishes to enter the stage of contemplation, he must let go of every thought as it rises, however high or holy it seems, for it is sure to bring associated thoughts in its train. However interesting or attractive these bypaths may be at other times, they are now just that—bypaths. He must rigidly seek the Void.(P)

163

Only in perfect stillness of the mind, when all discursive and invading thoughts are expelled, can the true purity be attained and the ego expelled with them.(P)

164

Every state other than this perfect stillness is a manifestation of the ego, even if it be an inner mystical "experience." To be in the Overself one must be out of the ego, and consequently out of the ego's experience, thoughts, fancies, or images. All these may have their fit place and use at other times but not when the consciousness is to be raised completely to the Overself.(P)

165

"The best form of meditation is to avoid thinking of anything. In the mind so kept clear, God will manifest Himself."—Shankara of Kanchi

166

It is not enough to make the mind a thought-free blank: his thoughts should expire in a state of deep fervent aspiration. After this achievement it must be held motionless, for then only can the touch of grace be felt, the authentic inner experience begin.

167

If he does not practise keeping himself—his body and mind—still, this presence which emanates grace is not given the chance to activate his consciousness. Here is the first secret of meditation—Be still! The second secret is—Know the I am, God! The stillness will have a relaxing and somewhat healing effect, but no more, unless he has *faith*, unless he deliberately seeks communion with God.

168

L.C. Soper: "The mind has to be still, not made still. Effort only leads to a rigid mind. When it realizes the futility of effort to penetrate to reality, the mind becomes still. There is only a self-forgetting attentiveness."

169

The thread of contemplation once broken, it is nearly impossible to pick it up again quickly enough that same time. This is why it is important to let nothing else, not even a change in bodily posture, come to interrupt the contemplation.

170

When the ego is silent, the Overself can speak.

171

When the last thought is absorbed and the mind left alone in its native stillness, if purification and preparation have been in some measure attended to, "then," as Chuang Tzu says,"the heavenly Light is given forth."

172

Hence he must let go of every single and separate thought which arises to bar his path, every sensuous image which memory or anticipation throws down as a gauntlet before him, and every emotion which seeks to detain or distract him.

173

When thoughts cease *of themselves* the stillness comes. When thinking rejects its own activity consciousness *is*.

174

When all movements are at an end, and all physical actions are suspended, he can enter into the most interesting of all states.

175

The catching of the breath happens partly by itself, partly is done deliberately to help bring the body into harmony with a deeper level of mental absorption.

176

"Be still, and know that I am God," sings the Biblical Psalmist. This simply means that the movement of thoughts and emotions is to be brought to an end by entering the deepest degree of contemplation. The same teaching is given in the *Bhagavad Gita*. "As the wick of an oil lamp placed in a wind-free spot is flickerless, so is the yogi of mastered mind who practises union with the God-Self."

177

What is called for at this stage is not so much a renunciation of the world as a renunciation of thoughts—of all thoughts, be they of the gross world or of the spiritual quest!

178

To give up the self means to give up what is ordinarily known as self—that is, personal thoughts and feelings—to the deeper self within. But the latter is pure awareness and void of all emotional or intellectual contents: nothing. Hence when the personal egoity gives up to, and enters, it, such thoughts and feelings become as nothing too. The mind is stilled and they are annihilated.

179

Mind purified of the image-making faculty's work—that is, free from visions, fancies and pictures, symbols, scenes, and every sort of imagination—can become quite silent.

180

There is no other way to discover the Pure Consciousness than the renunciation of thinking, then the willingness to go beyond it altogether.

181

It is the disentanglement of consciousness from its own projections, its thoughts of every kind, which is the final and first work of a would-be philosopher. Consciousness is then in its pure unconditioned being.

182

To the extent that a man is willing to empty himself of himself, to that extent he is providing a condition for the influx into his normal consciousness of a sense of the Overself's reality. It is like emptying a cup in order that it may be filled.

183

It is a fact that when the mind becomes perfectly controlled and thoughts are brought to a point and stilled, there arises a clear intuitive feeling which tells him about the mind itself.

184

The Surangama Sutra (Japanese title *Ryogonkyo*), Mahayana Zen text: "There are two methods to effect this entrance, practised conjointly. (1) By *Samatha* [tranquillization] the world is shut out of consciousness so that an approach is prepared for the final stage. When one's mind is full of confusion and distraction, it is no fit organ for contemplation. (2) By *Vipasyana* [contemplation] the Yogin is first to awaken the desire for enlightenment, to be firmly determined to live the life of Bodhisattvahood, and to have an illuminating idea as regards the source of evil passions which are always ready to assert themselves in the Tathagathagarbha [storehouse, all-conserving mind]. . . . When entrance is effected to the inner sanctuary, all the six senses are merged in one."

185

He must not only practise sitting perfectly still and thus stop squandering the body's energies, but also, and at the same time, practise emptying the mind of thoughts and thus conserve his mental energies, too. The whole effort is indeed intended to "stop the out-going energies," in the *Gita*'s phrase. This is why sports, long walks, protracted manual labour, and, especially, sexual intercourse are prohibited to the would-be yogi.

186

To put an end to this constant working of the mind, this manufacture of thoughts without apparent stop, is the purpose of yoga. But by the practice of philosophy, by the utter calm, thoughts end themselves.

187

It is the art of putting oneself into and, for experts, of remaining in the soul's consciousness. Therefore only one who is capable of doing this can write about it with either accuracy or authority. All other writers, viewing the state from outside, can get back only their own thoughts about it, not real knowledge.

188

To help mind attain the inner stillness, press the chest and "catch" the breath sharp.

189

Get away from your usual and habitual mental activities, your emotional drives and passional urges; get beneath them and you will come to pure mind, pure feeling, able to look, as from a far-off point, at God.

190

Both the world which his senses report and the thoughts which his mind creates must be left outside the door of Being. When that is done, consciousness is no longer lost in its states. Then only does the man know himself; then only does the eternal *I* manifest itself in the transient *me*.

191

E. Underhill, *Mysticism*: "The deliberate inhibition of discursive thought and rejection of images, which takes place in the 'orison of quiet,' is one of the ways in which this entrance is effected: personal surrender, or 'self-naughting,' is another."

192

Patanjali recommends a repeated effort to keep the mind steadily in a thought-free condition. This is a valuable method and not much known.

193

Patanjali said the idea is to vacuum thought from the mind.

194

The task which confronts the awakened man is nothing less than to free himself from this perpetual immersion in activity and thought. He already does it involuntarily during sleep. He must now do it voluntarily and therefore consciously during the waking state.

195

Whenever he is still, silent, concentrated, and reverent, he will be able to place his mind in rapport with the Overself.

196

A Japanese Master said: "If you try to get nearer to It, you will only get farther from It."

Deepen attention

197

When self-absorption is somewhat advanced and concentration fairly steady, we are ready for the third stage. Here, personal effort should cease. An intuition will gently make itself manifest and the moment it does we must let it affect us by being as inwardly submissive as possible. If we can follow it up, it will increase in strength and clearness. It is not at all easy to arrive at this profound submissiveness within ourself and let go of all the egoistic resistances which we unconsciously harbour. There should be a glad self-yielding to this intuition, which is a harbinger of the soul whose presence and power we had so long to accept on trusting faith alone. As it develops, some ethereal presence seems to come over us, a diviner happier nobler self than your common one. An ethereal feeling will echo throughout your inner being. It seems to come from some far-off world yet it will be like some mysterious half-remembered music in its paradoxical mixture of strangeness and familiarity. We are then on the threshold of that in us which links us with God.

198

The passage from the second stage to the third stage, from meditation to contemplation, from the activity of thought to the immobilization of thought, from the creation of mental images to their elimination, may take several years to effect. It calls for hard practice and hundreds of attempts. Even the person who has attained some proficiency in this art may find it requires at least a half or three quarters of an hour before he is able to attain the third degree.

199

At this advanced point, mentally dissolve each thought into undifferentiated Thought. Don't reason about the latter but try to be it and to feel it. Use imagination here rather than reasoned thinking. Reasoned reflections should have been pursued and finished during metaphysical studies and not carried into this contemplation. *Picture* it, instead of *reflecting* on what it is like.

200

When this stage is reached, when we can dismiss everything else from our attention, when the thought which flows through the sense-channels has been gathered in and turned around to face itself, we must grope within the heart with a strong determination for the essence of our consciousness.

201

As he sinks deeper after many relapses towards the undivided mind, as he calls on all the powers of his will and concentration to keep within focus the inner work of this spiritual exercise, he may get a sense of leading, of being directed by something within.

202

The idea around which his meditation revolved must now be used as a springboard from which to move to a higher level. Whereas he was before intent on working out his own thoughts, now he must abandon them altogether. Before he was positive; now he must be passive. The mind must become quiet, the emotions must compose themselves, before he can receive the sacred flux.

203

The particular idea upon which he is meditating may be dropped when concentration reaches its intensest point or it may then drop away of its own accord. He is embraced by pure consciousness, is immersed in the "contemplation without a seed" of the Yogis.

204

The second stage of meditation should be brought to an end the moment you become aware of a slowing down in the tempo of thinking and of a quickening of intuitive feeling; after that moment you are ready to attempt to enter the third stage of contemplation proper. Let your consciousness become quiet and still. In truth it has nothing really to do, except to permit that intuitive feeling to spread all over it and envelop it.

205

When a certain depth is reached and the concentration remains unflagging, the ego begins to sink back into its source, to dissolve into and unite with that holy source. It is then indeed as near to God's presence as it can get.

206

In this third stage all thinking is thrust aside. He simply looks directly at the Overself, remaining inwardly quite still until he feels himself being drawn into the Overself.

207

The contemplation deepens until it reaches a point where reasoned thinking and judgement, as well as memory, are suspended, so that only the mind's knowing faculty is left.

208

Trace consciousness back to itself, unmixed with bodily sense-reports, emotional moods, or mental thoughts. This can be done successfully only by withdrawing it inwards as you analyse. The process becomes a meditation. In the final term you are aware of nothing else, that is, of nothing but being aware. But at this point you cannot know it as a second thing, an object, but only by being it.

209

Take attention away from the everyday egoistic self and you may open a gate to the Overself. This is one method—and the harder one. Let attention be held by a glimpse so that the everyday self drifts out of focus. This is another method—and the easier. The first is yoga and depends on active personal effort. The second is passive and depends on absorption in art, music, landscape, or a visitation.

210

Follow this invisible thread of tender holy feeling, keep attention close to it, do not let other things distract or bring you away from it. For at its end is entry into Awareness.(P)

211

The student must for minutes deliberately recall himself from the external multitude of things to their single mental ground in himself. He must remind himself that although he sees everything as an objective picture, this picture is inseparable from his own mind. He has to transcend the world-idea within himself not by trying to blot it out but by thoroughly comprehending its mentalist character. He must temporarily become an onlooker, detached in spirit but just as capable in action.(P)

212

Contemplation is attained when your thinking about a spiritual truth or about the spiritual goal suddenly ceases of itself. The mind then enters into a perfectly still and rapt condition.(P)

213

He directs his attention inward, seeking the mind itself rather than its incarnation in thought-bodies.

214

The practice involves a search, a probe, made by directing both emotional feeling and mental concentration within the heart region.

215

Deeper and deeper attention is needed. It must draw all his forces, all his being, into the concentration.

216

The faculty of attention is interiorized and turned back upon itself.

217

Let the thoughts drift away into a state of harmony with the body, both getting more and more inactive. This is a practice which can be done whenever the time is convenient, and for as short or as long a period as desired.

218

He pushes the thoughts of the world farther and farther away towards the periphery of consciousness and sinks deeper and deeper into the centre of it.

219

We rise then from the working of imagination and from the activity of reasoning, which are but veils, to the pure reality itself, which is the void of pure thought.

220

Follow the "I" back to its holy source.

221

The mind undivided, that is, without a subject-object parting of it into two portions, passes into a deep contemplation.

222

He must pursue this faint feeling as it bears him into the inmost recesses of his being. The farther he travels with it in that direction, the stronger will it become.

223

None of these other ways of getting absorbed is absolutely prerequisite; the essential thing is to catch the delicate feeling of being indrawn and to go along with it.

224

He must let himself be entirely transported by whichever of these two feelings comes to him: indrawnness or upliftment.

225

Entry into the third or contemplative stage may be marked by a momentary lapse from any consciousness at all. Yet it will be such a deep lapse that the meditator will not know on recovery whether it has endured a few seconds or a whole hour.

226

Letting go all thoughts—the ego-thought, the world-thought, even the God-thought—until absolutely none is present in mind: it is as simple as that!

227

If he is sufficiently advanced he need make no verbal formulation or pictured image to prepare a point of concentration, but can begin straightaway in an abstract wordless pressure towards the heart.

228

This is one of the subtlest acts which anyone can perform, this becoming conscious of consciousness, this attending to attention.

229

Whether thinking of the personal God or of the impersonal God, one is still thinking of God. In the end he has to drop all thoughts, to *be* with God and not merely to have thoughts of God, whether they are personal or impersonal.

230

As he retreats from all the outer phases of experience, he comes to something which he can now identify as pure Consciousness.

231

What was named in *The Hidden Teaching Beyond Yoga* "The Yoga of the Untouch" can be literally translated as "The Yoga which Touches no Object," meaning—in plain English—the practice of turning attention away from every thought and image and thing in profound concentration and being utterly absorbed in pure Mind. This is a feat which obviously requires prior preparatory training. There is no attempt at self-improvement, self-purification, or mind-training here; nor any aspiration, or longing. It is a calm movement into the Silent Universal Mind, without personal aims.

232

Thinking is an activity which has its place in certain kinds of meditation—the kind which seeks self-betterment, moral improvement, or metaphysical clarification. It is an activity which occupies the generality of its practitioners in the earlier stages. In the more advanced stages and certainly on the Short Path, the attitude towards it must change. The practitioner must seek to transcend thinking so that he can enter the stillness where every movement of thought comes to an end but where consciousness remains.

233

A point is reached where the seeker must stop making a *thought* of the Overself, or he will defeat himself and ensure inability to go beyond the intellect into the Overself. At this point he is required to enter the Stillness.

234

We have to let our thoughts lose themselves for a while in the source whence they arose and not let them actively follow each other from the first moment of our awakening till the first moment of our return to sleep.

235

He must hold with unflagging concentration to this deep centre within his being.

236

Place the mind where it belongs—at the Centre.

237

Holding the high aspiration strongly but relaxing the thoughts and personal pressures opens the way.

Yield to Grace

238

He will understand the real spirit of meditation when he understands that he has to do nothing at all, just to sit still physically, mentally, and emotionally. For the moment he attempts to do anything, he intrudes his ego. By sitting inwardly and outwardly still, he surrenders egoistic action and thereby implies that he is willing to surrender his little self to his Overself. He shows that he is willing to step aside and let himself be worked upon, acted through, and guided by a higher power.

239

He has reached the subtlest area of the mind's journey. For what is to be done now must be done without bringing the ego into it, without the consciousness as a *background* that *he* is trying to do it. This may appear impossible and is certainly paradoxical. It is, however, accomplished by a process of letting go, negative rather than positive. It is a passive letting-do.

240

At this critical point consciousness shifts from forced willed attention, that is, concentration, to passive receptive attention, or contemplation. This happens by itself, by grace.

241

Nothing is to be held within the consciousness but rather consciousness is to let itself be held by the enveloping Grace.

242

The period of active effort is at an end; the period of passive waiting now follows it. Without any act on his own part and without any mental movement of his own, the Grace draws him up to the next higher stage and miraculously puts him there where he has so long and so much desired to be. Mark well the absence of self-effort at this stage, how the whole task is taken out of his hands.

243

This *anti*-technique must not be misunderstood. Without the quality of self-imposed patience, the student cannot go far in this quest. If he has only a tourist mentality and nothing more, if he seeks to collect in one, sweeping, surface glance all the truths which have taken mankind lifetimes of effort and struggle to perceive, he will succeed only in collecting a series of self-deceptive impressions which may indeed provide him with the illusion of progress but will lead nowhere in the end.

244

At this stage his business is to wait patiently, looking as deeply inward as he can while waiting. Any attempt to grasp at the Overself would now defeat itself, for the ego's willed effort could only get the ego itself back. But the willingness to sit still with hands metaphorically outstretched like a beggar's, and for a sufficient stretch of time, may lead one day to a moment when the Overself takes him by surprise as it suddenly takes hold of his mind. The much sought and memorable Glimpse will then be his. He has applied for discipleship and this is his sign of acceptance.

245

Thinking must be reduced more and more until it goes. But by no deliberate act of will can he bring on contemplation. All he can do is to be passive and wait in patience and keep the correct attitude—aspiring, loving, watching, but devoid of any kind of tension.

246

Look for the moment when grace intervenes. Do not, in ignorance, fail to intercept it, letting it pass by unheeded and therefore lost. There is a feeling of mystery in this moment which, if lingered with, turns to sacredness. This is the signal; seek to be alone, let go of everything else, cease other activities, begin *not* meditation but contemplation, the thought-free state.

247

He has to let himself become totally absorbed by this beautiful feeling, and to remain in it as long as possible. Work, family, friends, or society may call him away but, by refusing to heed them, he is denying his own will and abandoning it to God.

248

At this stage thoughts are removed by a higher power, even thoughts of higher things. This is a temporary experience but a very memorable one.

249

If a meditator shifts into passivity, the Overself must take over, provided the prerequisite qualifications have been fulfilled.

250

His own efforts at this stage will consist in removing from the field of concentration every mental association and emotional influence which distracts him from attaining the stillness. When he has succeeded in removing them, he is then to do nothing at all, only to relax.

251

Although it is the duty of the beginner who seeks to master concentration to resist this distraction of thoughts, this tendency to move endlessly in a circle from subject to subject, there is quite a different duty for the proficient who seeks to master contemplation. He ought not take this flow of thoughts too seriously or anxiously, but may let it go on with the attitude that he surrenders this too to the Overself. He lets the result of his efforts be in God's hands.

252

Withdrawn from the world's clamour to this still centre of his innermost being, waiting in utter patience for the Presence which may or may not appear, he performs a daily duty which has become of high importance and priority.

253

The more inert the ego can be during this exercise, and the more passively it rests before the Overself, the fuller will be the latter's entry. Obviously this condition cannot be achieved during the first stage, that of conscious effort and struggle with distractions.

254

His own power will bring him to a certain point but it will not be able to bring him farther along. When this is reached, he has no alternative than to surrender patiently, acquiescently, and wait. By such submission he shows his humility and takes one step in becoming worthy of grace.

255

He is beginning to master wisdom when he tries to learn how not to try.

256

It is almost impossible to throw all thoughts and all images out of the mind. But what we cannot do for ourselves can be done for us by a higher power.

257

Wait with patience for His Majesty the Inner Ruler to appear in the Hall of Audience.

258

It comes to this, that we have to learn the art of doing nothing! It would seem that everyone could practise this without the slightest preparation or training, but the fact is that hardly anyone can do so. For the expression "doing nothing" must be interpreted in an absolute sense. We must learn to be totally without action, without thought—without any tension or manifestation of the ego. The Biblical expression "Be still!" says exactly the same thing but says it positively where the other says it negatively. If we really succeed in learning this art, and sit absolutely still for long periods of time, we shall be given the best of all rewards, the one promised by the Bible: we shall "know that I am God."

259

Learn to free yourself from all the inner and outer bindings as the spirit wafts you into utter lightness and stillness.

260

What happens next comes from no effort on his part and depends on nothing that he does. He is simply to remain still, perfectly still in body and mind. Then from above, from the Overself, grace descends and he begins to experience the joy of feeling the divine presence.

261

Now that he has entered the blank silence he must be prepared to wait patiently for what is about to unfold itself. This next development cannot be forced or hurried; indeed, that attempt would effectively prevent its manifestation.

262

If it is true to say that in the earlier stages of his quest he holds *on* to the Still Thought-less stage, in the later and more settled stage he is held *by* It.

263

As he sits there, hieratically immobile, in peaceful surrender, his mind turned away from everyday matters, he feels the Presence little by little.

264

It was quite correct to seek in the earlier stages understanding of what is happening to him, but not in this later stage. Here he is to be like a dumb creature, letting the Overself do its cleansing, ego-stilling work in him.

265

It is no longer a matter of discursive thinking which flows by orderly and logical transition from one idea to the next—that was proper until grace came in—but of putting all thoughts aside and waiting passively, quietly, letting awareness sink deeper.

266

The significant moment in meditation begins when the man stops making efforts himself and when the mind begins to take him, to withdraw him into itself quite of its own accord. This is an amazing experience for he does not know how he came to stop doing what he was already doing, trying, using effort. He is somehow led into letting it all go, into yielding to the mood of passivity which gently, imperceptibly steals over him.

267

Before he can benefit by the Presence he must put himself in a receptive state, must be prepared mentally and emotionally and even physically. Rested and relaxed, self-cleansed and God-turned, humbled and involved, he is ready for the "touch."

268

Both mind and heart must be used in persistent effort to find the goal of this quest; but at a certain point the effort must cease, and both mind and heart must be stilled. For it is then that the divine can enter; it is then that the quester must cease trying and let the divine grace bless its preparatory work. Thus from a positive attitude he passes, eventually, into a passive one, not trying to force the issue any longer, but letting himself be receptive and relaxed.

269

The more deeply he lets himself sink into this attitude of receptivity—whether in meditation on God or admiration of art—the finer the result.

270

More than any other author, Lao Tzu has put in the tersest and simplest way the importance, the meaning, and the result of the sitting-still practice, the patient waiting for inner being to reveal itself, the submissive allowing of intuition to be felt and accepted.

271

There is nothing to do, no technique to practise when you already *are* in the Light.

272

Once these preliminaries have been fulfilled and the ego's active devotions have subsided, all that he can do is to wait, watchfully, for the arisal of intuitive feelings and then devote his utmost attention to them.

273

In the ultimate phase of meditation, he has mastered the art, finished his work, and relaxed completely. He is quite inactive, quite still in both body and mind, doing nothing. For now he is at his best level of consciousness—the holiest, calmest, widest one.

The deepest contemplation

274

When the mind is as clear as a purified lake and as still as a tree in the depths of a forest, it can pick up new transcendental perceptions and feelings.

275

"Here I am" is to be his attitude, "humbly receptive in the silence, submissively waiting with restrained ego and stilled mind for whatever guidance comes and however distasteful to personal emotion or however unwelcome to personal judgement it may be."

276

If after you reach the deepest contemplation, you then direct attention towards a particular problem on which you are seeking knowledge, knowledge which neither the senses nor the intellect has so far been able to supply, you may be able to perceive as in a flash what is the proper solution of this problem.

277

Observe how still our whole being spontaneously becomes when we want to be fully receptive just before some important announcement. If it is of the highest possible importance, we almost hold our breath; such is the intense stillness needed to take it in to the utmost degree and to miss nothing. How much more should we be still throughout every part of mind and body when waiting to hear the silent pronouncements of the Overself!

278

The truth germinates in Silence.

279

There is no better authority for a truth on which to rest than its own clear perception directly within oneself. But this statement is valid only if the ego has been put where it belongs, at least during the period of perception.

280

We not seldom find speech to be but the laryngeal medium whereby men convey lies to us; it is somewhat paradoxical, therefore, that silence should be the mysterious medium whereby someone should convey truth to us.

281

Out of this silence a voice begins to speak to him.

282

Advanced contemplation may lead to Revelation.

283

In the deeper phases, certain thoughts which come to him can be taken as divine guidance. "Thy will."

284

He has developed the capacity to open the door of his inner being. He has reached the stillness which envelops its threshold. But this is only a beginning, not the end. He has now to pass beyond it and find out what the light itself holds for him.

285

At such a time he is to put aside his own ideas and wait patiently for the Overself-inspired ideas to come to him.

286

A mind cleansed, centered, quietened, and emptied is what he must offer; the revelation and benediction are what he is given.

287

When attention is stilled, the mind void of thoughts and the desires at rest, it is possible *for the instructed person* to perceive truth much more clearly than before, and to feel Reality. But the instruction must concern what is the always-true and the ever-real.

288

It is only as he frees himself from all inward and outward pressures, all suggestions and impositions, that he becomes relaxed enough to receive what the Overself can present him with—ego-freed truth.

289

In the mind's stillness it is possible to find either nothing at all or clear understanding. It depends on the man's preparation for it, on his knowledge, character, and experience.

290

In the soft felicitous stillness he can wait expectantly for the answers to troubling questions.

291

Spiritual truth passes more easily into a mind emptied of its thoughts, its cares, its desires.

292

When the mind is brought to the quiescence of unstirring leaves in a windless garden, and when with this there is a habitual aspiration truthward, a devotion to the highest being, the Revelation may more easily come to it.

293

There, in the deepest state of contemplation, the awareness of a second thing—whether this be the world of objects outside or the world of thoughts inside—vanishes. *But unconsciousness does not follow.* What is left over is a continuous static impersonal and unchanging consciousness. This is the inmost being of man. This is the supreme Self, dwelling within itself alone. Its stillness transcends the activity of thinking, of the knowing which distinguishes one thing from another. It is incommunicable then, inexplicable later. But after a while from this high level the meditator must descend, returning to his human condition. He has come as close in the contact with the Great Being, the most refined ultimate Godhead, as is possible. Let him be grateful. Let him not ask for more for *he* cannot know or experience more. This is as far as any man can go, for "Thou shalt not see God and live."

294

The attainment of a certain experience marks the permanent attainment of a higher grade in the aspirant's evolution. When this experience comes to him, he will have "the universal vision," wherein he will actually *experience* whatever beings, persons, forms, and creatures in the world he thinks of. For a few minutes or a few hours he will forget his real ego and be universalized.

295

Said the Sage Arada: "Having obtained this ecstatic contemplation the childish mind is carried away by the possession of the new unknown ecstasy . . . he reaches the world of Brahma deceived by the delight. But the wise man, knowing that these thoughts bewilder the mind, reaches a stage of contemplation separate from this, which has its own pleasure and ecstasy. And he who carried away by this pleasure sees no further distinction, obtains a dwelling full of light, even amongst the Abhasura deities. But he who separates his mind from this pleasure and ecstasy, reaches the third stage of contemplation ecstatic but without pleasure. Upon this stage some teachers make their stand, thinking that it is indeed liberation, since pleasure and pain have been left behind and there is no exercise of the intellect. But he who, immersed in this ecstasy, strives not for a further distinction, obtains an ecstasy in common with the Subhakritsna deities. But he who, having attained such a bliss desires it not but despises it, obtains the fourth stage of contemplation which is separate from all pleasure and pain. But rising beyond this contemplation, having seen the imperfections of all embodied souls, the wise man climbs to a yet higher wisdom in order to abolish all body."—Asvaghosha: *The Buddha Karita*

296

If he is aware that he is aware, then he is no longer being aware!

297

"The priest concentrates his mind upon a single thought. Gradually his soul becomes filled with a supernatural ecstasy and serenity, while his mind still reasons upon and investigates the subject chosen for contemplation; this is the first Jhāna. Still fixing his thoughts on the same subject, he then frees his mind from reasoning and investigation, while the ecstasy and serenity remain, and this is the second Jhāna. Next, his thoughts still fixed as before, he divests himself of ecstasy, and attains the third Jhāna, which is a state of tranquil serenity. Lastly, he passes to the fourth Jhāna, in which the mind, exalted and purified, is indifferent to all emotions, alike of all pleasure and of pain."—Childer's *Pali Dictionary*

298

The Venerable Dr. Parawehera Vajiranana Thera: "The Buddha's own conclusion in regard to the practical methods of mind training has been developed into two complex systems known as 'cultivation of concentration,' and 'cultivation of insight.' Again, these two systems correspond to the two predominant faculties, faith and wisdom. Those who have entered into the religious life through strong faith and devotion are trained in the Samadhi path which appreciates the special practice of rapt, absorbed, concentrated thought called Jhāna, the ecstatic tranquillity of mind. The method of jhāna meditation is called 'the path of tranquillity,' and the disciple who has practised this path should enter in the end to the acquisition of that full knowledge which leads to Arhatship. Those who practise Samadhi meditation in the beginning, experiencing psychic powers as the aid of enlightenment, should practise insight at the end to attain Arhatship. Those who practise insight in the beginning, with or without Samadhi practice, will attain Arhatship. The Samadhi system, therefore, is optional in Buddhism, and is regarded as only a mental discipline preparatory to the attainment of full knowledge. But Vipassana being the direct path to full knowledge is indispensable and is universally imperative for the attainment of Nirvana. Hence insight meditation is the essential method of mental training in Buddhism and it is a unique system in Buddha's teachings. Thus ends an outline of the scheme of mental training explained in Buddhism as the only path to win the goal of man, the Eternal Happiness of Nirvana."

299

He should not be satisfied with a mere glimpse of the pacified mind. He should hold on to it long enough to make the meditation period a glorious success.

300

In the early stages of enlightenment, the aspirant is overwhelmed by his discovery that God is within himself. It stirs his intensest feelings and excites his deepest thoughts. But, though he does not know it, those very feelings and thoughts still form part of his ego, albeit the highest part. So he still separates his being into two—self and Overself. Only in the later stages does he find that God not only is within himself but is himself.

301

Psychologically the void trance is deeper than the world-knowing insight, but metaphysically it is not. For in both cases one and the same Reality is seen.(P)

302

The principle behind it is that once this contact with the Overself has been established during the third stage, it is only necessary first, to prolong, and second, to repeat the contact for spiritual evolution to be assured.(P)

303

"So by passing wholly beyond all consciousness of form, by the dying out of the consciousness of sensory reactions, and by turning the attention from any consciousness of the manifold, he enters into and abides in that rapt meditation which is accompanied by the consciousness of the sphere of unbounded space—even unto the fourth Jhāna (ecstasy)."—*The Dhamma Sangani* (a Buddhist scripture)

304

Meditation, absent-mindedness, abstraction, to be sunk in thought, trance "where both sensations and ideas have ceased to be"—these are Buddhist stages of progress.

305

Of those who reach the third stage, some go wrong at its critical point through inexperience or incomprehension. If they try to think egoistically about what has happened or even to draw an intellectualized meaning, message, or revelation from its silence, they lose the experience itself. It cannot be dragged down to these inferior levels. They must be content with its utter stillness, its sacred emptiness.

306

Sri Ramakrishna: "The mind ordinarily moves in the three lower chakras. But if it rises above them and reaches the heart, one gets the vision of Light. . . ."

"Even though it has reached the throat, the Mind may come down again (from utterly unworldly consciousness—PB). One ought to be always alert. Only if his mind reaches the spot between the eyebrows *need he have no more fear of a fall*, the Supreme Self is so close."

307

That desirable inner state is close to us, but its attainment is elusive to us. The mind is more slippery than an eel when one touches the fringe of the state, for usually the next minute one loses it in a flash.

308

During the course of a single session, the meditator may touch the transcendent consciousness quite a few times.

309

When man attains this state of harmony within himself and with Nature outside, it may be only a temporary experience or a permanent one. It is given to few to attain such a state permanently and even the hour of its temporary onset is usually unpredictable.

310

The most advanced person can enter immediately into the contemplative state.

311

He who has reached this stage of his meditation may well pray: "O Lord, grant the capacity to go deeper into Thy presence and to stay longer in it."

312

When the attempt at control is stopped, awareness arises that thinking itself has stopped. This stillness then continues by itself, effortlessly. If through inexperience, lack of instruction, unfamiliarity, or unpreparedness fear is felt, fear of death, annihilation of consciousness, this extremely subtle and delicate experience will suddenly come to an end. The opportunity is lost.

313

Consciousness must, and will, enter in the end into this unique activity—the contemplation of itself. But it can do so with much more understanding if it draws the world, along with its relation to the world—the two together—into that contemplation and then merges them there until they are dissolved.

314

The fear of annihilation which comes to a number of persons who meditate deeply enough, and which forces them to withdraw themselves from the practice for that session, is justifiable. There is an experience which seems to be equivalent to self-obliteration. Nevertheless it is not the end of existence, for it is followed by an entry into the beautiful white light, bringing an immense feeling of space and goodwill, of harmony and liberation from all that is low, of peace and compassion. The whole experience is so vivid, so real, so convincing—all through from beginning to end—that whether or not it recurs, it will remain forever in his memory. It has also a strange power when recalled years afterwards in moments of trouble and distress to provide inner help and support.

315

This transparent light-world is the source of creation, the cosmic birthplace, the home of dazzling primal energy. Galaxies, universes, suns, and planets come forth from here. The revelatory, blissful vision of God's Form may happen only once in a lifetime. Beyond it all is God without Form—the still void.

316

All these methods of establishing contact with the higher self may be dispensed with at a more advanced stage when it will suffice to have a simple turning of attention towards it or a simple remembrance.

317

He will attain a stage when he can sink in self-imposed rapt absorption at will.

318

We may know when we have entered into the awareness of the Self, for in that moment we shall have gone out of the awareness of the world. The spiritual records which have been left behind by the great mystics, and which evidence this rarer experience of the race, all testify to this.

319

The term "cosmic consciousness" is used rather loosely by different writers. It has been equated with different kinds of mystic experience and different grades of intuition and insight. Because of this ambiguity, it is best to try to avoid the use of this term; but, when found, it should be judged by the context wherein it appears.

320

One of the uses of the term "cosmic consciousness" is certainly to indicate what has been called "unitary" consciousness. Judging by the experience of at least one advanced mystic, its most appropriate application as a name would be to the experience whereby one is able to identify oneself with all other living creatures, in feeling and in intelligence. Many mystics are referring to this when they speak of "love."

321

The attention must be concentrated at this stage solely on the hidden soul. No other aim and even no symbol of It may now be held. When he has become so profoundly absorbed in this contemplation that his whole being, his whole psyche of thought, feeling, will, and intuition are mingled and blent in it, there may come suddenly and unexpectedly a displacement of awareness. He actually *passes out* of what he has hitherto known as himself into a new dimension and becomes a different being. When first experienced and unknown, there is the fear that this is death itself. It is indeed what is termed in mystical traditions of the West as "dying to oneself" and of the East as "passing away from oneself." But when one has repeated periodically and grown familiar with this experience, there is not only no fear but the experience is eagerly sought and welcomed. There I dissolved myself in the lake of the Water of Life.(P)

322

The novice must cautiously feel his way back from the divine centre at the end of his period of meditation to the plane of normal activity. This descent or return must be carefully negotiated. If he is not careful he may easily and needlessly lose the fruit of his attainment. An exercise to accomplish this, to bring the meditator slowly back to earth and to prepare him for the external life of inspired activity, is the following one: very slowly opening and shutting eyelids several times. Those moments immediately following cessation of meditation are equally as important as the period preceding. They are of crucial importance in fact. For in those few minutes he may have lost much of what he gained during the whole period. Hold the state attained as gently and preciously as you would hold a baby. Hold to the centre and do not stray from it. Such a state the yogis call *sahaja samadhi*: despite all moving about there is non-action, for the heart is free.

323

He finds that the peace generated, the will aroused, and the insight gained do not last longer than the period of meditation itself.

324

He should endeavour skilfully to keep active from one moment to another this wonderful faculty which lays the heart of reality open to his insight. He should keep the integrity of this insight quite unimpaired even when he is occupied with the shapes and is participating in the events of a space-time, relativity-stamped world. After he has learned to rest inwardly in the thought-free state at all times and amid all circumstances and not merely during meditation, it is not essential that he should keep permanently free from thoughts in order to keep always in the pure-Thought awareness. No mental or physical activity can interrupt this insight once it has been fully realized. For then whatever thinking the duties of earthly life may rightly demand of him will be done within the pure Thought and not with any feeling of being apart from it. He will feel that it is one and the same pure Thought which is able to play through all these separate thoughts without prejudice to its own self-identity.

325

Although its deepest meditation culminates in thoughts ceasing to exist, the man must eventually end his meditation. As he does so, his mind necessarily returns from this condition to the common one of continuously active thought.

326

For anyone to be able to hold the mind utterly free of all thoughts and absolutely cleared of all images is an uncommon achievement. Even when successful, the effort seldom lasts longer than a few minutes. But after that short space of time, those particular thoughts and those particular images which first rise up are important, valuable, or suggestive. They should be carefully noted or remembered.

327

The deeper he plunges in meditation, the less does worldly life appeal to him when he emerges from it; the old incentives which drive him begin to weaken.

328

If it is to be a continuous light that stays with him and not a fitful flash, he will need first, to cast all negative tendencies, thoughts, and feelings entirely out of his character; second, to make good the insufficiencies in his development; third, to achieve a state of balance among his faculties.

329

It was sweet to be in the temple of true consciousness, but I could not stay indefinitely. I roused myself to ordinary waking consciousness.

330

If he emerges from this deep state, he will recognize his surroundings by slow gradations only. His reluctance to leave that region of absolute delight may account for this slowness.

331

The end of a meditation which attains such a high state may find him unable to return at once to the body's activity. It is prudent in that case to wait patiently for warmth, force, and movement to return to it. There need be no concern about this condition, which is quite familiar to practising mystics.

332

Experience shows that if a sufficiently deep level—not necessarily the deepest level but one that corresponds to what the yogis call *savikalpa samadhi*, which is not as deep as *nirvikalpa*—if that can be attained and then prolonged sufficiently in time, an artist or a writer can draw from the experience creative power for his work.

333

When the mind has really plunged very deep in contemplation, when attention has travelled very far away from its normal plane, recalling oneself to that plane is best done slowly, gently, little by little.

334

It is a fact that contemplation can become so deep and the personality so lost for the time being that when the period of practice is over the meditator may need a little time to accustom himself to his surroundings, just as any ordinary person who awakens from a very deep sleep may need several seconds to become conscious of his physical surroundings. In this half-absentminded state he may even fail to recognize someone else in the room. This happened once to the famous professor D.T. Suzuki, the great

Zen teacher, after we had been sitting together in a private meditation in his study. Although the period was not at all long, when the silence was broken and he began to speak, he addressed the question to me, asking, "Who are you?" Of course after some seconds he came back into full consciousness and remembered.

8

THE VOID AS CONTEMPLATIVE EXPERIENCE

Entering the Void

All that he knows and experiences are things in this world of the five senses. The Overself is not within their sphere of operation and therefore not to be known and experienced in the same way. This is why the first real entry into it must necessarily be an entry into no-thing-ness. The mystical phenomena and mystical raptures happen merely on the journey to this void.(P)

2

At this advanced stage, Philosophy allows no idea born of the intellect or picture born of the imagination to come between the aspirant and the pure formless Divinity it would have him worship. All thoughts are to be absorbed into the Void, all mental images to be merged into Mind.

3

The highest and the last of the inward-bound stages is still to be reached, and this is the self-knowing Void of Being which can repeat the phrase "I am that I am" of Exodus 3:14, but which is without any other predicate.

4

The dividing frontier between the Void and Being, between utter emptiness and inner reality, is hard to find.

5

During self-absorption in the void, the ordinary functions of intellect are altogether suspended. This means that thinking comes to a standstill.

6

If he has succeeded in holding his mind somewhat still and empty, his next step is to find his centre.(P)

7

The inner movement is like no other which he has experienced for it must guide itself, must move forward searchingly into darkness without knowing where it will arrive. He must take some chances here, yet he need not be afraid. They will be reasonable and safe chances if he abides by the advice given in these pages.(P)

8

We must move from consciousness to its hidden reality, the mind-essence which is alone true consciousness because it shines by its own and not by a borrowed light. When we cease to consider Mind as this or that particular mind but as all-Mind; when we cease to consider Thought as this thought or that but as the common power which makes thinking possible; and when we cease to consider this or that idea as such but as pure Idea, we apprehend the absolute existence through profound insight. Insight, at this stage, has no particular object to be conscious of. In this sense it is a Void. When the personal mind is stripped of its memories and anticipations, when all sense-impressions and thoughts entirely drop away from it, then it enters the realm of empty unnameable Nothingness. It is really a kind of self-contemplation. But this self is not finite and individual, it is cosmic and infinite.(P)

9

When he attains the state of void, all thoughts cease for then pure Thought thinks itself alone.(P)

10

God as MIND fills that void. In being deprived first of his ego and then of his ecstatic emotional union with the Overself, the mystic who is thereby inwardly reduced to a state of nothingness comes as near to God's *state* as he can. However this does not mean that he comes to God's consciousness.(P)

11

We may now perceive a further reason why all great teachers have enjoined self-denial. For at this crucial point of perfected concentration, when the senses are still and the world without remote, the mystic must renounce his thoughts in favour of Thought. He can do this only by a final act of surrender whereby his whole sense of personality—all that makes up what he believed to be "I"—is let go as the last of his thoughts to vanish into a Void. He must make the abrupt leap into self-identification with the wide pure impersonal thought-less Thought. He must give up the last of all thoughts—which is the "I" thought—and accept in return whatever may come to him out of the great Unknown. A fear rises up and over-comes him for a time that with this leap he may so endanger his own existence as to plunge into utter annihilation. This naturally makes him cling all the more to his sense of personality. Shall we wonder then, that every student shrinks at this order?(P)

12

In the deepest state of meditation, the Void, there is utter calm. Joy cannot be felt there for it presumes the existence of someone equipped with an active emotional nature. The religio-mystical devotee who frequently enters ecstasies of bliss will lose it if and when he seeks to go deeper and succeeds in entering the Void instead. He will then feel perfect peace only.

13

He must convert himself mentally into nothingness, merge his being into emptiness, and put aside all other thoughts.

14

Attention is kept at the highest pitch, yet the whole direction of it is toward nothing—the Void.

15

"Well hidden and reached solely by arduous endeavour, is that subtle Void which is the principal root of Freedom. . . . Here is the Supreme Reality," says the *Shat Chakra Nirupana*, a Sanskrit medieval text.

16

"The state of emptiness should be brought to the utmost degree, and that of stillness guarded with unwearying vigour," says Lao Tzu.

17

He must wait in the stillness until there is a sudden catch at his heart, an abrupt intake of breath.

18

Lost within himself in utter self-absorption, numb to everything that traces back to the world of action, no longer held by the power and limit of the senses, he becomes pure mind, disembodied spirit.

19

All that consciousness holds must be reduced to nothing.

20

Courage to face and accept the unknown is needed at this deep level of meditation. But if there is insufficient information and insufficient purification, it might be well to pause at this point and make oneself better ready for this momentous step.

21

At this point he should turn *all* his inner attention on the "emptiness" and firmly hold it there.

22

It is only in the Stillness of the Void that he will find what he is looking for. But the Stillness is due to the shutting off of his own clamorous voices, his thoughts and feelings. It is *his* personal condition. He must look deep within it, lose himself in it, and come out on the other side as something else—real Being, not a being.

23

To sit silently in the Void is clearly the sequence of an act of meditation, the opened flower which bloomed after it.

24

Referring to nondual experience, Mahadevan said in a letter: "All that one can do is to prepare oneself to be ready to receive when the time comes."

25

Since no one can peer into the mind of God, finite-minded as we all are, the best we can do is to try to shift the idea of "I" over to the Stillness itself, where to lose itself as far as it can in our innermost being.

26

He himself, the experiencer of the meditation experience, must go, must lose himself, deny himself, if that which is beyond is to take over, that is, the true Reality.

27

Though he is without thoughts, he may still not have attained the highest level. For he may be *conscious* of their absence itself. This consciousness must be transcended next.

28

We cannot enter the Void if we carry any possessions—material or intellectual, emotional or social—with us. This is surely what Jesus meant when he said that the rich man could not enter the kingdom of heaven. It is not the bank book that can prevent anyone's entry, but rather the heart that is unable to leave the bank book.

29

At this crucial moment the mind must be utterly submissive, the self-will wholly relinquished.

30

He may enter, not into Nirvana, but at least next door to it, which is the "Void."

31

In the earlier stages of the Short Path he necessarily uses words to suggest something about the nature of his goal and to represent it by concepts. But in the advanced stages they lose their value and he rests calmly and patiently in the Void, identified with Mind, even though not yet realized as such.

32

Repose in this condition of vast emptiness is accompanied by intense and vivid happiness. He knows that he is with the living God. He understands that he has come as close to God as it is possible for a human being on earth to do and yet remain human and alive. But he knows and understands all this not by the movement of ideas—for there are none here— but by a feeling which captures his whole being. But it is during this final experience of the Void, when he passes beyond all relativity, that he experiences Mind to be the only reality, the only enduring existence, and that all else is but a shadow. Entry into this stage is therefore a critical point for every aspirant.

33

Those who can pass in to the Void with eager anticipation and glad acceptance of it are few. Those who hover at its brink, terrified, refusing to make the plunge, are inevitably more.

34

Men who are strongly attached by the cords of desire to the things of this world naturally find the very idea of the void repulsive. But even mystics who have loosed themselves from such things still hesitate when on the threshold of the void and often withdraw without taking the plunge. For with them it is the clinging to personal self-consciousness which holds them captive.

35

The first contact of the student with the Void will probably frighten him. The sense of being alone—a disembodied spirit—in an immense abyss of limitless space gives a kind of shock to him unless he comes well prepared by metaphysical understanding and well fortified by a resolve to reach the supreme reality. His terror is, however, unjustified. In the act of projecting the personal ego the Overself has necessarily to veil itself from the ego at the same time. Thus ignorance is born.

36

In the nihilistic experience of void, the mystic finds memory sense and thought utterly closed, he knows no separate thing and no particular person; he is blank to all lower phenomena but it is a conscious living rich blissful sublime blankness; it is simply consciousness freed from both the pleasant and the unpleasant burdens of earthly existence.

37

At some point his mind slips from its accustomed anchorage; an impersonal consciousness that is not his own and knows nothing of himself takes over, and all memories of experience in the world lapse as if they never were. He is isolated from everything and everyone. Only a knowingness remains. At first the loss of personality induces fear as he feels its onset but if he holds his ground and lies still, unresisting, quiet, trusting the beneficence of the process, the fear of it ebbs and vanishes. Then a calm, before unknown and now unutterable, replaces it. Such an experience will be remembered long after all others are forgotten.

38

Those who succeed in reaching this point in their meditation often withdraw just there, overcome by terror or gripped by panic. For the prospect of utter annihilation seems to yawn, like an abyss, beneath their feet. It is indeed the crucial point. The ego, which has lurked behind all their spiritual aspirations and hidden in disguise within all their spiritual thinking, must now emerge and show itself as it really is. For where, in this utter void, can it now conceal itself?

39

When he lets the last active thoughts go, the great Void may replace them. And if he is fortunate, the great Light will come and flash across the Void, as point, ray, shaft, or space, as pulsating dynamic energy or as focused stillness.

40

The womb of mysterious nothingness out of which the soul emerged is God, the World-Mind. When, in deep meditation, the ego faces the soul and is then led by it to that nothingness, the first reaction is, at worst, terrifying fear of annihilation, or, at best, an almost equally terrifying fear of utter aloneness.

41

In these first moments when he feels the Void opening up in the centre of his being, an intense expectancy thrills him.

42

He is to look for no support elsewhere and no light. Evidently the passage to such a unique position may frighten some aspirants to such a degree that they refuse to traverse it. This is not an ordinary kind of courage which is required here. All that ties him to his nature as a human being, to his very existence, must be let go. Nothing less than annihilation seems to confront him. Indeed, afterwards, when the experience is over, he thinks to himself that it was really "a kind of dying." He had been swallowed by death but disgorged again later. He had slipped into it so imperceptibly, so unconsciously, and so suddenly, that all this became known only after it was over.

43

Students draw back affrighted at the concept of a great void which leaves them nothing, human or divine, to which they may cling. How much the more will they draw back, not from a mere concept, but from an actual experience through which they must personally pass! Yet this is an event, albeit not the final one on the ultimate ultramystic path, which they can neither avoid nor evade. It is a trial which must be endured, although to the student who has resigned himself to acceptance of the truth whatever face it bears—who has consequently comprehended already the intellectual emptiness of both Matter and Personality—this experience will not assume the form of a trial but rather of an adventure. After such a rare realization, he will emerge a different man. Henceforth he will know that nothing that has shape, nobody who bears a form, no voice save that which is soundless can ever help him again. He will know that his whole trust, his whole hope, and his whole heart are now and forevermore to be surrendered unconditionally to this Void which mysteriously will no longer be a Void for him. For it is God.(P)

44

If the glimpse goes as far as an experience of the Void, it may leave him frightened or elated: the first, if he is utterly unfamiliar with everything esoteric and completely indoctrinated by conventional religious dogmas; the second, if he surrenders fear, trusts the Higher Power.

45

When all mental ideation is thus little by little brought to an end; when all mental forms are gradually eradicated by the suppressive power of Yoga, the container of those forms—Space—being itself an idea, is then also suppressed along with the ideas of ego, time, and matter. In the apparent emptiness which results, the Real is experienced in all its mysterious fullness. Man comes as close to God as he may. But few mystics have the courage to take this final step. Most falter on its very edge, stricken by fear of the Unknown or by unfamiliarity with this mental territory. They stop and withdraw. The chance to venture beyond is lost and often does not recur for many years.

46

Not only does the mind become utterly blank and lose all its thoughts, but it loses at last the oldest, the most familiar, and the strongest thought of all—the idea of the personal ego.

47

We have become so habituated to our bodily gaols that even in the deepest meditation, when we stand on the verge of the soul's infinitude, we draw back affrighted and would rather cling to our captivity than be liberated from it. These timidities and fears will arise but they must be overcome. *Bhagavad Gita* VI:25 teaches the meditation on the Void: "Let him not think of anything."

48

This is the Void wherein, as in deep sleep, the thought of world-experience is temporarily stilled. But here consciousness is kept, whereas in sleep it is lost.

49

The threshold of this inner being cannot be crossed without overcoming the fear that arises on reaching it. This is a fear of the unknown, the unfamiliar, the fantastic, and the illusory. The ego shrinks back from what is so strange to its past experience. It is afraid of losing itself in this emptiness that confronts it, and with that losing hold of the solid ground of physical life. Only by calling up all its inner courage and inner strength can these enemies be conquered.

50

But because the capacity to remain in the void for more than a moment imposes an intolerable strain upon a man's faculties and an almost impossible task upon his consciousness, his intellect or imagination will, in the very next moment, people this void with an idea or an image and thus end the tension. Thereafter a whole series of other ideas or images will naturally follow the primal one.

51

He stands on the very verge of non-existence. Shall he take the plunge? The courageous aspirant must not waver at this crucial moment. He must gather up all his force and draw the veil which conceals the face of Isis. A moment more—and he stands in the presence of the Unknown God!

52

What happens is not a passing-out of consciousness but a passing-into a vast consciousness, an all-space without any objects or any creatures, a Void.

53

If he is willing to accept this emptiness with all the annihilation of self that goes with it, he will succeed in passing the hardest of ordeals and the most rigorous of tests.

54

Without dramatic happening or sensational incident, the mind slips at long last into the Great Silence.

55

In this deep stillness there occurs the event which will hold his remembrance for long afterwards—the passage from his mere existence to his glorious essence. It is brief but transforming.

56

Out of his own large experience of meditation, "Fear not the stillness," wrote A.E. in a poem.

57

So many mystics are quite unnecessarily frightened by this concept of the Void that it is necessary to reassure them. They halt on the very threshold of their high attainment and go no farther, because they fear they will be extinguished, annihilated. The truth is that this will happen only to their lower nature. They themselves will remain very much alive. Thus it is not the best part of their nature which really dreads the experience of the Void, but the worst part.

58

The fear of losing individuality and dissolving in a mass consciousness, or of losing identity and disappearing as a personal self, comes up as an obstacle in a certain deep stage of meditation—but not the deepest. It has to be overcome, transcended.

59

Those who find that beyond the Light they must pass through the Void, the unbounded emptiness, often draw back affrighted and refuse to venture farther. For here they have naught to gain or get, no glorious spiritual rapture to add to their memories, no great power to increase their sense of being a co-worker with God. Here their very life-blood is to be squeezed out as the price of entry; here they must become the feeblest of creatures.

60

It is an experience which comes of itself, not constructed by the ego and not following the intake of a hallucinogenic drug. It leads into a consciousness where there are no objects, no activities, and no others. It is a zero, a nothing, yet simultaneously an utter intensity, clarity, and purity of consciousness.

61

The forms of meditation vary, but all in the end must lead the meditator beyond them. This is the crucial point when he must be willing to let them go: they have served their purpose. This is the crossing-over into *contemplation* (in Christian mystical terms) or *Nirvikalpa* (in Hindu yoga terms).

62

There is no need to yield to the fear of the void, which comes in the deepest meditation. That is merely the personal ego offering its resistance to the higher self. That same fear of never being able to come back has to be faced by all advanced mystics when they reach this stage of meditation, but it is utterly groundless and is really a test of faith in God to protect them in a most laudable endeavour: to come closer to him and to advance farther from their lower self. Having once yielded to the fear and failed to make the necessary advance, the aspirant has failed in the test and it may be a long time before a similar opportunity will present itself again, if at all. Nevertheless, the memory of that great experience should always be an inspiration toward a more impersonal life.

63

In that moment of utter emptiness the mind becomes a blank but the person becomes united with the unspotted and untainted Overself.

64

When the state of void is first attained, a trance-like stillness falls on the soul. The constant operation of thinking comes to an end for a time. The resultant freedom from this activity is marked and prized. The resultant feeling is memorable and pleasant.

65

A point will be reached in contemplation when the self makes immediate contact with, and is taken up into, the holy Void.

66

The ego finds itself chilled by the conception of nothingness, as if it had climbed to a Himalayan height.

67

Most men who are confronted with this concept for the first time shudder at the thought of annihilation, are terrified at the possibility of vanishing from existence altogether, and may even regard the quest of such self-destruction as madness.

68

He feels that to advance a single step farther is to place himself at the mercy of unpredictable forces and unfamiliar powers.

69

He feels himself to be on the very edge of existence, with a dark annihilating void just in front and the lighted, safe solidity of familiar ground just behind him.

70

In the deep waters of meditation, where self is absent and thoughts negated, he sinks into the Void. It is an indescribable condition and, to others, an incomprehensible one.

Nirvikalpa Samadhi

71

When he travels the course of meditation into the deep places of his being, and if he plumbs them to their utmost reach, at the end he crosses the threshold of the Void and enters a state which is nonbeing to the ego. For no memory and no activity of his personal self can exist there. Yet it is not annihilation, for one thing remains—Consciousness. In this way, and regarding what happens from the standpoint of his ordinary state at a later time, he learns that this residue is his real being, his very Spirit, his enduring life. He learns too why every movement which takes him out of the Void stillness into a personal mental activity is a return to an inferior state and a descent to a lower plane. He sees that among such movements there must necessarily be classed even the answering of such thoughts as "I am a Master. He is my disciple," or "I am being used to heal the disease of this man." In his own mind he is neither a teacher nor a healer. If other men choose to consider him as such and gain help toward sinlessness or get cured of sickness, he takes no credit to himself for the result but looks at it as if the "miracle" were done by a stranger.

72

For us—human beings—the Void is not so much a factual thing as a state of contemplation. Its deepest level is where the contemplator himself is so completely immersed, so utterly absorbed, as to vanish entirely—and the whole world with him. Selfhood has gone—where and into what? These things that were here, this world to which they belonged, suspended in space, unknown in time—were they hallucinations of consciousness, and is this Void a non-experience too?

73

Whoever succeeds in going down deeply enough into his own consciousness can find a phase where it passes away *as person*, as the limited little self, but is transformed into the Universal being and then, still farther, into the Void. This Void is not the annihilation of Consciousness but the fullness of it, not blankness but true awareness, unhindered by subsiding activities, not the adulteration of it by thoughts or imaginations but the purity of it. In this way he experiences his own personal self-nothingness. From this he can understand two things: why so many prophets have taught that self blocks our way and why the Mahayana Buddhists have taught the reality of the Void.

74

It is consciousness severed from all its objects, awareness with nothing other than itself.

75

Much of the writing of Plotinus is descriptive of the state Hindus call *Nirvikalpa Samadhi.* It is the total dispersal of the world from the field of awareness, a complete flight from sensations, thoughts, mental images, the physical body, and, above all, from any and every kind of activity. To an outside observer, it may seem to be a trance state, but he would not be correct in his observation, nor altogether wrong. It is as deep as contemplation can possibly go. It is Consciousness freed from any kind of personal admixture, staying only with itself. All these other things being removed, what is left is then true self-knowledge, *even if it is unconscious to the ego.*

76

When he experiences the deepest possible state, all mental acts are suspended, all mental activities ended. This includes the act of identifying oneself with the ego. There is then nothing more to prevent the coming of enlightenment.

77

Because the Real is also the One, and because thinking implies the existence of a thinker and his thought—that is, a duality—rapt absorption in the Real brings about cessation of thoughts.

78

In the deepest trance state we enter by introversion into the pure Void. There are then no forms to witness, no visions to behold, no emotions to thrill, no duality of knower and known. The experiencer of the world and the world itself vanish because the first as ego is idea and the second is also idea; both merge into their Source, the Mind.

79

In this awesome experience where the diverse world is annulled, even the experiencing self has its individuality annulled too. Yet, because both world and self reappear later, annulment is here not the same as annihilation.

80

This is the experience whose mystery as well as peace passeth understanding. It is incommunicable by or to the intellect. For with it we attain unity but lose personality yet preserve identity.

81

The culmination of these efforts is a thought-free state wherein no impressions arise either externally from the senses or internally from the reason. The consequence is that the felt contrast between the "I" and the "not-I" melts away like sugar in water and only the sense of Being remains—Being which stretches out wide and still like the infinitude of space. This is the Void.

82

This can be done only by entering the void of empty thought and being merged into its stillness. Because the Mind transcends the objective world, it transcends the manyness of this world. In it there is "no-thing." The dream-world is really a projection of the dreamer's mind. He is the subject and it is the object. But when he awakes the world vanishes. Where has it gone? It could only have gone back into his mind, for it is there that it originally arose. But this is something intangible, a veritable void. In the same way the external world as an object of thought is during this first stage deliberately retracted into the Mind-Void.

83

What we call here the Void, following the Mongolian-Tibetan tradition, is not dissimilar from what Spanish Saint John of the Cross called "complete detachment and emptiness of spirit." It is a casting-out of all impressions from the mind, an elimination of every remembered or imagined experience from it, a turning-away from every idea even psychically referable to the five senses and the ego; finally, even a loss of personal identity.(P)

84

In this experience he finds himself in sheer nothingness. There is not even the comfort of having a personal identity. Yet it is a paradoxical experience, for despite the total nothingness, he is neither asleep nor dead nor unconscious. Something *is*, but *what* it is, or how, or anything else about it, stays an unravelled mystery.(P)

85

In that sacred moment when an awed silence grips the soul, we are undone. The small and narrow bricks with which we have built our house of personal life collapse and tumble to the ground. The things we worked and hungered for slip into the limbo of undesired and undesirable relics.

The world of achievement, flickering with the activities of ambition, pales away into the pettiness of a third-rate play.(P)

86

When metaphysics speaks of the antithesis between subject and object, it means that between the ego and the world. When philosophy speaks of transcending them, it means entry into the Source of both in that still Void where they no longer appear.

87

Matter, form, and place collapse and vanish when you experience this endless emptiness; hence there is no world at all in the Void, no consciousness of persons, things, landscapes, or skies.

88

This mysterious experience seems also to have been known to Dionysius the Areopagite. It is definitely an experience terminating the process of meditation, for the mystic can then go no higher and no deeper. It is variously called *the Nought* in the West and *Nirvikalpa Samadhi* in the East. Everything in the world vanishes and along with the world goes the personal ego; nothing indeed is left except Consciousness-in-itself. If anything can burrow under the foundation of the ego and unsettle its present and future stability, it is this awesome event.

89

The world suddenly vanished from view like a morning mist. I was left alone with Reality.

90

This is the transcendental sight—that under all the multifarious phenomena of the cosmos, the inner eye sees its root and source, the great Void.

91

The old ego suppresses itself. There is only a liberated awareness of pure Mind, of something which he cannot speak of without feeling that it is the root of his own existence.

92

When the finite life surrenders to the infinite life, when it gives up self-will and earthly attachment for the sake of finding what is beyond self and earth, this unique experience comes to it. Everything is asked from it but everything is then given to it.

93

In this state he is no longer a thinking centre of existence, an individual human entity. For the intellect ceases to be active, the emotions cease to move.

94

The world abruptly vanishes from his ken. He is poised for a few minutes in No-thing, the same great Void in which God is eternally poised. His contemplation has succeeded and, succeeding, has led him from self to Overself.

95

Nirvana—by Sri Aurobindo:

All is abolished but the mute Alone,
        The Mind from thought released, the heart from grief
        Grow inexistent now beyond belief;
There is no I, no Nature, known-unknown.
The city, a shadow picture without tone,
        Floats, quivers unreal; forms without relief
        Flow, a cinema's vacant shapes; like a reef
Foundering in shoreless gulfs the world is done.
Only the illimitable Permanent
        Is here. A Peace stupendous, featureless, still
        Replaces all, what once was I, in It
A silent unnamed emptiness content
        Either to fade in the Unknowable
        Or thrill with the luminous seas of the Infinite.

96

It is not that personal identity was wholly lost but rather that it was immersed in the vast ocean of universal being.

97

The world, being for each of us a mental activity, vanishes as soon as that activity is wholly suppressed by yoga. It is only an appearance in time, space, matter, and form. The essence behind it is revealed when the idea of it is suppressed without consciousness itself being suppressed.

98

This condition, this entry into the Void, is a kind of death. Everything is taken away from him; he is nothing and has nothing; yet he still feels one thing which utterly compensates for this loss. He feels the presence of the Overself.

99

It is as if the world had never entered his experience and never even existed.

100

At this point he gets so lost in the Void that he forgets who it is who is meditating. Then and thus he receives a further answer to the question "Who am I?"

101

In the practice of Indian Yoga, *Nirvikalpa Samadhi* is considered to be the farthest point to which the practitioner can travel. *Nirvikalpa Samadhi* is the condition of the emptied mind, without any trace of thought, whether of the world or of the person himself; yet fully aware.

102

So many conversations on the words of Jesus have taken his sentence "I and my Father are one" to mean a kind of union like marriage. But they overlook the fact that married couples still remain couples, still express the number two. Jesus did not say, "I and my Father are two." The number one is definitely not two. For Jesus found, as every other man who attains that stage of consciousness finds, that when contemplating the Infinite Life-Power (which he named the Father) he himself vanished. There was then no other consciousness except that of the Infinite itself. For That was the substratum of his own "I." But what happened in his contemplation two thousand years ago still happens today; the same discovery is made when the illusion of egoity vanishes.

103

His own being mingles with the Great Being and vanishes for a while.

104

It is consciousness almost without content, what there is of the latter being perhaps the point from which all this began and rippled out.

105

No one can enter into the Absolute state as an individual entity and with an individual relation to it. It could not be what it is if the two could exist side by side on the same level. If a man is to approach it he can do so only by becoming as nothing, by casting out his personal ego.

106

If anyone says he has experienced the Void or if he says he has merged into the Absolute Spirit, then he must have been present to note that it is a Void or to know that it is Absolute Spirit. But clearly he was not present in his ordinary self, or he would not dare to deny its presence nor claim its complete merger.

107

Both self and universe vanish together. There is nothing and no one left during such temporary enlightenments.

108

Allama Prabhu, *gnani* of Northern Mysore State, probably fourteenth century, author of the book *Sunyasampadane* (*Attaining of the Void*), only half of which has (in the 1960s) been translated into English and published in Dharwar, thus describes the loftiest condition reached in mystical meditation:

> The motion of the will is still!
> All words are dedicated to Him.
> Nay, language has no trace of sound;
> Nor is there in all space a bound—

109

To enter this strange state, a primeval yet delightful void, where the ego, the intellect, the emotional desires, and the body do not intrude, is to be born again.

Meditation upon the Void

110

The Surangama Sutra chooses, as the best meditation method for the present historic cycle, the one used by Avalokitesvara. It disengages bodily hearing from outward sound, then penetrates still deeper into the void beyond this duality, then beyond ego and its object, until all opposites and dualities vanish, leaving absoluteness. Nirvana follows as a natural consequence. In other words, disengage consciousness from the senses and return to pure Consciousness itself.

111

Guhyasamajatantra: "The steady way of attaining enlightenment is to avoid any conception about the highest knowledge or its realization."

112

All other thoughts are banished by the single thought of the Void but this in turn cannot be got rid of by his own effort. The descent of grace is necessary for that.

113

When we contemplate World-Mind as existing in and for itself, not for its universe, not for the All, we have to contemplate it as the formless Void. And this can be achieved only by becoming for the time being indistinguishable from the ineffable Void, identified with it. There is then only the single and simple insight of Being into its own wonder. The circle has closed in with itself.

114

Through repeated contemplation of the void, the mind rids itself of the illusions of matter time space and personality and eventually the truth is reached.

115

A further result of this contemplation of the world as the great Void is that the work done by mentalistic study is advanced still further, for not only are the things experienced by the five senses seen to be only thoughts but the thoughts themselves are now seen to be the transient spume and spray flung out of seeming Emptiness. Thus there is a complete reorientation from thoughts to Thought. Instead of holding a single thought or scenes of ideas in perfect concentration, the practiser must now move away from all ideas altogether to that seeming emptiness in which they arise. And the latter, of course, is the pure, passive, undifferentiated mind-stuff out of which the separate ideas are produced. Here there is no knowing and discriminating between one idea and another, no stirring into consciousness of this and that, but rather a sublime vacancy. For the Mind-essence is not something which we can picture to ourselves; it is utterly formless. It is as empty and as ungraspable as space.

116

Lao Tzu: "Having once arrived at a state of absolute emptiness, keep yourself perfectly still. This stillness is going home to the First, the Origin."

117

The adverse force present in his ego will continually try to draw him away from positive concentration on pure being into negative consideration of lower topics. Each time he must become aware of what is happening, of the change in trend, and resist it at once. Out of this wearying conflict will eventually be born fresh inner strength if he succeeds, but only more mental weakness if he fails. For meditation is potently creative.(P)

118

We must withdraw every thing and thought from the mind except this single thought of trying to achieve the absence of what is not the Absolute. This is called Gnana Yoga: "*Neti, Neti*" (It is not this), as Shankara called it. And he must go on with this negative elimination until he reaches the stage where a great Void envelops him. If he can succeed in holding resolutely to this Void in sustained concentration—and he will discover it is one of the hardest things in the world to do so—he will abruptly find that it is not a mere mental abstraction but something real, not a dream but the most concrete thing in his experience. Then and then only can he declare positively, "It is *This*." For he has found the Overself.(P)

119

Mystic experience has its limitation. It still remains within the realm of duality. This is because the subject-object relationship still remains. How is this limitation to be removed? The answer is only by being Being, only by transcending this relation.

120

The meditations on All-is-Matterless, Empty-of-Form, and Nothing-but-Pure-Mind are so subtle that they will cause confusion to those persons who are quite unsubtle.

121

1. Do all meditation work with open eyes, with the Buddhic smile. 2. Keep attention inside on the No-thought state and refrain from unnecessary talk. 3. When residual impressions from the last incarnation come in, ignore them. 4. Kill out the mind. Be free from its activity. Stay in the Void.

122

Give four exercises of a highly advanced metaphysical character: (a) Meditation on the Void; (b) Meditation on Nonduality; (c) Meditation on Space; (d) Meditation on Ego's non-existence.

123

Knowledge of and deep meditation upon understanding the Void lead in the end, and more quickly than by wearisome yoga methods, to the dissolution of the thinking process.

124

The best meditation in forgetting our personal miseries is the meditation on the Void. For if we succeed in it to only a partial degree, we succeed to that extent in forgetting the ego, who also is the sufferer, and his miseries vanish with it.

125

Mind manifests itself in the most astonishing variety of forms and the most antagonistic array of oppositions. Its masked presence is the unity which binds them all together. Each man may prove this truth for himself, for each man may penetrate in contemplation to its void within himself.

126

If we make this discrimination between the Mind-essence and its products, between the Seer and the Seen—and we must make it at this ultimate stage—then we must follow it to the logical end. Not by adding more information, or more learning, or more study, can we now enter the Kingdom of Heaven, but rather by letting go, by ceasing this continual mental movement, and finding out what lies *behind* the movement.

127

One ordinary opposition between the experiencer and the experienced suddenly leaves him as they are both perceived to be one and the same "stuff"—Mind.

128

At one stage of meditation the student realizes that everything in the universe is the result of the activity of imagination and has no more if no less reality than an imagination itself has. At this stage the student realizes the nothingness of everything so that the incomprehensibility of this concept to the finite intellect vanishes.

129

It is not the *objects* of conscious attention which are to be allowed to trap the mind forever and divert the man from his higher duty. It is the *consciousness* itself which ought to engage his interest and hold his deepest concentration.(P)

130

When we comprehend that the pure essence of mind is reality, then we can also comprehend the rationale of the higher yoga which would settle attention in pure thought itself rather than in finite thoughts. When this is done the mind becomes vacant, still, and utterly undisturbed. This grand calm of nonduality comes to the philosophic yogi alone and is not to be confused with the lower-mystical experience of emotional ecstasy, clairvoyant vision, and inner voice. For in the latter the ego is present as its enjoyer, whereas in the former it is absent because the philosophic discipline has led to its denial. The lower type of mystic must make a special effort to gain his ecstatic experience, but the higher type finds it arises spontaneously without personal effort at all. The first is in the realm of duality, whilst the second has realized nonduality.(P)

131

This exercise requires us to imagine the Divine as, first, all pervasive and everywhere present, unbounded and limitless, and second, the hidden origin of everything in the cosmos.

132

In this exercise he first tries to comprehend that there is an immaterial and infinite Mind back of himself and, second, tries to identify himself with it. This he can successfully do only by an inner withdrawal in the one case and by a forgetting of personality in the other.

133

He may use the ocean or sky as a starting point for concentrating, its character being one of unlimited stretch, but he should think of it as being *within* himself.

134

He feels that he has touched something that always was even before his own body appeared on earth, something primeval and boundless.

135

He passes into all-engulfing space.

136

In itself, Thought is beyond thoughts. In himself, the Thinker is on a level different from all the activity of thinking.

137

He has to reject the *form* of the thought but seek out and keep what remains as its essence or being, Thought, which could never be rejected even if he tried a lifetime. He must fix—and he will need the utmost power of concentration to do so—his attention on this essence exclusively and steadily.

138

The mind thus turned inward upon itself can then discover what its own stuff is. It can comprehend how persons can be put forth and retracted through the incarnations while their basis remains ever the same.

139

For when awareness is retracted into its source, all thoughts fall away and no second thing other than Mind itself is known to us.

140

He must begin by ceasing to think of the Divine Being as if it were one object put among others, but preferred to them.

141

After one has meditated on the nature of Mind in itself, he must carry the same meditation into the thought of Mind's presence within himself. Thus he moves from its cosmic to its individualized character.

142

Suzuki: "Have your mind like unto space."

143

We have to seek Consciousness-in-itself, not those shadowy fragmentary and very limited expressions of it which are ideas. No collection of thoughts or combination of words can do other than misrepresent it.

144

How can we win this freedom of timelessness? There is one way and that is to step into the Void and to stay there. We must find, in short, the eternal *Now*.

145

The exercise of trying to break through the mystery of time, which is a mental state, into timelessness, which is not, belongs to the Short Path and is important, valuable, but admittedly difficult for beginners. It is practised by confining the thoughts again and again during spare moments and brief leisurely periods to the meaning of timelessness, of the eternal now, and of the everlasting Presence.

146

The aim here is to get at the very source of thinking itself, to penetrate to that deep ground whence it rises, it falls.

147

In this ultramystic state a man may verify the teaching that the Real World is a timeless one. For the sense of time can only exist when the succession of thoughts exists. But in this condition thoughts may be suggested at will and with them time itself.

148

He has to seek not merely another standpoint but that which is beyond all possible standpoints. He has to enter not just a different space-time level but that which is the base of all existing space-time levels.

149

The best form of meditation is that which lifts us above time and into the Eternal Now.

150

The longer you remain in this particular meditation the closer you will understand what the eternal Now means.

151

The student achieves the end of ordinary exercises when during the practice period his attention is able to rest introverted effortlessly naturally steadily and unswervingly. This by itself is an unusual achievement and brings with it an unusual sense of inner peace, an indifference to worldly attractions and moods of rapt ecstasy. We need not be surprised therefore that most students are content to stop here. But the philosophic student must proceed farther. He must use this interval of inward silence to attack the ego.

152

When all thoughts are extinguished; when even the thought of the quest itself vanishes; when even the final thought of seeking to control thoughts also subsides, then the great battle with the ego can take place. But the last scene of this invisible drama is always played by the Overself. For only when its Grace shoots forth and strikes down this final thought, does success come.(P)

153

Everything that intrudes upon the mental stillness in this highly critical stage must be rejected, no matter how virtuous or how "spiritual" a face it puts on. Only by the lapse of all thought, by the loss of all thinking capacity can he maintain this rigid stillness as it should be maintained. It is here alone that the last great battle will be fought and that the first great fulfilment will be achieved. That battle will be the one which will give the final deathblow to the ego; that fulfilment will be the union with his Overself after the ego's death. Both the battle and the fulfilment must take place within the stillness; they must not be a merely intellectual matter of thought alone nor a merely emotional matter of feeling alone. Here in the stillness both thought and emotion must die and the ego will then lose their powerful support. Therefore here alone is it possible to tackle the ego with any possibility of victory.(P)

154

He separates the thought of his own existence from all other thoughts, then attacks and annuls it by the most penetrating insight he has ever shown.(P)

155

Self is a tree with many branches—body, intellect, feeling, will, and intuition—but only one root. Aim at finding this root and you may control the growth of the whole tree. Hold your will (thoughts) within the leash.

156

The root-thought which underlies the ego that has to be slain is not that it is separate from all other creatures but that it is separate from the one infinite life-power.(P)

157

If meditation is ever to escape from the finite objects on which it is centered to union with the infinite subject which is its ultimate aim, it must find the meditator's real jailer and kill him; it must bring the ego out of its hiding place and face it boldly in mortal combat. If it is ever to transcend itself and become contemplation, by transcending all thinking whatsoever, it must catch the last thought, the "I" thought, and slay it.

158

Meditation on the void has, as one of its chief aims, the overcoming of egoism. It not only destroys the narrow view of self but sublimates the very thought of self into the thought of pure unbounded existence. Employed at the proper time and not prematurely, it burns up the delusion of separateness.

159

Hidden behind every particular thought there exists the divine element which makes possible our consciousness of that thought. If therefore we seek that element, we must seek it first by widening the gap between them and then dissolving all thoughts, and second by contemplating that out of which they have arisen.

160

This ultramystic exercise which enables us to slip into the gap between one moment and another, one thought and another, is the practical means of attaining enlightenment as to the true nature of Mind.

161

When thought is transcended, that moment—it may be one millionth of a second—he can comprehend the truth about Brahman's transcending thought. For then the idea becomes the mind. At that moment the mind negates all thoughts. This is called the lightning flash in the *Upanishads*. You must watch vigilantly for it. When between two thoughts you catch this brief flash you have to understand that the thoughts were still in your mind whether they had appeared or vanished. The thought-gap is hidden. That gap is the see-er of the thoughts, that is, *Drik*, Mind, Brahman.

162

During the gap—infinitesimal though it be—between two thoughts, the ego vanishes. Hence it may truly be said that with each thought it reincarnates anew. There is no real need to wait for the series of long-lived births to be passed through before liberation can be achieved. The series of momentary births also offers this opportunity, provided a man knows how to use it.(P)

163

The succession of thoughts appears in time, but the gap between two of them is outside time. The gap itself is normally unobserved. The chance of enlightenment is missed.

164

While the dualistic division of subject/object (self and non-self) is practised, there is ordinary physical sense-experience. But when consciousness is detached from this division, the real nondualist world as it is, and not as it is received by ordinary minds, reveals itself. (This can be done by entering the gap between two thoughts.)

165

The space of time between a man's two thoughts is quite infinitesimal so that he is not conscious of it at all. Yet it is real.

166

This is the indefinable middle point between consciousness and unconsciousness.

167

Time is for consciousness a succession of moments. It is at the end of the interval between the first two that we become aware of its passage and can call the measurement one second. If thinking stops but consciousness remains and we manage to stay with it without introducing the ego—which restarts the process, the movement—we are caught and held in the gap. This is pure consciousness.

168

The exercise of watching a thought arise and vanish and then intently holding on to the interval before the next thought arises, is a hard one. It needs months and years of patient practice. But the reward, when it comes, is immense.

169

When I wrote down the exercise in *The Wisdom of the Overself* of concentrating on the gap between two thoughts, I did not know that the Buddha had stated that Nirvana exists "between two mind moments." I take this statement to confirm the usefulness of that exercise—admittedly a very difficult one.

170

In *The Wisdom of the Overself* I gave an exercise for entering the gap in consciousness between two thoughts, as a means of entering the egoless state. Those who succeeded in mastering it at times went through this tremendous experience which follows, but admittedly few were able to find their way into this gap.

It is needful, when mentioning the subject again, to point out the significance that is given to holding the breath in the practice of yoga. This experience, although induced deliberately and artificially by the would-be yogis, can also come about involuntarily—of its own accord, by itself—purely through meditation or saying a prayer, when it is called "the catch in the breath." It can come unexpectedly. When the grace descends, one falls into utter stillness, a great deep silence, and the breath seems to stop of itself. Of that moment is written, in an age-old sacred work belonging to a period far earlier than the times of Plato and Buddha, that it is the soul of man.

Emerging from the Void

171

The moment he emerges from the void, he regains his individuality. For with this he has to live and move in this lower world. But it is not the personal ego which is regained. That is already dead. It is his soul.

172

The "great void" mentioned in my book is not synonymous with death. Death conveys the idea of the loss of consciousness. There is no loss of consciousness in this state, but the consciousness is transformed indescribably. The state is so blissful, moreover, that there is no worrying about the loss of the ego. However, it is a temporary state because so long as we are living in the flesh we are unable to sustain it and are drawn back by the forces of nature—first to the ego and then to the body. But anyone who has been through that experience even once cannot possibly regard the ego and the body ever again in the same way, because their limitations are clearly felt.

In any case, one need not worry about this absolute condition but rather should await its arrival—then judge whether it is worthwhile or not.

173

If he has once passed through the experience of the Sacred Nothingness, the Eternal Emptiness, and understood its correct meaning, he will be ready to pass discerningly tranquilly and securely through every experience that the world of activity and movement may offer him.

174

Could an individual succeed in stopping these thoughts of the manifested universe from overpowering him, he would attain to a knowledge of the Void. This can be done by yoga, and the consequent state is technically termed "the vacuum mind." Naturally there is nothing in the void to suffer the pains of illness, the decay of old age, the transition of death, and the miseries of ill-fortune. Therefore it is said that he who succeeds in attaining mentally to it, succeeds also in attaining the blessed life of exalted peace.

175

Paradoxically enough, tremendous forces lie latent here. Indeed the law is that the deeper a man penetrates into the void and the longer he sustains this penetration, the greater will be the power with which he will emerge from it.

176

When these powers come into his possession, there also comes a deep sense of responsibility for their right use.

177

Paradoxically, it is in the trancelike state of self-absorption that the degree of passing away from the personal self is completely achieved. But when nature reasserts herself and brings the mystic back to his normal condition, she brings him back to the personality too. For without some kind of self-identification with his body, his thoughts, and his feelings, he could not attend to personal duties and necessities at all.

178

We are meditating on something which will not arise and disappear, as ideas do and as material forms do, on something which is not ephemeral. Because that which vanishes contradicts its own arisal, we seek for that which does not contradict itself. Hence this kind of meditation which brings contemplation into action, sleep into wakefulness, has been called by the ancients "The Yoga of the Uncontradictable."(P)

179

It comes as a state of intense bliss, and then you are your personal self no longer. The world is blotted out; Being alone exists. That Being has neither shape nor form. It is, shall we say, coexistent with space . . . in it you seem to fulfil the highest purpose of our Being. It is not the Ultimate, but for the sake of your meditation practice you nevertheless may regard it as the Ultimate. You will come back after a while. You cannot stay in it for long. You will come back and when you come back you will come back to the intellect; then you will begin to think very, very slowly at first, and each thought will be full of tremendous meaning, tremendous vitality, tremendous beauty and reality. You will be alive and inspired and you will know that you have had a transcendent experience. You will feel a great joy, and then for some time you may have to live on the memory of this glorious experience. Such experiences do not come often, but they will provide a memory that will act as a positive inspiration to you from time to time.(P)

180

He who passes through these deeper phases of the Void can never again call anything or anyone his own. He becomes secretly and spiritually deprived of all personal possessions. This is because he has thoroughly realized the complete immateriality, spacelessness, timelessness, and form-lessness of the Real—a realization which consequently leaves him nothing to take hold of, either within the world or within his personality. Not only does the possessive sense fall away from his attitude towards physical things but also towards intellectual ones.(P)

181

All desires are naturally quenched in the void because nothing that is relative can coexist with it. This ever-renewed contemplation of our infinite Root will in time dissolve our lower tendencies and give the quietus to our animal passions. Thus it is not merely a theoretical exercise but a practical one yielding valuable fruit.

182

He must learn not only to identify himself with the Void but to remain immovably fixed in such nihilistic identity. He must not only learn to regard everything as Mind but to remain unshakeably certain that it is so. When no doubt can penetrate this insight and no experience can dislodge him from this inner vacuum . . .

183

There are two ultimate experiences open to the meditator. Both share in common a contentment and calmness that is supernormal in quality and an absorption in superphysical states. The mystic attains this by religious devotion and the concentration practice alone. But where the latter is accompanied by philosophical discrimination and knowledge, the consciousness is carried almost twice as far into still subtler states and values until it reaches the second ultimate experience. This is near to indescribable, so it has been called "the plane of neither perception nor non-perception." This is because the ego, the conscious observer, is no longer functioning; the experience, the object observed, is no longer there; the residue is a Void. Yet it is not total annihilation; consciousness of some kind must have been held there: for on returning to the normal state, it is picked up again. This raises the interesting question: what, then, is the Void? Ordinarily the term is used for that state where personal, physical, and mental experiences come to a stop but with a rarefied consciousness still remaining. There is no-thing to be known and no-one to know it, certainly no personal memory. This, in the understanding of most students, is the end of the matter: after all, it is too abstract a conception to have any bearing on the lives of those, most of us, who are not monks or hermits with the time and opportunity for prolonged meditations in depth or for intensive analysis of such subtleties. But to complete the record before it is too late, let it be said that there is another kind of Void, seldom studied by the monks and less known among them. In the first kind, there is what might be called "the awareness of awareness." In the second kind, even that ceases. It might be called "death in life." Once experienced, it need not be gone through again, for it leaves its mark permanently on the man. But in the ordinary circumstances of worldly life, especially today, there is little chance for a safe approach to it. Nor is it necessary. For us non-monastic Westerners, the practice of philosophy is the best way.

184

The Void which he finds within frees him for a while from all attachments without. The more deeply and more often he penetrates it, the freer will he become on the surface of his life.

185

One may be fortunate enough to have a most uncommon mystical experience. His desire to experience it again may be fulfilled if he attempts the exercise in the fourteenth chapter of *The Wisdom of the Overself* in which this experience is given as one of the results. It is inevitable that such a high, advanced experience usually occurs at rare intervals. Had he been able to sustain and prolong it for as much as five hours, he would permanently and unbrokenly have entered into the consciousness of his divine soul.

186

The Void must not be misunderstood. Although it is the deepest state of meditation and one where he is deprived of all possessions, including his own personal self, it has a parallel state in the ordinary active non-meditative condition, which can best be called detachment.

187

After all, even the Void, grand and awesome as it is, is nothing but a temporary experience, a period of meditation.

188

The awareness of what is Real must be found not only in deep meditation, in its trance, but when fully awake.

Why Buddha smiled

189

I have often been asked what I thought was the secret of Buddha's smile. It is—it can only be—that he smiled at himself for searching all those years for what he already possessed.(P)

190

Gautama's face, set in a half-smile indicative of being transported in consciousness to a transcendental world, is unforgettable.

191

Two-and-a-half thousand years ago Gautama attained peace more completely than our sense-bound, intellect-confined contemporaries can imagine. On the statues which have come down to us from near his time, there appears the flicker of a smile. Yet this was the man who formulated the tragedy of human existence, the everlasting frustration of human desire.

192

The bland secret smile of a Buddha, cobra-canopied and legs curled under him . . .

193

The Buddha's face is passionless but not expressionless. If its skin is taut like a mask, that is due to achieved serenity and not to hard cold stoniness. The lips are just beginning to break into the smile of Nirvana's joy and compassion's feeling.

194

What does Gautama's quiet smile mean? It means that here is a man who has found a benign relation with all other people and an assured one with himself.

195

The contemplative inner work of a Buddha, as exemplified by his seated statues, is a gentle one, not like the austere determined self-combative yogi's. It is also a patient one, as if he had all the time in the world.

196

Those little figures and large statues of the Buddha which are to be found in some Western homes, museums, and art galleries of quality, show us perfect examples not only of the power of concentration, but also of the meaning of contemplation. For in them we behold the sage utterly absorbed in the Void's stillness, ego merged in the universal being, consciousness empty of all moving thoughts.

197

Why did Gautama smile? Nothing outward had happened to him; all remained as it had been! Yet his lips and mouth formed the tenderest, gentlest, happiest shape.

198

What does the faint, half-hidden smile of Buddha tell us? That he came from Nirvana, assured of peace and hope for mankind's *inner* future.

199

The small, slowly beginning, and delicately mysterious smile of Buddha is full of meaning. But the happiness which it points to does not belong to the simple carnal pleasures or the egoistic intellectual ones.

200

The Buddha's delicate half-smile, pathetically self-deceptive to the cynic, beautifully compassionate to the devotee, is not impenetrable to the man who can let his ego go, however briefly. For then there is utter relaxation, freedom from tension, the disavowal of negativity, and the clear perception of the Good, the True, and the Beautiful.

201

The knowledge that all things are moving toward all-good keeps a quiet smile around the corner of his lips.

202

When the West was first confronted by these pictures and statuaries of the Buddha, it could make nothing of his inward smile. Today it knows better.

203

The traditional Buddhist belief that all happiness must in the end change into unhappiness is not a cheerful one. It need never be taken too literally as being universally true, nor by itself alone, for there are counter-weighting truths. When Buddha brought to an end the meditation which culminated in final enlightenment, dawn was just breaking.

The last star which vanished with the night and the first one which he saw as he raised his head was Venus. What was his inner state, then? Did it synchronize with the reputed planetary influence of Venus—joyous and happy felicity—or with the gloomy view of life which tradition later associated with Buddhism? Who that has had a glimpse of those higher states, felt their serenity, can doubt it was the first? The Overself is not subjected to suffering. But this is not to say that it is bubbling with happiness. It is rather like an immensely deep ocean, perfectly tranquil below the surface. That tranquillity is its ever-present condition and is a true joyousness which ordinary people rarely know. This is what Buddha felt. This is what he called NIRVANA.(P)

204

As I gaze upon the rigid rapt figure of the Buddha upon my desk, I realize anew how much of Gautama's power is drawn from the practice of contemplation. It ties wings to the mind and sends the soul soaring up to its primal home. Gautama found his peace during that wonderful night when he came, weary of long search, dejected with six years of fruitless effort, to the Bo-tree near Gaya and sat in motionless meditation beneath its friendly branches, sinking the plummet of mind into the sacred well within. The true nature of human existence is obscured by the ceaseless changes of human thought. Whilst we remain embroiled in the multitude of thoughts which pass and re-pass, we cannot discover the pure unit of consciousness which exists beneath them all. These thoughts must first be steadied, next stilled. Every man has a fount within him. He has but to arise and go unto it. There he may find what he really needs.

Part 2:

THE PEACE
WITHIN YOU

For the person who is not a complete beginner, who has attained a modest proficiency in the inner life, there is no real contradiction between the inner and the outer life. The one kind of existence will be inspired by the other. Neither despising the world nor becoming lost in it, he moves in poised safety through it.

Outwardly we live and have to live in the very midst of cruel struggle and grievous conflict, for we share the planet's karma; but inwardly we can live by striking contrast in an intense stillness, a consecrated peace, a sublime security. The central stillness is always there, whether we are absorbed in bustling activity or not. Hence a part of this training consists in becoming conscious of its presence. Indeed only by bringing the mystical realization into the active life of the wakeful world can it attain its own fullness. The peaceful state must not only be attained during meditation, but also sustained during action.

1

THE SEARCH FOR HAPPINESS

The limitations of life

Where is the person who has gained total satisfaction of all his needs, let alone his wants and desires? Therefore no one is totally happy. It is better not to be a candidate for happiness and suffer frustration. Then what is the next goal worth seeking? It is peace within oneself.

2

It is in the World-Idea that the living creature is made to undergo so many varieties of unhappiness along with its experience of so many varieties of happiness.

3

It is not really that Gautama declared life to be misery, as the earlier translators told us: the correct version is that he declared life to be unsatisfactory, insofar as limitations are imposed upon each separate person—limitations which bring loss, pain, disappointment. There is so much that he does wrongly through ignorance, so many things he wants but cannot have. Moreover no person finds himself in a perfect situation, a flawless environment, or a faultless set of circumstances. There is always something in each one which offsets to some extent the satisfaction it yields.

4

When people seek excessive entertainment and amusement what are they doing but confessing their lack of happiness and their need to forget this fact?

5

The more persons one observes, the wider one's acquaintance, the more one must conclude that few of them enjoy real happiness for long without some complementary source of unhappiness.

6

Too often does desire gain its object only to find that it still has not gained its happiness.

7

The frustration of our desires happens much more often than the satisfaction of them. The disappointment of our expectations of other people is more frequent than the fulfilment of them. The brevity of our happy periods when compared with the length of dull or distressed ones can be seen when viewed from the vantage of elderly age.

8

He has learned through the experiences of many births not to cling desperately to anything, not to hold on stubbornly when life's clear indication is to let go, not to get so attached to persons or objects that all his happiness rests solely upon them.

9

A happiness that is continuous and unbroken, we find nowhere among men: the circumstances of their lives simply do not permit it to exist, as Buddha saw.

10

The wisdom of experience teaches us that all things change. Friendship wanes and realized ambition brings its own new troubles or disappointments. A fixed and unalterable worldly happiness based on outward things is sought by many but found by none.

11

Whatever he grasps at in his search for happiness, it is only a substitute for the real thing and therefore must one day leave him discontented with it or bored by it.

12

The man who follows his ego's lead in his pursuit of happiness treads circles without end. He may attain fleeting pleasure but never lasting happiness.

13

A satisfaction which is substantial and lasting cannot be found in human life. Existence largely amounts *in the end* to some kind of disappointment. This was Gautama's discovery 2500 years ago and it is the same today.

14

The satisfaction, even happiness, got from any thing, situation, or person is certainly there. But it is only there for a limited time and in a limited way and to a limited extent. For by relaxing from the desire when it is first gained, the tension is dropped and there is inner peace. This may last a short or a long time, but other situations will arise which oppose, reduce, or even destroy and remove it. Whatever satisfies him now may bore him later on.

15

When one has received a terrible blow—such as losing someone very dear to him—he will understand better why the Buddha taught that all living is suffering. In pleasanter times, this truth goes unrecognized. It is only through heart-rending sorrow that many finally arrive at the gates of the Quest, for they have learned at last that only in seeking some knowledge of the Higher Power can they obtain an enduring measure of inner peace. In the calm heart of the inner life—in its strength and understanding—compensation may be found for our outward hardships, griefs, and losses.

16

Young souls look for happiness, older ones for peace, calm, and equilibrium.(P)

17

No other person can bring us happiness if he or she does not possess it in himself or in herself. The romantic urge to seek in a second individual that which neither of the two has, can never find successful fulfilment.(P)

18

You may make yourself happy, by spiritual or other means, but will other human beings let you remain so? Not having accomplished this feat themselves, they are notorious for their interference in their neighbours' lives.

19

Gautama succeeded in making a religion out of disillusion, as Schopenhauer succeeded in making a metaphysic out of it.

20

If it be true, as the pessimist says, that life moves us from one trouble to another, it is also true that it moves us from one joy to another. But it is a question whether the anxieties and miseries of life are sufficiently compensated by its pleasures and satisfactions.

21

To rest the whole of one's happiness upon the physical existence, the close presence, the emotional response, or the personal loyalty of a single individual is risky. If anything changes adversely, the happiness will change with it.

22

It may well be asked how could it be possible to find happiness if harrowing experiences and terrible griefs have been one's lot in the past? Or, for the more fortunate, if seeing or knowing of others who suffered them creates a sympathetic sadness not to be erased?

23

There is so much pain—mental, emotional, physical—in human life that the joy which is also in it is discounted by the Buddhist or Schopenhauerian pessimists.

24

If happiness is to depend on the caprice, the whim, or the desire of some other human being, it will not escape having uncertainty at the core.

25

One day the violence of hate, war, and revolution will spend itself and man will find by his own experience the meaning of peace of mind.

26

The Buddha tried to teach men to look only on the decay and death and suffering inherent in existence on this physical plane. This is as unfair and as extreme—if isolated—as the teaching of modern American cults which look only on the growth and life and joy which are also inherent here.(P)

27

"Life could not be endured were it seen in reality," wrote Sir Walter Scott in his private diary, echoing Buddha, whose words he may never have heard, and anticipating Schopenhauer, whose writings appeared shortly after. We may flinch at this truth, but it is not the whole truth. Perhaps the great artist or composer who rises to incredible beauty offers a counterbalance.

28

It is pleasant to be so optimistic by temperament as to see a rainbow in every sky. But is it always TRUE?

29

Did Gautama magnify the sorrows he came across during his first free explorations of the world outside his palace? Was it fair to concentrate on them alone?

30

Gautama's assertion that "life is suffering" may be matched with Socrates' assertion that "life is terrible." But both Indian and Greek sage referred solely to life in the ego. Is it quite fair to stress the misery of human existence without pointing to its mystery? For that is just as much there, even if attention is seldom turned toward it. Man, in order to complete and fulfil himself, will and must rise to life in the Overself with the ego put into place, belittled and broken.(P)

31

If some good fortune comes your way, before accepting it remember that *everything* has to be paid for, so it will be well to pause and enquire the price.

32

Sometimes they feel on the verge of suicidal despair. Lucretius' poems have been food for such people, as well as for those who, like the nineteenth-century English agnostic George Gissing, could find God neither in nature nor in themselves. His belief in, and following of, Epicureanism doubtless supported him for a time but in the end he returned to his melancholy and, if Jerome is to be believed, killed himself.

33

The criticism of life which the pessimists like Gautama and Schopenhauer make, is too negative. This is not because it is not true but because it is not complete and hence is lopsided.

34

Those who can concentrate their thoughts *only* on the difficulties of the problems which confront them, the dangers of the solutions which are offered to them, or the sacrifices which are demanded of them, will never solve their problems.

Philosophic happiness

35

"Sadness does not befit a sage" is the reminder of an ancient Confucian text. "He is a man inwardly free of sorrow and care. He should be like the sun at midday—illuminating and gladdening everyone. This is not given to every human—only one whose will is directed to 'The Great' is able to do it. For the attribute of 'The Great' is joyousness."(P)

36

Because he is seeking the ultimate source of true joy, he is more likely to find it if he searches for it with a cheerful heart than if with a miserable one.

37

The attitude of Emerson, which induced him to call himself "a professor of the science of Joy," is more attractive than that of Schopenhauer, who taught the futility of life, proclaimed the vanity of existence, and spread the mood of despair. Emerson declined to accept the massive Oriental doctrine of melancholy resignation along with the Oriental gems of wisdom which he treasured. "This world belongs to the cheerful!" he said.(P)

38

Gautama Buddha thought that even mere existence was needless suffering whereas Emily Dickinson thought it to be one of the greatest gifts. "The sense of living is joy enough," she told a visitor.

39

Happiness is not to be hoarded but to be shared. This is not only a responsibility but also a joy.

40

If man's innate nature is exalted peace, then it is logical to presume that melancholy and pessimism are but alien accretions which do not properly belong to him. The smile is man's true expression and not the scowl.

41

"I enjoy life and try to spend it in peace, joy, and cheerfulness," Spinoza wrote to a correspondent.

42

It is easier to solve problems and overcome difficulties if they are met positively and courageously, and that means, or leads to, meeting them cheerfully and hopefully.

43

Buddha continually recurred to his tragic theme whose ending is gloomy for some of his readers but starbright for other ones.

44

Han Suyin writes, "Sadness is so ungrateful."

45

He who preached the misery of life is, despite that, depicted on the ancient statues with a faint beatific smile—Buddha.

46

Despite the prevailing pessimism of today, he may find a peace and steadiness that will well support him.

47

Hung Chou often said: "Since I received enlightenment in the infinite wonders of truth I have always been cheerful and laughing." (Zen)

48

If anyone wishes to practise the inner life, he should try to reflect its quietly joyous character. Father John of Kronstadt—a priest who was a true mystic, an instantaneous healer, and beloved by thousands whom he helped—went so far as to say that to sorrow is to fall away from God.

49

Whether he is sad because of his troubles or sullen because of his temperament, the gloomy man is not in touch with his Overself.

50

The man who knows and feels the Overself's bright light and beneficent love cannot go about habitually gloomy, cannot show a dreary face to the world, cannot hold a wretched pessimism as his leading thought.

51

There is sufficient reason for Confucius' saying: "The superior man is always happy."

52

If some people find an underlying melancholy in life, a few find an underlying joy in it.

53

He will cultivate not only an equable mind but also a sunny one.

54

When this happy peace is real, so that it does not depend on ideological or emotional moods, and is permanent, so that it does not depend on fortune's changes, it is entitled to the designation of "philosophic happiness."

55

It is a quiet kind of happiness, not so apparent as the gay and exuberant kind but much more worthwhile because much more solid and permanent.

56

It is not a boisterous hearty optimism but a quiet perceptive calm.

57

It is a hopeful faith which neither war nor revolution, calamity nor retrogression, can destroy or even diminish.

58

It is not a hysterical bliss nor a wild delight; it is a serene, beautifully balanced happiness permeating a mind that effortlessly keeps itself in amazing equilibrium.

59

Philosophic happiness has its own sense of humour and bears its own signs. But these do not include noisy guffaws and cackling laughter.

60

Must he wear the fixed automatic smile of a Hollywood celebrity to show that he has found happiness?

61

It does not mean looking for hope in a hopeless situation. Philosophy is more sensible and more practical than that.

62

All previous experience should teach him that it is not safe to be too happy, that he cannot live on the heights of joy for too long with impunity. It is not safe to exult too freely in the good fortune which comes in the summers of life; it is not safe to forget the hours of bad fortune which came in the winters of life. Fate cannot be trusted to bring in only such pleasant hours, for it may equalize itself by hurting him now and then. He should temper his delight at fate with fear of it. But even this is not an ideal attitude. Serenity, which leaves him above both delight and fear, is immensely better.

63

It is seldom noted that the Buddha taught a disciple that his advance from the third degree to the fourth and final one depended upon "the passing away of any joy, any elation" he had previously felt. This is a curious statement but it is quite understandable as a resistance to the one-sided emotionalism which is carried away by the pleasanter states *of the ego.*

64

The joys have flapping wings but the sorrows have leaden feet. To bring himself to inner equilibrium, the midpoint of balance is the better way for a man.

65

He may still feel the need of certain things, he may even like to have them, but he will not feel that they are essentially important to his happiness.

66

He will accept the pleasant things of life if they come his way, but he will not long for them or be unhappy if they never come.

67

Without a peaceful mind and a healthy body, happiness must remain at a distance.

68

The man of deep thought and sensitive feeling cannot be happy in a world like ours. But he can be serene.

69

He enjoys a peace which is above passion, above many a desire, so that what the world runs after has no power to attract him. Indeed, the peace itself holds him because it has a greater power and gives a greater enjoyment.

70

The serenity inside a man's mind, the faith inside his heart—these can contribute to his happiness as much as his material surroundings or his way of physical living.

71

If peace, deep inner peace, is not found, then sooner or later moods of elation will reign for a while, only to be succeeded by moods of depression. As fresh events arrive or circumstances change, so the human being is pushed emotionally and mentally from one side to the other.

72

When one finds a constant happiness within oneself, the pleasures of the senses will not be missed if they are not there. They are no longer necessary to stimulate him, although they will still be appreciated if they are there.

73

Whereas the mystic rapture comes only at intervals, the mystic peace may be found forever.

The heart of joy

74

If you investigate the matter deeply enough and widely enough, you will find that happiness eludes nearly all men despite the fact that they are forever seeking it. The fortunate and successful few are those who have stopped seeking with the ego alone and allow the search to be directed inwardly by the higher self. They alone can find a happiness unblemished by defects or deficiencies, a Supreme Good which is not a further source of pain and sorrow but an endless source of satisfaction and peace.(P)

75

Pleasure is satisfaction derived from the things and persons outside us. Happiness is satisfaction derived from the core of deepest being inside us. Because we get our pleasures through the five senses, they are more exciting and are sharper, more vivid, than the diffused self-induced thoughts and feelings which bring us happiness. In short, pleasure is of the body whereas something quite immaterial and impalpable is the source of our happiness. This is not to say that all pleasures are to be ascetically rejected, but that whereas we are helplessly dependent for them on some object or some person, we are dependent only on ourselves for happiness.(P)

76

He will be honest enough to admit that he *does* care if things are going wrong, if possessions are falling away, and if his desires are ending in frustration instead of fulfilment. But he will also be wise enough to declare that he knows that peace of mind is still worth seeking despite these disappointments and that intuitions of the Overself are no less necessary to his happiness and well-being than are the comforts of this world.

77

If the mind can reach a state where it is free from its own ideas, projections, and wishes, it can reach true happiness.(P)

78

The earth moves its cargo of four billion human creatures through space, but how few of them taste the Overself's peace and enjoy its happiness?

79

In those moments when he touches the still centre of his being, he forgets his miseries and enjoys its happiness. This provides a clue to the correct way to find real happiness, which so many are seeking and so few are finding. It lies within.

80

Letting himself be borne along by this inner rhythm of life will yield a contented happy feeling.

81

If his efforts to procure happiness have ended in frustration, discontent, or failure, what more sensible thing can he do than draw a line through them and try a different approach?

82

Buddha promised an "abounding bliss" to those who would give up their "little pleasure." These are his own terms.

83

There is immense joy in being released from the close-knit web of the ego, in escaping from himself.

84

Jules Renard: "I am a happy man because I have renounced happiness."

85

Artificial pleasures are not the same as enduring happiness. They come from outside, from stimulated senses, whereas it comes from within.

86

Out of these labours at self-elevation, he can create and keep a joy of the heart not less intense even though it is not derived from outward things.

87

The man who is not inwardly free cannot be inwardly happy.

88

No environment is ideal. Not in outward search but in deeper self-penetration shall we find true lasting happiness.

89

Any man can say he is happy, but few men are competent to appraise the quality of their happiness accurately.

90

He who has learned how to enter at will into this silent inner world will return to it again and again. In no other way can such calm holy joy be felt, such deep meaning be known, such release from personal problems be secured.

91

We think that this or that will bring us to the great happiness. But the fortunate few know that in meditation the mind is at its most blissful when it is most empty.(P)

92

Galatians 5:22 says that joy is a fruit of the spirit.

93

He is happy even though he has no blessed consciousness of the Overself, no transcendental knowledge of it, but only secondhand news about it. Why, then, is he happy? Because he knows that he has found the way to both consciousness and knowledge. He is content to wait, working nevertheless as he waits; for if he remains faithful to the quest, what other result can there be than attainment? Even if he has to wait fifty years or fifty lifetimes, he will and must gain it.

94

The fully satisfying joy he is searching for in this or that thing, which always yields it coupled with disappointment in some way or at some time, is forever waiting for him deep within the heart's deepest silence. But he comes to it only when all else has failed him.

95

One of the oldest Hindu philosophic texts, one of the *Upanishads*, tells us that joy comes out of the deep inner peace of the Overself.

96

Only one who has intimately felt this divine peace, however briefly, can know its inestimable worth. Only one who has felt this divine love, however seldom, can know that its indescribable joy is above all earthly ones.

97

Whether or not he is living in a mystical fool's paradise or a genuine heaven depends upon how much ego and how little truth-seeking are present.

98

When we find the still centre of our being, we find it to be all happiness. When we remain in the surface of our being, we yearn for happiness but never find it. For there the mind is always moving, restless, scattered.

99

The Overself is present with man, and life is nothing more, in the end,

than a searching for this presence. He engages in this activity quite unconsciously in the belief that he is looking for happiness.

100

Hidden under its miseries, life keeps incredible happiness waiting for
one who will search and work for it.

101

Happiness is the desire of man but is it also the goal of life? So far as it is
only an emotional condition, like misery, it cannot be the goal, for evolution keeps leading us upward to control and eventual conquest of all
emotions. Therefore the true goal must be in those rarefied regions and
the true happiness must be there too.

102

If suffering brings moods of dejection, it is only fulfilling its intention.
This is part of its place in the scheme of things, leading to the awareness
that underneath the sweet pleasures of life there is always pain. But
thought would present only a half-truth if it stopped there. The other half
is much harder to find: it is that underneath the surface sufferings which
no one escapes, far deeper down than its counterpart, is a vast harmony, an
immense love, an incredible peace, and a universal support.

103

In the universe there is joy and suffering: in that which transcends it
there is only a higher pure joy. The pairs of opposites cannot be escaped *in*
the universe.

104

Joy and sorrow are, after all, only states of mind. He who gets his mind
under control, keeping it unshakeably serene, will not let these usurpers
gain entry. They do not come from the best part of himself. They come
from the ego. How many persons could learn from him to give up their
unhappiness if they learnt that most of their sorrows are mental states, the
false ego pitying itself?(P)

105

They find relief in its explanations of compensatory knowledge or new
qualities extracted from their suffering; they take refuge in its promise that
somewhere along the route, if they remain faithful, grace will manifest its
benign help.

106

If the divine presence is dwelling at the core of his mind, then the divine
bliss, peace, and strength are dwelling at the core of his mind too. Why
then should he let outward troubles rob him of the chance to share them?
Why should he let only the troubles enter his consciousness, and withdraw

all attention from the bliss and peace and strength? The conditions of this world are subject to the cosmic law of change. They are temporary. But the bright core within him is not. Why then give a permanent meaning to those conditions by a total surrender to the sadness they cause?

107

If the Overself is beyond all human conditions, it will be asked, how can the term "happy" be applied to it?

108

It is always hard to watch others who are near and dear to him suffer, but he must not let go of his own inner faith and peace, however little they be, because of having to witness such suffering. It ought not to take him by surprise if he remembers that earthly life is usually a mixture of pleasure and pain, and that only in the Overself is there lasting happiness.

109

The incentive to seek happiness will always be present so long as the consciousness of the Overself is absent. But so soon as that is found, the incentive vanishes. For then we *are* that which was sought—seeker, search, and object blend into one.

110

There is peace beneath life's pain and peace at the end of its pain.

111

He will see that no affliction and no misfortune need be allowed to take away his happiness.

112

It is not enough to achieve peace of mind. He must penetrate the Real still farther and achieve joy of heart.(P)

113

Both grief and joy claim their shares of a man's life, do what he will to avert the one and secure the other. But by renouncing them emotionally he may find the supreme tranquillity. Gautama sought refuge from the searing sun under a branching leafy tree. There he found the secret which he had sought for six years. "There is no happiness higher than tranquillity," he announced later.

2

BE CALM

After the brief hour of peace come the long months of storm: its purity is then contested by opposition, its light by the world's darkness. It is through the varying episodes of experience that he must struggle back to the peace and purity which he saw in vision and felt in meditation. True, he had found them even then but they were still only latent and undeveloped.(P)

2

Settled serenity which can be unaffected by the disorder of our times seems theoretically unfindable. Yet some have found it!

3

We cannot hope to achieve such calm in a day. It must be worked for, the obstacles to it must be struggled through, before it can be won.

4

"Time must elapse between sowing and harvest—nay, even in the growth of such wild grass as the holy Kusa and the like, reflection on the SELF ripens into self-realization by degrees, and in the course of time."— *Panchadasi*

5

Is the search for inner peace a hopeless one? There is enough testimony to prove that it is not.

6

Sceptics refuse to believe that passion is unable to intrude itself into that peace-filled mind.

7

Once this sublime equilibrium of mind is reached, there is then the further need and practice of not letting it get upset.

8

Peace in the hearts of men, with peace in their relations with one another: is this an idle dream?

9

We do not have to fall asleep to experience this truth. Everyone has been momentarily flung into the peace-fraught vacuum state by the unexpected removal of a great fear or by the sudden satisfaction of a great desire. But very quickly other thoughts, desires, or fears rush in to fill the vacuum and the glimpse of peace is lost.

10

It is in the very nature of things that the good should ultimately triumph over the bad, that the true should dissolve the false. This understanding should bring him patience.

11

He will find that whereas there is a quick road to agitation, there is no quick road to serenity.

12

How can this peace become continuous and uninterrupted? That is a question often asked by many who have felt and lost it.

13

It is useless to expect that those who are insufficiently receptive by temperament and development will be able to feel this benedictory calmness.

14

Many years are needed for a man to gain this composure of self, this sureness of purpose.

15

Is it possible to attain such inner calm that negative thoughts and the baser emotions swirl against it in vain?

16

It is easy to attain a kind of artificial serenity while seated in the comfort of an armchair and reading a philosophic book, but to keep calm in the midst of provocation or peril is the test. So the would-be philosopher will try to keep an even mind at all times, to chill its passions and control its agitations.

The goal of tranquillity

17

A peaceful life does not merely mean the absence of troubles and strifes. It means this uncommon thing, but it also means something entirely different: a peace-filled mind.

18

I have written and spoken that this inner work should start with cultivating a calm, peaceable temperament. The Brahmin boy in India who is initiated into his caste and given the symbolic sacred thread to wear at the age of thirteen is also given this same instruction: "Be calm!" And five hundred years before Jesus started his public work, Lao Tzu in China earned a personal compliment from Confucius, who observed, "He is a man of great peaceableness." Two hundred years later, Mencius was practising and gaining the Unperturbed Mind; later, as an honoured Confucian moralist, he was teaching others, in his turn, the same method.

19

He should set up as his goal this mood of sustained inward tranquillity and train himself to allow no wave of emotion or upsurge of passion to dispel it.

20

The longing for peace may be kept inside a man for many years, repressed and ignored, but in the end it has to come out.

21

Seek the centre of inner gravity and try to stay in it. Try to avoid being pulled out of it by emotions and passions, whether your own or other people's, by anxieties and troubles—in short, by the ego.

22

He who lives in the higher levels of his being comes into a beautiful serenity as part of his reward. This is a pointer to us. By consciously cultivating such a serenity, we prepare the way for entry into such a level.

23

In the end and after many an experience, he will come to see that peace must take the place of passion, truth must banish falsity, and reality must come through the illusion which covers it.

24

To attain knowledge of Brahman, the mind must be held in the prerequisite state of being calm, tranquil, and in equilibrium—not carried away by attachment to anything. *After* this is established, and only then, can you begin enquiry with any hope of success. Unless the mind is balanced you cannot get Brahman.(P)

25

The importance of cultivating calmness is well known in India. The Brahmin youth at puberty when initiated into his caste status and given the sacred thread is taught to make the first sought-for attribute calmness. Why is this? Because it helps a man to achieve self-control and because without it he becomes filled with tensions. These tensions come from the ego and prevent him from responding to intuitive feelings and intuitive ideas. For the student of philosophy it is of course absolutely essential to achieve a composed and relaxed inner habit.

26

It is not to be a forced calm, imposed from without and liable to break down, not a suppression of feelings on the surface while letting them rage within.

27

The Psalmist's advice, "Be still, and know that I am God," may be taken on one level—the mystical—as a reference to the ultimate state achieved intermittently in contemplation; but on another level—the philosophical—the reference can be carried even deeper. For here it is a continuous state achieved not by quietening the mind for half an hour but by emptying the mind for all time of agitation and illusion. Towards this end the cultivation of calmness amid all circumstances makes a weighty contribution.

28

Half of Asia holds this faith, burns its sweet-scented incense before the firm conviction that the search for inner calm and emotional freedom is the highest duty of man.

29

Chinese wisdom verified Indian experience. "Perfect calm with gentleness makes Tao prosper," wrote Tze Ya Tze.

30

It may be possible to achieve only seldom, but it is worth trying for: let nothing shake your composure.

31

The quest of the deeper calm that is ordinarily experienced only occasionally by some people becomes important for him.

32

Hold on to serenity amid all circumstances until it becomes an abiding quality.

33

This is to wrap the mantle of peace around himself.

34

What is it that Lao Tzu says? "The disciplined man masters thoughts by stillness and emotions by calmness."

35

The Persian Sufi Attar's advice to the quester to "go thy way in tranquillity" amid all his fortunes and frustrations on this venture is very practical, and not only very sensible.

36

He sets up the ideal of meeting events, be they favourable or adverse, with equanimity.

37

He must practise an invariable calm, sheathe himself in its protective power.

38

He should learn to cultivate the feelings of peace whenever they are strongly present. He should give himself to them completely, putting aside everything else. For they will bear to him something hidden inside of them that is even still more valuable.

39

If at any time he feels the touch of Peace, he should stay where he is, forget all else, and surrender to it.

40

This inner emptiness, its equipoise, serenity, is neither deviated by passions nor pushed by extremes. Take Nagarjuna's mid-view and also the early Gautama's middle path.

41

Cultivate calmness; try to keep the balance of your mind from being upset.

42

If this kind of thought and life is followed, there comes by slow degrees a stable calmness throughout the whole being which nothing ever upsets.

43

These quiet moments may enter his life with greater frequency. If so, he ought to welcome them gratefully and respond to them wisely and sensitively.

44

The moments when a sudden stillness falls upon a man must be carefully tended, for they are as delicate as a tiny sprout of grass. Thus treated so hospitably and reverently, they will expand and lengthen and turn into a blessing.

45

One can keep the mind as serene as an undisturbed temple and hence be happier than when amid the mob. We must learn to treasure such moments when we think grandly, and surrender our laboured hearts to sublime peace.

46

Whether stricken and humbled in penitence or uplifted and exalted in meditation, one should come back to the central calm.

47

Great balance is needed. This can be achieved only if steadfast calmness is cultivated.

48

These moments when negatives are non-existent and peace within is vivid can only be called delicious, exquisite, and he will do well to linger over them and stretch out their time.

49

Let the mind find its repose in this delicious and desirable tranquillity.

50

He who has entered this balanced state has found peace.

In daily life

51

If his daily life makes him feel that it is taking him farther away from this peace, this inner harmony, he may have to reconsider his situation, environment, and activities.

52

No pleasure which is brief, sensual, and fugitive is worth exchanging for equanimity and peace, not even if it is multiplied a thousand times during a lifetime's course.(P)

53

Nothing matters so much that we should throw ourselves into a state of panic about it. No happening is so important that we should let ourselves be exiled from inner peace and mental calm for its sake.

54

So long as a man cannot live at peace with himself, so long will he be unable to live at peace with others.

55

The fidgety, restless movements of the moderns merely betray their neurotic lack of self-control. The Buddhist seeker and the Taoist sage value and practise calm.

56

The worst result of all this hurry and tumult and preoccupation with externals is that it leaves no time for intuitive living.

57

Those who live in a world of turmoil need this serenity not less but even more than the yogis do.

58

It is never worth paying the price of losing one's inner calm to attend to any matter or to do any job. If he cannot cope with the matter or master the job without fraying his nerves, he had better drop the one or the other, if he can.

59

Tranquillizers and antidepressants sell by the million in highly advanced countries such as England and the U.S., but peace of mind is no nearer; indeed, this enormous sale is a sign of how far away it still is.

60

He must find and keep a centre within himself which he is determined to keep inviolate against the changes, alarms, and disturbances of the outside world. Human life being what it is, he knows that troubles may come but he is resolved that they shall not invade this inner sanctuary and shall be kept at a mental distance.

61

The serene life is not subject to emotional crises. It has clearly worked out, in the hours of contemplation, its wise attitude towards life and men so that no situation that arises can sweep it off its feet.

62

Take your experiences with as much equanimity as you can muster. Like Buddha, keep no illusions about life's delightful side: observe its imperfections and inadequacies, lament its transiency; but, unlike Buddha, enjoy its offerings while they are still here. Only—value your peace of mind above all amid the good and the bad; keep the precious inner calm.

63

But such calm, such satisfying equanimity, can only be kept if he does not expect too much from others, does not make too many demands on life, and is not too fussy about trifles.

64

Even when a situation becomes quite critical, a here-and-now matter, he should not give way to panic. The first move after the first shock should be to restore and maintain calm, the second to consider what he is to do—a question for which he should look not only to thinking for an answer but also to intuition.

65

However adverse or difficult a situation may be, it is not only in conformity with the Quest to keep one's equanimity but in the end it is to one's advantage.

66

A great mind is not distressed by a little matter.

67

He learns by practice to live within a measure of inner peace while working in the closely packed, crowded world.

68

He will learn by practice to discipline his own emotional reactions to every situation, however provoking or irritating it may be. The cultivation of inner calm, the growth of mental equanimity, will be set up as a necessary goal.

69
If the world tires you, if the evil deeds of others torment you, you can find blessed peace and healing refuge by turning within.

70
Marcus Aurelius: "When you happen to be ruffled a little by any untoward accident, retire immediately into your reason, and do not move out of tune any further than you needs must; for the sooner you return to harmony, the more you will get it in your own power."

71
Patience is needed, and confidence in the path chosen; resignation is better than rebellion.

72
He does not need to turn his back on the world to find peace.

73
In the stillness we find the perfect shelter from the unease brought by so many human presences, with all their radiating auras.

74
Remember to recess back into consciousness, to the centre, when other persons are present. This instantly subjugates nerve strain and self-consciousness.

75
To remain in obscurity and to pass unnoted assists inner peace. For the contrary attracts other persons' thoughts which beat against one's head and buzz in one's mind like flies—this is an annoyance.

76
He will develop a rhythm of response to intuitive feeling and reaction to outward environment which will be in faultless harmony and put no strain of conflict upon him.

77
It is easier to feel the fine excitement of a sacred presence, and most especially the Overself's presence, than to relate it to and unite it with the prosaic everyday human routines.

78
When confronted by turmoil, he will remember to remain calm. When in the presence of ugliness, he will think of beauty. When others show forth their animality and brutality, he will show forth his spiritual refinement and gentleness. Above all, when all around seems dark and hopeless,

he will remember that nothing can extinguish the Overself's light and that it will shine again as surely as spring follows winter.

79

The belief that this kind of beatitude is valueless for practical life can only be expunged by personal experience.

80

When the evils or tribulations or disappointments of life become too heavy a weight, if he has made some advance he has only to pause, turn away and inward, and there he can find a radiant peace of mind which offsets the dark things and counterbalances the menacing depressions.

81

This truth, taught by Greek sage and Zen master, that action is best done from a tranquil centre, is logical in theory and provable in practice.

82

If trouble comes, first take refuge in the Void, then do what reason and practicality suggest.

83

That some unexpected and unpleasant event may surprise him to the extent that his composure breaks down, is another possibility to which the same rule applies—rise after *every* fall.

84

He is to cultivate a smooth calmness under all conditions until his emotions are never taken by surprise. He is to keep self-possessed at all times so that no contingency finds him inwardly unprepared for it.

85

The better he is poised, the more easily he will adjust to unexpected situations.

86

Such great serenity gives an effect of great reserves dwelling behind it.

87

He who has enough confidence in himself to be at ease can keep his nerve, his emotional equilibrium, in the most varied situations.

88

The changes and happenings around him, the temptations and tribulations he encounters will not affect his precious inner calm.

89

Amid all the vicissitudes of human affairs, and the distractions of historical upheaval, he will keep this central peace.

90

The more he gathers in this peace, the less he feels the need of artificial stimulants like drugs or tobacco or alcohol.

91

Amid the chances and changes, the happenings and episodes of everyday life, he practises keeping unaltered within—in temper and temperament.

92

He is never disturbed by untoward events or perturbed by untoward personal events. His mind floats in a sea of calmness.

93

He walks on his serene course, kept to it by remembering where his true allegiance lies.

94

There is serenity and certainty of the mind when he is in this state.

95

The wise man cannot spare a single hour for repining as he cannot spare a single word for recrimination. He will maintain his imperturbable calm, his reserved air, his refusal to dispute any question.

The qualities of calm

96

Tranquillity—the first psychological quality taught at his caste-initiation to the Brahmin youth; much admired by Benjamin Disraeli because seldom met with in society; prized by Marcus Aurelius and his Stoic sect as the best of virtues—this is to be practised by those who would become philosophers and sought by those who would become saints. Yet for others, who must perforce stay, mix, and work in the world, it is not less valuable to smooth their path and reduce their difficulties. The first it does by putting men at their ease, the second by bestowing clearer sight. For them too it is the defense against rancour, the preserver of humour and peace, and, lastly, if they desire, the way to be in the world but not of it. As Lao Tzu wrote: "There is an Infinite Being which was before Heaven and Earth. How calm it is!"

97

He who attains this beautiful serenity is absolved from the misery of frustrated desires, is healed of the wounds of bitter memories, is liberated from the burden of earthly struggles. He has created a secret, invulnerable centre within himself, a garden of the spirit which neither the world's hurts nor the world's joys can touch. He has found a transcendental single-ness of mind.(P)

98

As his centre moves to a profounder depth of being, peace of mind becomes increasingly a constant companion. This in turn influences the way in which he handles his share of the world's activities. Impatience and stupidity recede, wrath at malignity is disciplined; discouragement under adversity is controlled and stress under pressures relaxed.(P)

99

How soothing to the nerves, how healing to the wearied mind is this quality of utter calm.

100

Depression cannot coexist with this realization of the presence.

101

That state is a joyous one which brings with it freedom from lusts and passions, wraths and resentments, servitudes to cravings, and enslave-ments that prevent growth.

102

Vasistha: "To those who have gained internal composure, the whole world becomes calm."

Sruti: "Whoever has his standby in Self—all desires harboured in his mind turn away." (P.B.: He has freedom of the spirit.)

103

The inner calm which philosophy preaches and the philosopher prac-tises, while not an anodyne to assuage the pains of living, does help the struggle against them and the endurance of them.

104

When this peace falls upon him, equilibrium establishes itself spontane-ously in emotion and thought.

105

The great calm which now *holds* him absorbs and thus causes the disap-pearance of passions, negative emotions, and fears.

106

The fruits of the Spirit are several but the list begins with inner peace. The agitation and anxiety, the desires and passions are enfeebled or ex-tinguished.

107

It is said in the ancient texts that constant *sama* (calmness) and *sa-madhana* (equanimity) provide conditions out of which knowledge of truth can arise.

108

The man who has found this wonderful serenity cannot be tormented by the denial of desires and longings or excited by their satisfaction.

109

It is a peace so complete as to lift him beyond the world.

110

Such is the peace which he attains that he can say with Chuang Tzu, "Within my breast no sorrows can abide; I feel the great world's spirit through me thrill."

111

In those high gathered moments when truth and beauty become loving allies to possess us, we ourselves become inwardly aloof from tormenting desires.

112

Here, within this delicious calm, he will find the inspirational source of such diverse qualities as courage and benevolence, poise and honesty.

113

The man who is established in the Overself cannot be deflected from the calm which it gives into passions, angers, hatreds, and similar base things. Calmness has become his natural attitude.

114

Those desired moments of the mind when peace falls are rare, but they exist and are still to be found. The solace they can confer becomes with time the most prized possession of those few who have touched it.

115

It affords a satisfaction free from anxiety, unmarred by painful changes.

116

If he can attain this inner poise, no event can bring him unhappiness, no person can bring him harm.

117

From this deep calm, certain valuable qualities are born: courage when tragedy confronts him, strength when battles must be fought, and wise perception when problems arise.

118

Wise action comes out of composure, not out of passion or lust, which put the mind in a feverish state and blur, even falsify, its vision.

119

Whoever achieves this gemlike serenity will no longer be sensitive to criticism, however vulgar it be, or susceptible to insult, however venomous. This does not mean he will always ignore them. He may even humbly study the one to learn about his shortcomings and calmly reply to the other to fulfil his public duty. But he will not feel personal resentment nor express emotional anger about them.

120

Right judgement is more easily made in a calm atmosphere. It is confused, upset, or even blocked by passion or tension or strong negative moods such as depression.

121

Where this attitude of philosophic detachment is lacking, one's sufferings under the blows of karma will inevitably be more intense.

122

This freedom from inner conflict, this disburdenment of troubling complexes, this liberation from gnawing unrest, releases his mental and emotional energies for concentration upon his work.

123

A serene, cool mind is more likely to grasp the truth of any situation in which it is personally involved than is a turbulent, excited one.

124

Caruso: "It is essential that the singer should bring to his study a complete calmness. Unless he is calm, how can he hope to control his will? Moreover, a calm mind facilitates the task of completely relaxing the vocal organs."

125

He becomes established in a calm when dealing with the world or when alone with himself, a calm which leads to freedom from moods, which remains the same whether he is provoked by someone's nasty sneers or flattered by pleasant compliments.

126

Suzuki always kept imperturbable, always calm, whenever and wherever we met. As Herman Hesse said of him, when Arthur Koestler's criticism of Suzuki appeared in *The Lotus and the Robot*, "He does not allow himself to be touched."

127

If he puts up a curtain of equanimity between himself and his troubles, this is not to evade them but rather to deal with them more effectively.

128

If he has real inner peace he will never know the mental shock and nervous collapse which come to numbers of people when bereavement or loss of fortune comes. Such a calamity may not be preventable, but the emotional suffering it causes may be cut off at the very start by a philosophic attitude toward life generally.

129

If a man can train himself to keep calm not merely in pleasant periods but also in distressing ones, he will be in better form to do what can be done to mitigate his trouble. Without such self-training and with panicky nerves or fear-stricken mind, he will be in worse form. A calm man's actions when calamity besets him are more likely to be right than a frantic one's.

130

If he is to keep this inner peace, he must keep no care on the mind. But this does not mean that he is to become casual, indifferent to responsibility, and neglectful of duty.

131

As the inner peace advances, the outer problems recede; as truth permeates the mind, harmony re-arranges the life.

132

He will then be able to endure with unruffled mind what the average man can only endure with exhausted emotions.

133

In this desirable state cares are forgotten, agitations are lost, and a godlike peace descends on the man.

134

The problems that once tormented him do not seem to exist any more. But have they really been dissolved by the exaltation, by its calmness and satisfaction?

135

Present troubles are mentally put at a distance so that inner calm may be restored: then they can be more properly attended to.

136

The more you can let yourself stay in this wonderful mood, where the sacred presence becomes so vivid and so positive, the less will you be troubled by, or at the mercy of, negative moods or other people's negative thoughts about you.

137

Not to lose this inner peace amid difficulties which may crush others to the ground in despair, not to lose faith in this deeper source of fortitude and support—if this should be called for at a certain time in a quester's life, he will only grow inwardly by taking the challenge, even if he fails outwardly by the seeming result.

138

The work of the day will be better cared for if it is done in an atmosphere of serenity than if it is done in an atmosphere of anxiety.

139

The attainment of inner peace does not guarantee the freedom from outer conflict. But it does reduce the likelihood of such conflict.

140

He will gradually build a habit of applying this balanced and poised attitude to all his problems, be they worldly or intellectual. It will be a habit that will bring them to a quicker and better solution.

141

To practise being calm at the onset of troubles, whether one's own or someone else's, is not the same as to practise being callous.

142

Does the phrase "peace of mind" suggest that he will not suffer in a suffering world? This can hardly be true, or even possible. As actual experience, it means that his thoughts are brought under sufficient control to enable him to repel disturbance and to retain sensitivity. The sacred stillness behind them becomes the centre.(P)

143

It is easy to misunderstand this deep unfathomable calm of his and regard it as a chill, impassive, impersonal, and remote attitude. But in reality if one could explore its heart, it would be found to be a beautiful benevolent and wise *feeling*.

144

It is not that he has no likes and dislikes—he is still human enough for them—but that he knows that they are secondary to a true and just view, and that his inner calm must not be disturbed by them.(P)

145

It is not that the years pass by unregarded, nor that he is dead to human feelings, but that at this centre of his being to which he now has access, there is utter calm, a high indifference to agitations which compels him to treat them with serene dignity. He is a dweller in two worlds more or less at the same time.(P)

146

A frozen calm, which chills with its iciness, is not what is meant.

147

His calm is inscrutable to those who themselves know only agitation.

148

He himself, though utterly calm, can sympathize with, and fully understand, those who are agitated or worried.

149

It is not a dull apathy, this equanimity.

150

It is not correct to believe that the stricken body of a sage suffers no pain. It is there and it is felt, but it is enclosed by a larger peace-filled consciousness. The one is a witness of the other. So pain is countered but not removed.

151

While within himself remaining imperturbably calm, he will yet be sensitive enough to register the moods and feelings of all others who cross his orbit.

152

Some people mistake philosophic calm for fatalistic resignation. This is because the philosopher will seem to endure some situations stoically unperturbed. They do not know that where he finds that he cannot work outwardly to improve a situation, he will work inwardly to extract the utmost spiritual profit from it.

153

To keep contained within himself and thus preserve the precious treasure which he has won, and yet not withhold sympathy from others nor interest in them, is another balancing act he learns with time.

154

The more he practises this inward calm, the less he shows concern about outward situations. If this seems to lead to a kind of casualness, it actually leads to inner peace.

155

To say that outer events will not affect him at all is to say something untrue. What happens in him is that they do not affect him in the same way as they do others.

Staying calm

156

This state of mind and heart is attainable by regulated life, purified emotions, and the practice of mystical exercises.

157

This calmness comes partly from this self-imposed training of thoughts and feeling during the day's activity, partly from practice of meditation, and partly from knowledge of the World-Idea and the profound trust in the World-Mind which it engenders.

158

Holding on to the future in anxiety and apprehension must be abandoned. It must be committed to the higher power completely and faithfully. Calmness comes easily to the man who really trusts the higher power. This is unarguable.(P)

159

He teaches and trains himself to feel the peace beneath the tension.

160

Think of the Overself as an ever-deepening calm. It may seem to come spontaneously after you have practised it much and found the helpfulness.

161

With sufficient intelligence, reverent devotion, and personal purification, it is possible to enter one day into this experience of being enclosed within the divine mystery, enravished by the divine peace.

162

This moving of consciousness to a higher level will come about by itself, if the calm is patiently allowed to settle itself down sufficiently, and if there has been preparation by study, aspiration, and purification.

163

The mind which is purified from desire may easily be calmed. The mind which is calmed may easily be abstractly concentrated. And, concentrated, it may then easily be turned upon itself.

164

Before the Overself can stay with you, the feelings must be brought to a condition of calm, the thoughts must be turned inwards and centered there. Otherwise the outer difficulties will not let go of your attention. All this often includes the disengagement from strong desires and sensual passions. This inner work leads the practitioner—if he is willing to go so far—deeper within the self. What does he find there if efforts are successful? A beautiful quietude, an unearthly sense of having moved to another plane of being, a closer communion with spirituality. It is true that at its deepest points the working of intellect gets suspended. It is, however, a temporary condition.

165

Passion of any kind is a bad counsellor; and in its blind mood nothing drastic, nothing irrevocable, should be done.

166

When desire is quenched, peace is found.

167

He has brought over from earlier births a number of subconscious memories, tendencies and complexes, unfulfilled desires and unexpressed aspirations. These have to be dealt with, either by increasing eradication or by diminishing satisfaction, so that they no longer interrupt the calm tenor of the mind.

168

The closer he comes to the source of his being, the farther he goes from depression and despair.

169

One consequence of inner rule is inner peace. The more there is mastery over lust and thought, the more there is peace.

170

There is no room in that complete inner quiescence for vain useless emotions or violent disturbing passions.

171

The impulses which arise within and the temptations which come from without may attack his peace. If he would keep it, he must overcome the desire to gratify the one and to yield to the other.

172

The unclouded evenness of his mind is precious to him: he tries to keep it undisturbed by frenetic passions.

173

This preliminary injunction to nourish calm is given very seriously. The student is expected to practise it as if he were never short of time. Both lack of patience and the hurrying attitude—so marked in the modern West—are condemned.

174

Seek continually the deepest tranquillity possible—this also is a yoga path.

175

Haste is not only vulgar, as Emerson noted, but it is also irreverential.

176

Peace reigns within him because desires do not reign there.

177

One secret of preserving the stillness after returning to outward activity is not to let oneself be hurried, not even to seem hurried. Cultivate a leisurely approach.

178

How can a man obtain dominion over an unfavourable environment from which he is unable to escape? There is but one way and that lies entirely within himself. He must turn away in thought from its contemplation and fix his mind firmly upon the radiant Power within. Thus he will be uplifted.

179

That deep inner state keeps him calm and deliberate: it makes hurrying seem a kind of madness and impatience a kind of vulgarity.

180

At this stage of inner development take care of the *hara*, centre of balance, by not moving abruptly and hastily but slowly and sedately. He should walk more gently than before among his fellows yet not less purposively or determinedly.

181

This evenness of temperament comes gradually of itself as he lives more and more with the deeper part of his being.

182

We gain more by learning to depend upon the silent mind within rather than the noisy rituals without.

183

If calmness is the friend of the quester, haste is the enemy of calmness.

184

The man in a hurry is the one who is more likely to commit an error than the man who is not.

185

By assiduously learning to live inwardly, he may develop slow deliberate and unhurried movements, while his eyes develop a far-away look.

186

The man who has learned the art of staying within himself finds peace.

187

There is an inward way to that stillness.

188

When one knows that the Real always is and that all disappear back into it because there is nowhere else to go, then one ceases his terrific hurry to get somewhere and takes events more calmly. Patience comes with the fragrance of the eternal. One works at self-improvement all the same, but there need not be any desperate bother about the task. There is plenty of time. One can always do tomorrow what one needs to do today.

189

The practice of philosophy brings more peace, more freedom from frantic passions of every kind. Calm reigns within the walls of a true philosopher's mind.

190

If philosophy does not help him meet each troubling situation as it arises with inner calm and without destructive agitation, then it is not true philosophy.

191

Because an even mind is necessary if inner peace is to be reached, philosophy instructs us to take both the troubles and the joys of life with calmness.

192

When the I is no longer felt then all the problems and burdens associated with it are also no longer felt. This is the state of inner calm which philosophy seeks to bring about in a man.(P)

193

If you would become a philosopher in practice, then the first step is to cultivate calmness.

194

It is this deep calm which especially marks out the philosopher and makes him what he is. In most cases it has not come to him easily.

195

The tensions inside himself and the circumstances outside himself combine to determine what kind of mood prevails at any given time in the average man. But the philosophic aspirant needs to achieve a deeper stability than this, a greater fixity of attention.

196

The first fruit of philosophy is to bring the calm repose of the soul into the activity of the body.

197

With the passage of well-spent time and the coming of well-deserved Grace, he will finally reach the serenity and mastery that characterize the last stages of the path.

198

It is often not easy to preserve one's calm amid provocative or passion-filled events, but that is precisely what a philosopher must set himself to do.

199

The first thing to note about an attained philosopher is that he constantly stays in his innermost calm being, a condition generally reflected in his outermost active physical self.

200

Philosophy places a high appraisal upon this quality. It says, blessed is the man who can keep serenely balanced and inwardly progressive amid the carking troubles and exciting pleasures of the modern world.

201

It is the business of philosophy to show us how to be nobly serene. The aim is always to keep our thoughts as evenly balanced in the mind as the

Indian women keep the pitchers of water which they may be carrying evenly balanced upon their heads. A smugly self-satisfied, piously sleek complacency is not the sort of exalted serenity meant here. It would indeed be fatal to true progress, and especially fatal to the philosophic duty of making one's personal contribution toward the betterment of human existence. When such equilibrium of mind is established, when the ups and downs of external fortune are unable to disturb the inner balance of feeling, reason, and intuition, and when the mechanical reactions of the sense-organs are effortlessly controlled, we shall achieve a true, invincible self-sufficiency.

3

PRACTISE DETACHMENT

Even while you share in the life, the work, and the pleasures of this world, learn also to stand aside as a witness of them all. Learn how to be a spectator as well as a participator; in short, let detachment accompany your involvement, or rather let it hide secretly behind the other. You may say that this is an impossible task, a contradictory one, a pulling in two opposite directions at one and the same time. Yes, it seems so in theory; but in practice you will find that, given enough time, enough understanding, and enough work at it, it can be fulfilled. For you do not stand alone with it; behind is your own higher Self. From its resources and by its grace, the way to this wonderful attainment may be found. Learn how to pass into mental quiet, inward stillness, and you may intuit this higher Self.

2

What has been called "purgation of the intellect, memory, and will" actually happens in the deep contemplative state. The faculty of thinking temporarily ceases to function, the awareness of personal identity vanishes for a time, and the ability to direct the muscular movements of the body stops as in a paralysed man. These changes last only for the hour of his meditation practice and are responsible for much interior growth in the shifting of consciousness from the lower nature to the higher self. But there is a more enduring state wherein the "purgation" reappears in another form, better suited to the aspirant's active everyday existence. He finds that the more he inclines to detach himself from worldly things, the less firmly do they lodge themselves in his memory. In this way, and little by little, neither the dead past nor the active present can overcome him and make his mind their prisoner. So, too, the unrealized future does not do the same in the form of fears or anticipations, anxieties or desires. Thus he "purges" memory, he loosens himself from immersion in time and begins to live in the blessedly liberated and liberating Eternal Now. The purgation of intellect shows itself in this active form throughout the day as a perfect tranquillity of the mind which instantly comes into logical thinking activities as and when needed but otherwise remains at peace in the Eternal Stillness. The purgation of the will manifests in a continuous freedom from enslaving passions, from bodily directives and egoistic impulses.

3

There are two different ways of being detached: the ascetic's, which dissociates itself from the world and tries to live outside the world's activities; and the philosopher's, which accepts those activities but not the dependence which usually comes with them.

4

In that once locked-up land of Tibet there dwelt a spiritual teacher named Marpa. He wrote a text for his disciples. Therein is the piece "Be Content":

"My son, as a monastery be content with the body, for the bodily substance is the palace of divinity. As a teacher be content with the mind, for knowledge of the Truth is the beginning of holiness. As a book be content without things, for their number is a symbol of the way of deliverance. As food be content to feed on ecstasy, for stillness is the perfect likeness of divinity. Companions, be content to forsake, for solitude is president of the divine assembly. Raging enemies be content to shun for enmity is a traveller upon the wrong path. With demons be content to meditate upon the void, for magic apparitions are creations of the mind."

5

How trifling all his earthly successes must seem to a dying man! Such is the state of mind which may be called inner detachment and which the aspirant needs to cultivate.

6

Only he is able to think his *own* thought, uninfluenced by others, who has trained himself to enter the Stillness, where alone he is able to transcend all thought.(P)

7

He cultivates detachment, for this is a means to becoming a truly free man.

8

Is detachment a condition of mummified or half-tranced living? If wisely practised, with balance and common sense, it need not be anything of the sort.

9

What man can live entirely immune from troubles? Where is he? I have never met him and know no one who has.

10

"Independent of" seems a better term than "detached from" (outside things).

11

In this matter I must take my attitude from Epictetus when he asked, "Who, then, is the invincible man?" He himself answered it thus: "He whom nothing that is outside the sphere of his spiritual purpose can dismay."

12

Not everyone can reach such heights of complete detachment. Most usually feel it to be far beyond their capacities . . . yet it often comes by itself when they are old dotards. But then the credit is hardly theirs, neither karmically nor personally.

13

The term *fana* is associated in origin with the Sufi Abu Yazid (or, Bayazid) Tayfur ibn Isa ibn Sharushan al-Bastami (ninth century). It first came into prominence in eastern Persia. The person who practises it becomes, in Inayat Khan's words, "independent of all earthly sources and lives in the Being of God by the denial of his individual self."

14

Loneliness vanishes completely in the Stillness. He is then with the power behind the entire universe, with the Mind behind all human consciousness. He returns from the Stillness welcoming the condition of being free, unattached, unjoined—this is no longer the condition of being lonely.

15

When this equanimity becomes *of itself*—for it is in the end a grace—a deeply settled state, he finds that detachment is a part of it.

16

By detachment I mean something less in the Hindu sense and more in the Taoist. Do not ask me to define this with more sharpness.

17

He is always himself, undetracted by the worldly turns, undeterred by the worldly difficulties.

18

As for the detached man, happenings pass him by. He knows them for what they are: transitory, coming and going, ever moving. And to what are they moving? They are moving until they are finally gone into death.

19

The detachment which comes to the old through weariness and fatigue is in some ways similar to the detachment which comes to much younger people through the study of philosophy and the work upon themselves. However, in the latter case it is a positive quality whereas in the case of the old it is merely a passive one.

20

He will live leisurely in the moment yet not aimlessly for the moment. He will take things as they come, yet a steady purpose will underlie this calm detachment. He will establish within himself a retreat from the furor and rush of modern existence yet not be apart from it.

21

That mind is truly free which has emerged from the common state of being conditioned, distorted, unbalanced, and physically sense-bound.

22

Although there are some points where they touch one another, there is a fundamental difference between philosophic detachment and the unassailable insensibility cultivated by the lower order of Hindu yogis or the invulnerable unfeelingness sought by the ancient Stoics. Some part of the philosopher remains an untouched, independent, and impartial observer. It notes the nature of things but does not allow itself to be swept away by the repulsiveness of unpleasant things or lost in the attractiveness of pleasant ones. But this does not prevent him from removing himself from the neighbourhood of the first kind, or from finding pleasure in the second kind. It is the same with his experience of persons. He is well aware of their characteristics; but however undesirable, faulty, or evil they may be, he makes no attempt to judge them. Indeed, he accepts them just as they are. This is inevitable since, being aware of his and their common origin in God, he practises goodwill towards everyone unremittingly.

23

Until you arrive at the stage of development where you can be content to let others find their own heaven or make their own hell, you will not be able to find your own peace. Until you learn not to mind what they say or how they behave, you show that you have yet to reach philosophic maturity.

24

Philosophy does not ask you, nor ought it ask you, to become perfectly indifferent towards your personal concerns. It is not wildly idealistic. Attend properly to them, it enjoins, but do so in a transformed spirit.

25

He has been brought by experiences of life and studies in philosophy to a point where the personal life has become much of a dream. He sees everything as the Buddhists say, as subject to change, coming, and going, and he sees no exception to this universal law. Consequently he attaches himself to nothing, but accepts everything that is worth accepting, without, however, so tying himself to the need of it as to suffer too grievously should destiny remove it again.

26

He will mentally be in control of every situation, yielding no reaction to it which is not in accord with philosophical principles.

27

There is a difference between the watchful patience which philosophy inculcates when adversity falls and the mute resignation which fatalism commands.

28

For a sensitive person, living in the world is difficult: he is tempted to renounce, desert, or hide from it and go his own way. But if he gains this inward peace and is practised enough to stay in his centre, then worldly life turns into a sacrament, is known for the passing spiritual drama that it is, and is borne philosophically.

29

The notion that the fortunes and misfortunes of life should be of little importance to a philosopher is not a correct one. To practise a calm detachment is not to ignore worldly values.

30

He will find, with time, that this increasing detachment from his own person will reflect itself back in an increasing detachment from other persons. Consequently, irritation with their faults, quarrels with their views, and interference with their lives will show themselves less and less. It is pertinent to note, however, the difference between the ordinary mystic's detachment from personalities and the philosophical mystic's. The first tends finally to become mere indifference, whereas the second always becomes compassionate.

31

Will this atmosphere of impersonality have a chilling effect on him? It might be thought so and in some cases it does happen so. But in a well-controlled, well-balanced person it need not be so. There is no real need to withdraw from the more affectionate or more intimate human relationships. They can be taken into the larger circle.

32

To be detached from the world does not mean to be uninterested in the world.(P)

33

Do not confuse inner detachment with callous indifference. Do not search after impossible results. A worthy goal for human beings cannot be devoid of human feelings, however elevated they may be: it cannot be a glacial one.(P)

34

He may become detached without becoming dehumanized. He may live inwardly apart from the rest of the world without lessening his goodwill and good feeling for others.(P)

35

Does this practice of detachment chill a man's nature to an inhuman degree? It sets him free from enslavements—a freedom which he comes to enjoy, which enjoyment makes him happier, with the result that he shows a happier front to others. He does not become frozen.

36

A person who has brought his feelings under control with a view to detachment is likely to be an undemonstrative person. That is true but it is also likely to lead others to misjudge him.

37

The world is told of the inner detachment which philosophy bestows, the deeper calm which it puts into a man's existence. Too often this is misread to mean a chilling remoteness from life's inescapable concerns, a feeble response to the personal demands which duty lays upon him.

38

It might be thought that at such an inner distance from most of mankind he is in danger of becoming a misanthrope. But the presence of a positive quality of goodwill is inalienably associated with awareness of Overself.

39

This emotional detachment seems unnatural and frigid, if not suicidal, yet it is really a capacity to see things as they unromantically are.

40

The practice of detachment need not destroy, perhaps not even weaken, our enjoyment of the arts, the entertainments, the comforts, and the gadgets which human genius creates.

41

Calmness and detachment should not be practised to the point of fanaticism, so that they become cold, unfeeling. To prevent this imbalance, the practice of cheeriness and the cultivation of goodwill are to be called in.

42

Whoever comes close to this uncovered goodness within his heart—can he have any other feeling towards others than that of goodwill?

43

Philosophic serenity in the midst of civic commotion is not the same as, and therefore is not to be confused with, religious fatalism or sceptical rashness.

44

That such profound detachment can coexist with normal human feelings of liking or disliking may seem impossible, yet experience proves it—for some persons.

45

Anger cannot upset his peace, nor can hate be projected towards someone else; virtue comes of itself and kindness is an inevitable attribute.

46

The kind of emotional neutrality where there is no more aversion to pain or attraction to pleasure is not quite the detachment sought by philosophy.

47

It is an error to believe that being detached is equivalent to being callous, that the change of values and the control of thoughts leads to an icy, emotionless composure.

48

Whoever lives in the spirit lives in its perennial peace. It is a happy peace, a smiling peace, but he is not lost in it. He is aware also of the suffering which exists around him and in the world at large. In just the same way, if he is responsive to the beauty which nature offers and man creates, he is also aware of the ugliness which exists.

49

None of those humanist qualities which are really worthwhile need be discarded. They ought indeed to be preserved. But they are put into their proper place by philosophy, evaluated at their correct price. For they, as everything else, must be subordinated to, and coordinated with, the life divine.

50

When detachment is overdone it becomes a cold bloodlessness. The man then moves and acts like a marionette.

51

In a sense he becomes depersonalized but he need not become dehumanized.

Turn inward

52

He who attains this inner equilibrium is neutral to all the ideas thrown at him by books and men, unresponsive to all the suggestions dumped on him by social trends and institutions. His mind dwells in vacuity—free, happy in itself and with itself. His is the centered life.

53

To turn one's mind instantly towards the divinity within, when in the presence of discordant people, is to silence harsh thoughts and to banish hurtful feelings. This frequent turning inward is necessary not only for spiritual growth, but for self-protection. Everything and everyone around us plays a potent influence upon our minds, and this is the best means of detaching oneself from this ceaseless flow of suggestions.(P)

54

By expecting nothing, he avoids disappointment. By refraining from effort, he avoids defeat. By clinging to inner calm, he avoids anxiety.

55

If he is to keep this wonderful inner calm, he must be vigilant that he does not accept from others the pressures they would put upon him. That is, he must be true to himself, his higher self.

56

One form of self-training to help acquire this inner detachment is to practise seeing and hearing no more of what is happening around one than is absolutely necessary for one's immediate purpose, duty, or activity.

57

If such a man is to live in untroubled inner peace, he can do so only if he no longer worries—not only about himself but also about others.

58

Like Liu Ling, third-century philosophic Taoist and poet, who "dwelt without having any domicile," he is detached even in his activities and not detained even in close friendships.

59

The happiness he finds in certain persons, events, things, or places may pass away with time or with them, and leave him feeling so empty that it is as if they had never been in his life, or as if they had appeared only in a dream. This is because he left them where he found them—in the world of illusion—instead of bringing them where they become transformed—in the world of Reality.

60

This is an art, indeed, to live alone in the midst of the multitude.

61

It is not that he takes a neutral position in all controversies—he sees only too well for that—but rather that he prefers to be disinvolved and detached by attending to his own business, where alone he can do the most good!

62

He tries to put himself beyond the power of other persons to suggest thoughts, wishes, actions, or feelings to him, even when they do it unawares. A detached attitude is of much help for this purpose.

63

When a man needs nobody and possesses nobody, he is much closer to peace and strength.

64

Song—author unknown: Look not thou on beauty's charming/ Sit thou still when kings are arming/ Vacant heart and hand and eye/ Easy live and quiet die.

65

The itch of curiosity which wants to know other people's private lives, the urge to meddle in their affairs or tamper with their lives, must be suppressed if one's own peace is ever to be found.

66

Whoever accepts praise must also accept blame. Whoever is inwardly unaffected by the first will likewise be inwardly unaffected by the second. What action he may then take outwardly depends on his individual circumstances.

67

When we arrive at such a state of impersonal understanding, we begin to see friends in our enemies and sometimes even enemies in our friends. For we begin to seek without emotion the causes in ourselves which arouse antagonism in others. Thus we learn more about our weaknesses, our incapacities, and our faults, even though we have to sift many falsehoods, many exaggerations, distortions, and even wickednesses to get at this knowledge.

68

The serenity which possesses his heart permits him to regard the shabbiness, the injustice, or the meanness of the treatment which he may receive from others with lofty indifference—with resignation, too, it ought to be added, for he realizes that nothing better need be expected from such characters and such perceptions as theirs.

69

He must train himself to become so accustomed to bearing the injustice of surface judgements that he will expect few of the other kind.

70

How much better to live in dignified silence, ignoring the petty printed sniping and the jealous vocal yapping of those who incarnate the dog, the reptile, or the flea!

71

Nothing that his enemies say will ever have the power to wound him if he listens to it with the ear of inward detachment.

72

While outwardly and resolutely doing all he can to foil the evil designs of his opponents, he must inwardly and resignedly detach himself from his troubles.

73

Human frailty being what it is, human conduct should never surprise us and never amaze us. By not expecting too much from it, we save ourselves unnecessary bitterness or disappointment.

74

He will get a lot of fun out of life when he can sit indifferent to its ups and downs, when he can pity his enemies and laugh at their libels.

75

He will look for no approbation from others and no reward from society. How could he if he is really detached?

76

He will see the faults in those he has to deal with just as before, but now they will not seem to matter and will not be able to irritate or upset him.

77

When a campaign of invective grew, Ananda suggested to the Buddha that they should go elsewhere. But the Buddha refused to do so, saying, "I am like the elephant that has entered the fray: I must endure the darts that fall upon me."

78

Not for him should be the vanity which demands to have its ego built up by others, by their praise or flattery.

79

Jesus did not answer when malignment and malediction were hurled upon him. Buddha kept silence when vilification and abuse were uttered against him. These great souls did not live in the ego and therefore did not care to defend it.

80

It is part of the price that may have to be given by the aspirant to separate himself from friends who are constantly critical of his quest, social groups that are time-wasting hindrances to it, or relatives who are virulently antagonistic to it. This is not to say that he must always do so, for each case is individual and needs to be carefully judged. Sometimes he will be better advised to bear sneers in patience and bear mockery of clacking tongues in resignation.

81

Thank heavens we do not have to carry with us to the Divine Arbiter any certificate of character drawn up by the mob that does not know our hearts: He, and He alone, can read our true worth and reckon our human faults with accuracy and with mercy.

82

While others avidly seek publicity, he is indifferent both to popular acclaim and to popular criticism.

83

The more successfully he can keep himself free from worldly ties, the more extensively he will be able to serve mankind.

84

As I was studying him one wintry evening in the snow-covered streets of St. Albans where I first met him, strange thoughts filled my head. Under those tattered rags dwelled a spirit of purest sapphire. The inscrutable writ of destiny had put him upon this path. But as he spoke to me, in calm happy tones, of diverse spiritual matters, I felt my mind being steadily raised by the tremendous power of his dynamic thoughts to a sublimer state. I sensed his amazing peace, his godlike realization, his cosmic outlook, his profoundly impersonal feeling, and I knew that the man before me would not willingly change his lot for that of any millionaire on earth. Hard to understand, this, but there are a few who will grasp my meaning. I do not preach poverty as a path to peace. But I do say that unless you have found *inner* wealth, unless your success exists within your heart and thoughts and conscience also, the external symbol of an all-powerful checkbook is a mockery and may even prove a curse as well.

85

He who has attuned himself to the egoless life and pledged himself to the altruistic life will find that in abandoning the selfish motives which prompt men he has lost nothing after all. For whatever he really needs and whenever he really needs it, it will come to his hands. And this will be equally true whether it be something for himself or for fulfilment of that service to which he is dedicated. Hence a Persian scripture says: "When thou reachest this station [the abandonment of all mortal attachments], all that is thy highest wish shall be realized."

86

Out of the continued practice of this inward detachment from his own actions and their results, there develops within him a sense of strength and mastery, a feeling of happy peace and being at ease.

87

The cool detachment which he feels in the presence of temptations is a very satisfying feeling, a worthwhile reward for the struggles to attain it.

88

No man can try to hold this detached attitude toward his own activities without getting a continuous and excellent training in self-control. Mental equanimity, emotional stability, and a better knowledge of his self are also among the fruits of success.

89

If he establishes himself *first* in this vital creative centre, all else will be added unto him inevitably and inescapably.

90

The *Gita* enjoins unconcern about the results of activity not only because this leads to calm detached feelings as the large general result, but also because it leads to better ability to keep meditation continuously going on in the background of attention as the special result.

91

If you want to enjoy inner peace, you must practise inner detachment.

92

Those who can bring themselves to give up all, will receive all. Those who can dare to lift themselves out of emotional oscillation will find "the peace which passeth understanding." Those who can perceive that they are their own obstacles in the way will in no long time perceive the truth.

93

The man who practises this spirit of detachment is no longer the victim of conflicting emotional states. He feels free inside himself.

94

Temptation as such disappears at this advanced stage and becomes a means of increasing his strength of will.

95

Whatever you really need inheres in, and may be drawn from, that stillness.

96

The man who knows how to live in his centre and not stray away from it, frequently finds that he need not make any move towards satisfying a need. It will often come by itself at the right moment drawn by the magnetic central power.

97

The results of this inner freedom are many. Thus he who feels this inward peace which he has won through deep renunciation is likely to feel a cynical dislike for politics, for the sharp debates it fosters, the personal abuse it suggests, the selfish conflicts it engenders, and the harsh polemics it creates.

98

Just as the leaves of a sapless tree dry up and fall off, so the desires of such a man wither away of themselves.

99

Such cool detachment has its uses at a time when passions are violent, emotions are explosive, and destructive ideas or persons run wild among us.

100

Because he can see straight through it, because he can penetrate its true nature, reaching Reality through the Appearance that it merely is, he can deal with the world, negotiate its transactions, and experience its ups and downs all the better now that he is detached and nonchalant.

101

Ananda Coomaraswamy on the doctrine of the Tao, the path of non-pursuit: "All that is best for us comes of itself into our hands but if we strive to overtake it, it eludes us."

102

When in the end the ego gives up its struggle because it sees that the better way is the higher way, however much that may involve resignation and renunciation, the reward comes quickly in the peace that falls upon the soul.

103

If a man understands that life is like a dream and is mental at bottom, and if as a result he practises a certain kind of detachment, there will descend upon his character a calmness and a serenity for which he will not even have to work, given sufficient time.

104

If he can transcend himself, can rise to independence from the ego's attachments and desires and emotions, utter peace awaits him.

Solving difficulties

105
It is a quality not easily come by, this detachment, and moreover one which is too often falsely assumed. He will have to test himself from time to time, or co-operate with life's own testing of him, to find out how authentic his detachment really is.

106
There is a materialistic serenity and a spiritual serenity. The first comes from the possession of money, property, position, or affection. The other comes from no outward possessions but from inward ones. The first can be shattered at a single blow; the other soon recovers.(P)

107
Can he keep his mind unruffled amid bad times as well as good ones, under catastrophe as well as victory? The capacity to sustain such indifference is the ideal; the circumstances are the test of what he is, as well as the opportunity to become better than he is.

108
Nor is it a question of choosing between being self-important and being humble, for the ego can be strong in both cases. It happens in the second case if accompanied by exhibitionism, and in the first case if accompanied by total concentration upon itself. The practice of detachment avoids both errors.

109
If he has truly attained this peace, he will also have died to the flesh, and its unruly urges, at the same time. This is one of the tests for him to know just where he is.

110
If his inner peace is only a spurious one, it will crumple at the first thorough test. And be sure life will provide this test.

111
These professionals of spirituality make it such a self-conscious affair that the constantly reiterated references to "giving up the ego" or "standing aside from the personal self" seem like a kind of play-acting, not to be taken seriously, not real, not authentic, only make-believe, a pretense.

112
His unruffled calmness and dispassionate outlook will show itself not only in the day-by-day events of ordinary life but also when tested in the rigorous crises of fate. He will be as detached towards them as if they had happened a half-century before and he was viewing them from afar.

113

Can he detach himself from the personal aspects of the situation? Can he refuse to be guided by them or influenced by the feelings of the moment? This is his test.

114

To live and work in the world as it is today, strenuous, materialistic, and sensual, and still keep vivid an intuitive feeling of its own dreamlike mentalistic nature, is a balance quite hard to find.

115

People get uneasy when they are asked to practise detachment, as if it would take the joy out of life if they followed this rule.

116

It is a difficult art, this, to live in one's Spirit-centre simultaneously with existence in the Body-circumference.

117

This question is often asked: How is it possible to keep the mind constantly engaged in the inner life when it has also to give attention, and, quite often, unswerving attention, to the necessary tasks involved in earning a livelihood?

118

It is not easy, this twofold attitude, which lives alertly in what is taking place around it, yet as detached from the present as from the future.

119

It is easy to look at the past with detachment and to judge it with calm, but to do both during the flow of current events is very much harder.

120

It is not easy where there are duties and commitments to adopt an attitude of renunciation.

121

It is perhaps not true to write that the man must become utterly detached. No one who is yet embodied, yet compelled to deal with the world without him and traffic with it for his necessities, can be called that— however free he has made his heart and however firm he has made his mind.

122

The attitude required of him is a detachment from his emotions as impartial and as disinterested as that of the mathematician from his figures. This attitude may seem not only too impossible to attain, but also too frightening, too bleakly abstinent to retain. It would seem that no human creature could deliver himself up to it, or would want to do so.

123

Whether it is possible for anyone to achieve a total impersonality may be questioned; but if the ideal of it is set up, at least right direction will be gained and some progress will be made.

124

Detachment as ordinarily proposed seems virtually impossible except in smooth talk about it or glib writing of it. What is possible and indeed preferable is a commonsense indifference or a better *balanced* detachment.

125

Is it at all possible that a human being, with flesh blood and nerves, living in a world and time like ours with all the inflamed discussions, the tensions and frictions, the sufferings and violence, can keep an inner aloofness?

126

Desire only to be desireless. Be detached even from efforts to be detached. It does not seem humanly possible to follow such rules.

Training mind and heart

127

The mind must be hardened until it can rise, to whatever extent its endurance allows, above circumstances. It can do this only by habitually cultivating equanimity, indifference, detachment.

128

Whatever mental-emotional clouds the day may bring, he does not detain them but lets them pass over him. This would seem a superhuman feat, but it becomes possible when he turns them over to the higher power.

129

No disappointment in expectations can lead to embitterment in heart. His own tranquillity is worth more to him than that.

130

He will little by little adjust himself to his handicaps and live in emotional peace despite them.

131

It is true that he can quickly recover his serenity and steadiness. But he is able to do so only by sheer force of habit and by deliberately returning in reflection and meditation to the universal and eternal truths which blot out the temporal and particular grief.

132

No man can get out of his own sorrows unless he can get out of his own thoughts.

133

When he can smile at his disappointments and forget his desires, he is learning detachment.

134

"Now what can harm me who, even while living, shall be as dead?" Thus sang Lalla, a fourteenth-century Kashmiri yogini.

135

It is not only that he must remove the impurities, the faults and the weaknesses, which obstruct the divine entry or prevent the divine settlement, but also that he must, by continually training himself to remain undisturbed by troubles and unexcited by good fortune, keep mind and heart always calm so that the divine guest may be able to remain permanently.

136

He will know inner calmness, true peace, when he knows nevermore any emotional agitation. And this is true of its pleasurable as well as its painful forms. Both have to be risen above. Both the attraction which attaches him to a thing or person and the repugnance which prevents him from seeking it, are to be felt without any movement of the emotions, much less of the passions.

137

To cultivate equanimity when life is full of splendours is as necessary and as much our duty as when it is full of miseries.

138

If you will take care not to become too depressed when things go wrong, nor too elated when they go right, you will gradually achieve an equilibrium which later will assist you to remain always in touch with Reality.

139

The inner security and ineffable peace of this state cannot be got for the asking. They have to be fought for by refusing to be unduly elated by good fortune or unduly depressed by misfortune, by allowing no attachments to touch the heart and no entanglements to hold the mind.

140

If good fortune comes he may rejoice at it, but he should not either optimistically count upon it or pessimistically discount it.

141

He tries to recall the experiences he underwent during a period of great difficulty, danger, calamity, or illness, and to do so calmly, impersonally.

142

This way of looking at all experiences for their inner meaning, of learning from all alike, causes him to reject nothing and to express tolerance. For all are valuable—even if not equally valuable—in serving his higher purpose and fulfilling his spiritual quest. The tension between good and evil disappears, and it is no longer necessary to favour one above the other since he puts himself on a level where *the One* rules.

143

The Overself is never hurt.

144

It is better to be above moods which spread over an ultrasensitive man and either light up the day with joy for him or darken it with dejection.

145

When the frustration of past privation turns into the elation of present fortune, he needs to be careful—to cultivate as much detachment now as he should have cultivated then.

146

There are disagreeable elements in our experience of life as well as pleasurable ones; but if we are ever to find peace of mind we must learn to put a reserve behind these feelings, to stand aside and scrutinize them, even in the midst of the events which produce them.

147

He will not be led astray from this deliberate cultivation of inner tranquillity. He will take worldly failure with recognition of its true causes and worldly success with utter humility.

148

A man is not necessarily unspiritual if he lives fully in the world, engaging in its activities and appreciating its satisfactions. Only, he must remember constantly who and what he really is and never forget his ultimate purpose.

149

Although he should give his best to external life, he should not give the whole of himself to it. Somewhere within his heart he must keep a certain reserve, a spiritual independence. It is here, in this secret place, that the supreme value of the Overself is to be cherished, loved, and surrendered to.

150

Those activities which belong to a human existence in the world may still go on, and need not be renounced, although they may be modified or altered in certain ways as intuition directs. His business, professional, family, and social interests need not be given up. His appreciations or creations of art need not be abandoned. His intellectual and cultural life can remain. It is only demanded of him that none of these should be a self-sufficient thing, existing in total disregard of the Whole, of the ultimate and higher purpose which is behind reincarnation.(P)

151

However busily active he may have to be to fulfil his worldly duties, inwardly his mind will repose in perfect placidity. It is this ideal state that enables him to remain secretly detached from and emotionally uninvolved with the world. Without it, he would be caught up by temptations and tribulations, and affected by them as most men are affected.

152

He will carry on the busiest daily work with such profound composure as can arise only from the realization that it does not exhaust the whole area of living.

153

He need not despise the perishable and ephemeral, for he needs must live with them. In that sense they surely are important. And insofar as he has to work with his body and take part in earthly activities, there is no spiritual reason why he should do his worst. They, too, deserve his best effort. What he should really guard against is their demands' becoming excessive and consequently encroaching upon time that ought to be reserved for higher things.

154

Practical activity must run side by side with inner detachment.

155

Is isolation from every physical expression of nonphysical experience, thought, and feeling a proper goal? Is being entirely shut up within one's inner self without actualizing its revelation to be the last state of one's aspiration?

156

He has to live inside the world with worldly people, as most of us have to do, and yet be able to keep alive the awareness of its divine background, not losing the feeling of godliness deep within his heart. He has to function as a physical being while sensitive to underlying transcendental nature.

157

Finding the Overself's stillness does not necessarily mean withdrawing from the world's bustle.

158

Whatever happens he is to stay centered.

159

He is not asked to abandon his social aspirations, for instance, in favour of his spiritual aspirations, but to balance them sanely. He is asked not to seek the one at the cost of the other, not to desert worthy ideals at important moments. The major decisions of his life must be grounded on a reconciliation of being in the world with not being of the world.

160

Let the body be there, let the worldly life go on; there is no need either to deny their existence or to neglect their requirements; but do not let either dominate you.

161

The sense of being inwardly detached from all his daily activities, the consciousness of deep power kept in reserve, will be present.

162

We must plunge into the life of the world but we need not be drowned in it.

163

There is nothing wrong in the daily contact with the world, attending to duties, being practical, effective, even successful in profession, business, or other work, and rearing a family, provided all this is done within the remembrance of the higher power.

True asceticism

164

We must use the material things, yes, and not abandon them; but we must do so without attachment. We may love the good things of life like other men, but we ought not to be in bondage to this love. We should be ready to abandon them at a moment's notice, if need be. It is not things that bind us, not marriage, wealth, or home, but our *craving* for marriage, wealth, or home. And what is such craving in the end but a line of thinking, a series of mental images?(P)

165

Where others get caught in this whirlpool and spend themselves, their energies, and their years in the piling-up of earthly possessions or the exhausting of earthly pleasures, he says to his instincts: "Thus far, and no farther." For him there is satisfaction in a restrained enjoyment of this world, with enough time and thought and strength for study of the great gospels and the practice of going into the Silence.(P)

166

The detachment to be practised is not a denial of necessary things or a refusal of beautiful things, but a rejection of superfluous life-burdening things. I suggest that this statement be compared with what was taught and done in India.

167

He will appreciate the comforts and conveniences which money provides, he will enjoy the aesthetic pleasures and physical satisfactions of life, but he will not be dependent on them. They are becoming to his developed human status and needs, but inessential to his real welfare. He can let them go at any time, if circumstances demand it.

168

The first price which he who would cultivate serenity has to pay is inward detachment. He must bring himself to the right answer of an age-old question: Do I want to possess things or to be possessed by them?

169

It is a reasonable act to reject whatever hinders the attainment of one's ideal. The rejection of personal possessions, of physical goods and worldly powers which become such hindrances, is therefore not wrong. But we ought to distinguish between the mere external symbol of possession and the real internal attachment to it. The latter is solely mental. True asceticism must be practised inside the heart. A publicly advertised asceticism has no intrinsic value.

170

Our relation to possessions, and even to persons, should be one which does not put dependence upon them to such an extent that any change will rob us of inner tranquillity.

171

If he takes care to own nothing in his deepest heart, he cannot experience the mortification of losing anything.

172

It is true that a number of men find peace of mind in abundance of wealth, but it is also true that they do not find the greatest peace of mind. This comes from, and can only come from, the abiding tranquillity of the Overself.

173

He can achieve this state by *secretly* standing aside from every possession which he has acquired, every honour he has won, every relationship he has entered into or has inherited by Nature. In this way, he casts off what is outside himself and is made free to receive what is inside himself.

174

It is not necessary to disown all one's property and material possessions in order to qualify for the "poverty" to which monks vow themselves or to enlist oneself in the ranks of "the poor" whom Jesus described as being blessed. Correctly understood, the state of poverty is a spiritual one, and means inner detachment from outer things. It is the state of being *free at heart* from materialism and worldliness, ambition and egoism.

175

He must begin by mentally surrendering all personal claims on all things and all persons.

176

I once knew a man who followed Jesus literally. What he received with his right hand he gave away with his left—such was his utter indifference to possessions or his complete charitableness to the needy, call it as you wish.

177

Desirelessness is the last test of the mystic's moral strength and practical sincerity. Can he give up without undue bitterness this thing which he most treasures because he seeks a higher value? Can he cut the last attachment to the world for the sake of reaching that state which is beyond the world? If his thinking and behaving can survive this test, great will be his reward.

178

What is it that injures your Mind? It is Desire. When desires are many, what we can preserve of our Original Mind is inevitably little; and when they are few, it is much. If desires were eliminated, the Mind would automatically be preserved. If scholars could refuse to follow passions and desires, they would be successors to the ancient sages.

179

In the end, man has to arrive at this conclusion: that there is no resting place for him in any earthly desire, and that the satisfying and enduring peace of desirelessness is immensely superior to the always partial and transient fulfilment of such desire.

180

He must learn to keep the equable detachment of his mind undisturbed and the clear sight of his intuition unclouded.

181

He must achieve a disinterestedness in motive and a dispassionateness in mentality.

182

There comes a moment in the life of the earnest disciple when he will be impelled to draw the sword of Detachment from the sheath of Aspiration, and with it cut the last hankerings for the alluring things of sensual life.

183

When Christ taught that he who would find his life must first lose it, he meant simply that one must first lose his attachments.

184

Jesus declared clearly that those who could not forsake their earthly attachments could not become his disciples.

185

Jesus' saying "Come unto me, all ye that labour and are heavy laden, and I will give you rest" means: "Cast aside your burden of attachments, desires, thoughts; then the real I-nature will alone be left, and you will have true peace, rest from the ego's heaviness."

186

His mind is to achieve a complete poise and his heart a complete placidity which no passion can ruffle and no desire excite.

187

A man may fall into the sin of vanity because of the facility with which he is able to work up the devotional feelings or excite the spiritually rapturous ones. But those who enter into the Void because they are able to enter into the innermost part of themselves cannot fall into this sin. They are detached not only from the emotions but also from themselves. This is why they live in so great and so constant a peace.(P)

188

If you try to hold to the thought that all this turmoil is after all an idea and to be valued accordingly, it will be easier to find and retain your inner calm. If you can look upon the present era with the detachment with which you look upon the Napoleonic era, the trick will be done; but of course, humanly speaking, it is impossible to do this except by minute-to-minute effort and day-to-day practice carried out over a period of years to discriminate what is real and what is merely an idea. It is this long-continued striving which really constitutes *gnana yoga*, and it eventually brings success in the form of a settled and unshakeable understanding of the truth behind life.

189

He becomes detached when he frees himself from the universally prevalent tendency to connect every experience with the personal ego. Detachment takes him out of himself and saves him from getting emotionally involved in his environment.(P)

190

He is able to hold himself up to the light, as it were, able to remain impartial and detached even in dealing with matters which greatly concern him.

191

He has reached a point where contact with the Stillness is now possible, where its glorious blessing is now available. But he soon finds that on returning to the everyday world, as return he must, the contact swiftly vanishes. Is there anything he can do here to reduce and delay the loss? The real obstacle is, as always, his ego. If he cannot remove it, he can practise temporarily suspending it.

192

Turn away from your self. Leave your ego behind. Do this in thought and deed and in emotion and mood. Change your attitude—and thus change your life.

193

He must bring the whole edifice of ego-built attachments to the ground: either abruptly and courageously with a crash or slowly and fragmentarily with time.

194

He will learn to see the acts of others from this impersonal angle. In this way he instructs himself by their experience.

195

The way forward from here is travelled by cultivating the quality of being impersonal in his reactions to outer experiences, contacts, and surroundings. He must recognize and accept the truth that the Spirit is utterly impersonal and unegoistic.

196

More and more the World-Idea becomes a background for the ego-idea in habitual thinking. Thus he gets more and more out of the attachment to the personal "I."

197

He is beginning to detach himself from his own ego when he is experiencing a strong self-distrust and a great doubt about the value of his own judgement.

198

What he has to learn is to extend this indifference to the world—which he professes—to his own personal affairs in the world.

199

Those who try to grasp Tao, lose it, declared Lao Tzu. Why? Because they are using willpower, personal willpower, instead of becoming passive and letting the Tao *use them*, their minds and bodies, as if they were its instruments. This elimination of the self-will is what Jesus meant when he counselled his followers to lose their life in order to find life.

200

As he advances in the idea of being detached from results and possessions, he will inevitably have to advance in the idea of being detached from concern about his own spiritual development. If he is to relinquish the ego, he will also have to relinquish his attempts to improve it. This applies just as much to its character as to its ideas.

201

The aspirant who does his best at self-improvement, however poor it may be, may leave the results to the higher power.

202

To wish to get rid of desires is itself a desire. Therefore the superior way would be not merely to change the desire alone, but to cease desiring in every way, and that is only possible by entering the inner stillness, and staying there.

203

Some Tibetan sage has said that the best course is to be neither enlightened nor non-enlightened, and thus to rise above this pair of opposites. A Hindu sage advised the Brahmin to let go of his scholarship first, then of his meditativeness, and finally of his non-meditativeness; then only would enlightenment appear.

204

Don't occupy yourself with things or thoughts, not even with the search for inner experiences, but be quiet and desireless.

Becoming the Witness

205

To witness what is happening around him without being influenced by it, or what is happening to him without being concerned about it—this is part of the practice of inward detachment.

206

He becomes not only a spectator of others, but also of himself. If such detachment is seldom seen, it may be because it is seldom sought.(P)

207

To practise living in the world and yet not being of it involves becoming a spectator not only of the world but also of oneself. To the extent that he gets lost in the world-experience, to that extent he loses this deeper self-awareness.

208

To say that he becomes a detached spectator of the world is not wholly true, for a part remains there but he keeps a certain distance from it. This is not possible for the materialistic man, as his personal involvement with the world is complete. I use the term "materialistic" here as referring to one who has not awakened to the truth or once experienced a glimpse. The situation is plainly to be seen in most theatrical actors. They become the part they play during the time of a performance but they do not wholly forget who they really are.

209

Men who are too close to themselves cannot really understand themselves.

210

One part of him must remain untouched by the outer happenings—calm, watching observer, emotionally distant and secretly unreachable.

211

It is a strange feeling, a sensation of being away from himself, something deeper than and different from being away from his body.

212

When he can mentally withdraw at will from a situation where he is involved with others, so as to regard all the parties, including himself, with calm impartiality, he will have travelled far.

213

Dissociate yourself from the person who has to go through with the dream-drama of life. He is forced to act, but you can inwardly practise this dissociation.

214

He feels as if he were a mere spectator at a theatrical play, with the whole world for a stage. More, he feels himself to be a ghostly spectator.

215

He may come in time to feel a certain amusement at watching his own performance on the stage of life.

216

He sees his personality playing its role on the world stage and, although he recognizes its connection with him, it is felt as an object, as an "other."

217

Again and again he will have the extraordinary sensation of looking down at the game of human life as from a peak-like mental elevation. He will see the players—millions of them—vehemently struggling for trivial aims and painfully striving for futile ones. He sees how paltry is the sum-total of each individual life-activity, how bereft of mental greatness and moral grandeur it is. And, seeing, aspiration will re-dedicate itself to un-faltering devotion to the Quest within his own mind.

218

Whether he evokes the past or dreams the future, he will stand aside from his own ego and judge the one or plan the other with impersonal, detached wisdom.

219

From this higher level of existence, it is immeasurably easier for him to solve all problems of conduct and settle all questions of appraisal.

220

The mind rests on the summit of this Olympus wherefrom it gazes on the sorrows and cares of this burdened existence and wonders why they were ever permitted to disturb it. For on this mountaintop, life seems so clear, so right, so tranquil.

221

He does not shrink from problems but rather rises to a higher level where he can see them in truer perspective.

222

By adopting a witness attitude he puts a distance between the day's activities and himself. This helps him bring them under control, prevents them from submerging his quest altogether, and preserves whatever inner peace he attains.

223

In refusing to identify himself with the surrounding scene, but remain-ing its spectator, he saves himself from emotional involvement and retains a mastery of himself which would otherwise be hard to secure.

Timelessness

224

The peace in such a man's heart is as measureless as his trust in Infinite

Mind. Indeed the peace is there because of the trust. He has no need to open the door of the future. The experience he needs or the thing he must have will, he knows, emerge from its obscurity before his eyes at the proper time. So he is patient enough to let circumstances ripen of themselves, when patience is necessary.

225

Partly because Life is a perpetual transition, we do not know how we shall behave the day after tomorrow. Let us not give pledges, then, but rather honour the law of life instead, and be free.

226

So far as past errors are concerned, forget them and start afresh, as if it were your first day in this body; but so far as your present contacts are concerned, be kind to them, as if it were your last day in this body.

227

The personal history which has gone before—let it really go and be free of the past, which can become a mental prison for unwary persons; learn to abide in the timeless, coming out of it as duties call but holding on to it as the background.

228

Do not give a single glance backward to the error-filled past, for the education given by it and the suffering from its consequences have led to the strength and wisdom of the Present.

229

The past has furnished its lessons, so why need there be regrets? Drink, sex, ambition, money, travel—they were all stations on the way to understanding. If they robbed, they also gave. If they disappointed, they also trained you. If the past showed weaknesses, it also showed you could tear them out.

230

It is useful to look at the past by this new and clearer light, to review it from this impersonal angle.

231

Every animal except man is mentally free from anxieties, fears, and worries about its future. No animal except man makes itself miserable with regrets and laments over the past.

232

How can he have fears for his future who knows that he is related to God, and that God is the same yesterday, and today, and forever?

233

Both anxiety about the future and regret about the past are inconsistent with the state of serene detachment. It is uplifted beyond them, and free even from being affected by the day's changes and pressures.

234

Don't let the past suffocate you. Try to be in complete control of thought and mood and bring both into the sacred peace of the Eternal Now.

235

To put anxiety aside, which follows naturally when our personal attachment to results and the eager desire for ends are laid aside, is to have the fullest faith that the higher power will take care of our true needs.

236

If men refuse to see the transiency of person and possessions or acknowledge the inevitableness of change in mind and body or recognize the duality of pleasure and pain in all things, then Life itself will come and teach these lessons directly and definitely in some way or other. Sickness may invade their flesh, bereavement their families, loss their fortunes, or darkness their minds. Is it not better, prudent and wise, to remember the eternal in this present moment, to understand the mentalistic nature of their world-experience, to hold all things as "idea" and thus, freed from inner conflicts and false hopes, attain an unruffled tranquillity?

237

Kenshin, a great general of the eighteenth century and a Zen adherent, wrote the following verses in both Chinese and Japanese: "Even a lifelong prosperity is but one cup of wine. A life of forty-nine years is passed in a dream; I know not what life is, nor death. Year in, year out—all but a dream. Both Heaven and Hell are left behind: I stand in the moonlight dawn, free from clouds of attachment."

238

The wise man lives secretly in the even, sorrow-soothing knowledge of the Oneness, and remains undisturbed by the inevitable and incessant changes in life.

239

From this lofty standpoint, the tenet of rebirth sinks to secondary place in the scale of importance. What does it matter whether one descends or not into the flesh if one always keeps resolute hold of the timeless Now? It can matter only to the little "I," to the ignorant victim of ephemeral hopes and ephemeral fears, not to the larger "I Am" which smiles down upon it.

240

Past, present, future become mere dreams when considered against the background of THAT. If man could switch his thought of self over to the Source, and keep on identifying it with that, his consciousness would be transformed.

241

We finish off particular desires or ambitions as we get wiser, or older in reincarnatory experience. We dissolve certain attachments to possessions, places, persons.

242

Finally, he may remember those lines by Ernest Dowson: "They are not long, the weeping and the laughter,/ Love, desire and hate." And he cannot forget those other versed lines of Dowson: "They are not long, the days of wine and roses;/ Out of a misty dream,/ Our path emerges for a while, then closes,/ Within a dream."

243

What is the use of getting attached to a particular form when all forms are transient?

244

The more you can succeed in detaching yourself from things, from individuals, and from time's content of past, present, and future, the more will you feel peace.

245

Time progresses but the *pure* spirit stands still, motionless.

246

Time itself is erased by the mysterious power of the mind's stillness.

247

Here is a serenity so deep that it draws him out of time.

248

He feels that time has utterly ceased, that the whole world and its movement has become the mere shadow of a thought, that he has entered an untellable and unstrained silence.

249

Who is the visionary, anyway? Is it the worldling who worries himself through the years hoping to find calm in a settled but problematical old age, or is it the philosopher who gains his inner calm here and now?

250

A man without the sense of time is a man with the feeling of peace.

251

Thinking can only approach but cannot enter this timeless condition.

252

Living in measured time as he does is the consequence of living in the movement of thought. But when this vanishes into the still centre of his being, he finds timelessness as its attribute. If there is any surprise, it is a flash only, for in the new consciousness he feels at home.

253

The stillness is beyond conflicts and unbroken by emotions. It is aware and even alert, authoritative and even timeless. For it does not measure the passage of moments, the seconds or the minutes.

254

The actual situation in which he is now becomes a point where this transcendence is possible.

255

When this turning inwards completes itself in the final state of contemplation so that thought is stilled and breath is quiet, the sense of succession is dispelled, a kind of continuous now takes its place, and a stillness of the body corresponds with a stillness of the mind.

256

In this moment here and now, letting go of past and future, seeking the pure consciousness in itself, and not the identifications it gets mixed up with and eventually has to free itself from—in this moment he may affirm his true being and ascertain his true enlightenment without referring it to some future date.

257

If he can penetrate deep enough into the stillness he reaches a state of consciousness that is actually timeless. That must be the reference in the New Testament declaration that there shall be no more time.

258

He tries to transcend both future and past, to live in the immediacy of the present. But it will not be the "ever-moving present." It will be the still Eternal Now.

259

He must cultivate a great patience and see through the illusions bred by the time-sense.

260

The *Mahabharata*: "Let man fix his mind on the reality and, having done this, he will transcend time."

261

Do not be anxious about making provision for the future, if you are in a state of surrender to the Overself; but if you are not, then indeed you need to be anxious. The first relies on a superior power, the second on an inferior. If you will trust the Overself today, it will provide for you tomorrow. If you repose trust in the Overself, it will never let you down and you may go forward in surety. It is indeed the "Father who gives us each day our daily bread."(P)

262

To be at peace means to be empty of all desires—a state the ordinary man often ridicules as inhuman or dismisses as impossible. The spiritual seeker goes farther and understands better, so he desires to be without desire—but only to a limited extent. Moreover, some of his desires may be hidden from consciousness. Only the sage, by which I do not mean the saint, is completely free from desires because the empty void thus created is completely filled by the Overself.(P)

263

He can find the Overself even if he is caught up in the work of earning a livelihood. But his participation in the world's activity and pleasure will have to be a limited one. Not other men's voices but his own inner voice should say how far he should go along with the world.(P)

264

The complete happiness which people look forward to as the objective of their life on earth can never be attained. For it is mostly based on things and persons, on what is outside the seeker, and on what is perishing. The happiness which they can truly attain is not of this kind, although it may include and does not exclude this kind. It is mostly based on thoughts and feelings, on what is inside the seeker, and on what is abiding.

The disciple's serenity must remain unbroken whether he succeeds in any enterprise or not, and whether he is able to do so soon or late. For it must not depend on these outward things; it must depend on inward realization of truth. He should do all that is humanly possible to succeed. But, this done, he should follow the *Gita* counsel and leave the results in the hands of God or fate. Thus, whatever the results may be, whether they are favourable or not, he can then accept them and keep his peace of mind.

Even if he is doubtful about a favourable result, he must resign himself to the situation as being truly the Overself's will for him just now. By this acceptance, the sting is removed, and patient resignation to the divine will is practised. He will then have no feeling of frustration but will retain his inner peace unshattered. He should remember, too, that he is not alone. He is under divine protection, for if he is a true disciple he has surrendered himself to his higher self. Therefore let him cast out all worry in connection with the matter, placing it in higher hands and leaving the issues to It.

Let him refuse to accept the depression and anxiety. They belong to the ego which he has given up. They have no place in the quest's life of faith, trust, and obedience. Let him resort to prayer to express this humble resignation and trust in superior guidance, this belief in the Overself's manipulation of the results of this matter for what will be really the best in the end.

Fate provides him with difficulties from which it is often not possible to escape. But what *must* be borne may be borne in either of two ways. He may adjust his thinking so that the lessons of the experience are well learnt. Or he may drop it, for he need not carry the burden of anxiety, and remember the story of the man in the railway carriage who kept his trunk on his shoulders instead of putting it down and letting the train carry it. So let him put his "trunk" of trouble down and let the Overself carry it.(P)

265

"Diogenes could surrender anything with equanimity because he knew the source from which he had received them."—from a journal of philosophy

266

The *Jivanmuktaviveka* teaches that only after the adept has attained the knowledge of his true being, of his identity with *Atman*, does he become free of the fleshly desires and worldly attachments.

267

It is not easy to know a peace undisturbed by anxiety, unbroken by fear; but whoever finds and stays in the timelessness of the Overself as his inner background will be able to know it. Not only that, but it will protect him against the self-made miseries of impatient unsatisfied desire.

268

The presence of any other thing or being, emotion or even thought, between a man and his Overself represents an obstruction to it.

269

Those who know how to work internally in the deep ground of the Overself may trust all to its kindly care.

270

He should dismiss fears and anxieties concerning the present state or future destiny of anyone he loves. Let him do what he reasonably can to protect the other, then place him or her trustingly in the care and keeping of the higher power.

271

He does not need to support a shaky ego by taking stimulants, talking loudly, or drawing attention to his past achievements. He has no need, and feels no need, to impress others, whether they be single persons or whole groups of persons, nor to ingratiate himself with them, nor to prop up their egos by pretending to agree with their opinions or to accept their actions. He cannot let them live off his integrity, and thus be a traitor to himself. His confidence in the higher laws and the Overself's power is complete.

272

If a higher power can be trusted to arrange my affairs for me, it is unnecessary to be constantly thinking about them, much more so to be often worrying about them. A little thought may still be required of me, a little planning of details, but in the main the affairs will be taken care of, and that better than I could do alone.

273

He cannot depend upon outward circumstances alone for his security, though he will not fail to give them their proper value and place. He knows that for total security he must also have, or at the very least have, the certitude of the Overself's protective presence.

274

As his interest in the Overself increases in depth, so his attachment to the things of this world decreases in passion and his interest in them becomes more serene.

275

However anxious or worried, turn aside to the Overself. Ask first that your fears be forgiven and then that you be helped.

276

The belief that perfect security exists is certainly a vain one so far as worldly life is concerned. But so far as the inner life is concerned, there is a full basis for it.

277

"The Power that made the world will mend it. . . . Why should you upbear the world? Are you Atlas?"—Israel Zangwill

278

Whatever the trouble be which distresses any man—be it physical or mental, personal or public, worldly or spiritual—there is one sure refuge to which he can always turn and return. If he has learnt the art of being still, he can carry his trouble to the mind's outer threshold and leave it there, passing himself into its innermost recess of utter serenity and carefree tranquillity. This is not a cowardly escapism or a foolish self-deception, although with the unphilosophical mystic it could be and often is. For when he emerges from the inner silence and picks up his trouble again, he will pick up also the strength to endure it bravely and the wisdom to deal with it rightly. This will always be the case if his approach is through *philosophical* mysticism, which makes inspired action and not inspired dreaming its goal. Furthermore, his contact with the inner Mind will set mysterious forces working on his behalf to solve the problem quite independently of his conscious effort and knowledge.(P)

279

From the moment that a man begins to look less to his changeful outer possessions and more to his controllable internal ones, he begins to gain the chance for real happiness. When this truth breaks upon the intelligence, he learns to keep his final reserves hidden in his heart. Then whatever happens, whatever course fortune takes, no one and nothing can take it from him. So long as he can carry the knowledge of truth in his head and the peace of God in his heart, he can carry the best of all his possessions with him wherever he may go. Not having lodged his possessions—whether material things or human affections, capitalized wealth or social honours—in his heart but having kept them outside it where they belong, he can remain calm and unmoved when Fortune's caprice disturbs or even destroys them. He has learnt to keep within his heart only inalienable possessions like wisdom and virtue, only what renders him serenely independent of her revolutions.

He who depends on externals plays dice with his happiness. He who depends on his own Overself attains unfailing serenity.(P)

Free activity

280

Whoever acts by becoming so pliable as to let the Overself hold his personal will, must necessarily become inwardly detached from the personal consequences of his deeds. This will be true whether those consequences be pleasant or unpleasant. Such detachment liberates him from the power of karma, which can no longer catch him in its web, for "he" is not there. His emotional consciousness preceding an action is always enlightened and characterized by sublime composure, whereas the unenlightened man's may be characterized by motivations of self-centered desire, ambition, fear, hope, greed, passion, dislike, or even hate—all of which are karma-making.

281

If he can act attentively and yet stand aside from the results of his actions; if he can discharge his responsibilities or carry out his duties without being swept into elation by success or into misery by failure; if he can move in the world, enjoy its pleasures and endure its pains, and yet hold unwaveringly to the quest of what transcends the world, then he has become what the Indians call a "karma yogi" and what the Greeks call a "man."

282

Life in the busy world should be a continuation of life in the meditation sanctum and not an interruption of it.

283

Even when the period itself has come to an end, even when he perforce returns to the world's turmoil, something of its precious joy still lingers on, inspiring him to greet others with goodwill and events with detachment.

284

"The fifth paramita 'dhyana' [meditation] means retaining one's tranquil state of mind in any circumstance, even when adverse situations present themselves. This requires a great deal of training."—D.T. Suzuki

285

Go out into the world, act and do your duty. So long as you are the impersonal *Witness* of them, your actions will not add to your karma.

286

He has to learn to carry something of this consciousness from the world within to the world without. He left the stage to find the secret of meditation: now he must return and rejoin the ego's play.

287

He is not yet perfect in his development at this stage—"Application" is still being practised—but enlightenment is a very real thing to him. It results in this, that although his first reactive feelings toward a person, an event, or a situation may be negative or passionate, he is not carried away by them and they are swiftly checked.

288

Desires die of themselves without struggle, karma comes to an end, the stillness of the Overself settles in him.

289

When all action comes to an end, when the body is immobile and the consciousness stilled, there is achieved what the Chinese have called *Wu Wei*, meaning non-doing. This brings a wonderful peace, for tied up with it is non-desiring and non-aspiring. The quester has then come close to the end, but until this peace is thoroughly and permanently established in him, the quest must go on. Let go of all negative thoughts, especially those which concern others. Cease from condemnation and criticism except where it is a necessary part of one's obligation, duty, or position in the world, such as a magistrate's.

290

Do not strain yourself unduly; let the ego be passive to the intuitive influences so that actions are dictated by them without interference from it, rather than by aggressive desires, and hence become karma-free. This is the meaning of the Chinese expression *Wu Wei*, associated with the teaching of Taoism.

291

The man who is so detached from his own actions is detached also from the making of any karma that could darken his future.

292

Wu Wei, no-doing, is free activity, done for its own sake and not for that of a reward. This is possible to creative minds intent on bringing the needed new into existence, or to inspired artists working for pure love of beauty and not for glory, or to saints obeying a higher will.

293

The power to gain what we really need, subject to the operation of God's laws, is within us. Why run hither and thither for what we already embody? We have only to take our need into the Silence—and wait. We have nothing further to do unless the Inner Voice directs us to do it.

294

Just as a flat-surfaced mirror will correctly give back an image of whatever is presented before it, so a properly quieted mind will register objects, creatures, and persons such as they are and will not disturb them by distortions, prejudices, or expectations. One whose inner being is purified, controlled, and concentrated is able to live in the world and yet not be of the world, is able to go through worldly experiences and happenings and yet not be pulled out of his tranquil centre by them.

295

Somewhere within his interior self he must keep a circle fenced and reserved against the exterior world. No desire may cross it, no attachment may enter it. For it is his Holy of Holies, his surest guarantee of peace and happiness, his sole certitude in an uncertain life.

296

To find the correct equilibrium, through knowledge and practice, which enables one to deal with the affairs at hand but never deviate from staying in the Presence—that is the art of life. That also is to become "natural" in the best sense, to possess an unself-conscious unadvertised spirituality.

297

This is what he has to learn—and it can be learned only by personal practice, not from any book—how to keep in beautiful equipoise receptivity to his sacred Centre and efficiency in attending to the world's demands. This is answering Jesus' call to be in the world but not of it. This is the union of busy actuality with central tranquillity.(P)

298

In the foreground of his thought he deals with practical affairs in a practical way; in the background he remembers always that they are only transitory manifestations of an Element beyond all transitoriness, an Element to which he gives his deepest self. But only when his power of yogic concentration is complete and his knowledge of philosophic truth mature, does the possibility of achieving such harmony arrive—not before.(P)

299

If he is to keep his inner peace he must always keep the innermost part of himself aloof and deny the world any intimacy with it.(P)

300

Chinese poet T'ao Yuan-Ming (365–427 A.D.):

> I have built my cottage within men's borders,
> But there is no noise of carriage or horses.
> Do you know how this is possible?
> When the heart is remote, the place becomes like it.

301

Thus he builds a mental cloister out of which no work, however pressing it be, can drive him. It will be superior to and safer than any physical cloister or earthly ashram.

302

The ability to keep established in the Consciousness while engaged in the world's affairs is acquired by practice. It is a form of skilfulness acquired as bicycle-riding is acquired.

303

If the peace and enlightenment are to persist at all times so that they become a natural state, they must be philosophically induced.

304

The shrill voices of the vulgar break into the peace as if in opposition to one's spiritual well-being, but to the established philosopher the interruption passes away with the sound.

305

With mind absorbed inside itself, the noisy sounds of the world seem to come from a far distance.

306

Han Shan, Chinese Tang Period: ". . . My mind at peace, undusty and undeluded: It is pleasant to need no outer support. To be as quiet as the autumn waters of the river."

307

Though he may never put on the brown robe of the Yogi, he may consider himself every whit as real a Yogi in the thick of London's activity as that Indian prototype who sits in seclusion by the Ganges.

308

There is a fixed centre deep within every man. He may live in it, if he can find and keep to it, so tranquilly that all else in his thoughts and feelings and actions will be affected by its magic without being able to affect it.

309

The agitations of the emotional and passional nature prevent a man from attaining this mental quiet. If he has not built up its power by practice, or got it by grace, they cause him to lose it. These include both the pleasant and the unpleasant feelings, the desires and the cravings as well as the sorrows and anxieties and lusts, excessive pleasure and excessive pain. The art of mental quiet can be pushed to a deep inner stillness and by practice can be inwardly maintained in the midst of outward activity. This is why the value placed on keeping calm is very high in both yoga and philosophy.

310

The Real can't be merely static, actionless; this aspect is one of its faces, but there are two faces. The other is dynamic, ever-active. On the path, the discovery of its quiescent aspect is the first stage; this is mysticism. But the world is always confronting him and its activity has to be harmonized with inner peace. This harmonization can only be established by returning to the deserted world (while still retaining the peace) and making the second discovery—that it, too, is God active. Only then can he have unbroken peace, as before it will be intermittent. He then understands things in a different way.

311

If the One Reality alone *is*, if even the world-illusion vanishes in deepest contemplation, how is he to deal with the world, since it awaits his attention whatever its status be? The answer is that he is to act in the world AS IF it were real: this is to be his working rule to enable him to carry on with everyday existence and perform all duties. This same practical rule was stated by Jesus in his succinct sentence: Be in the world but not of it.

312

How to put his knowledge into practice, how to be able to cope with the world, its pressures, strains, trials, temptations, while inwardly centered upon the Overself is a feat for which man must train himself. This requires periods of withdrawal during which he works upon himself, his character and concentration, renews his aims and strengthens his will, and, especially, restores his balance. The periods may be brief or long, as his circumstances allow: a few hours or days or weeks.

313

When everything within, when thoughts, emotions, and desires are silenced, it is inevitable that the personal will shall also be silenced. What then has to be done will be done, but it will be done through him.

314

The student should always remember that just as the World-Mind does not lose or alter its own nature even in the midst of world-making, so he also should hold reverently and unalterably to the thought of his own true mystical identity even in the midst of worldly activity. What he does outwardly must not for a moment detract from what he has to do inwardly. It is a matter of self-training.

315

He has gone far when he can live in this remembrance and this presence without constraint even while occupied in the affairs of this world; when it all becomes a settled, easy, and especially *natural* attitude entirely free from superior airs, from a holier-than-thou or even a wiser-than-thou attitude. For humility grows side by side with his growth, of itself, unbidden. (How different from the arrogant egoistic pride of the self-conscious intellectual whose real worship is only himself!) By "natural" I mean not a self-conscious thing and certainly not a forced one. It is no supernatural experience either, but human consciousness put at a better level where it has harmony with World-Idea. It is easier to withdraw from the world, where people portray so widely and so often all their inadequacies, than to return to it and apply positively what is learned during withdrawal. It is more possible for the spectator to appraise the passing show and evaluate its offerings than to come back, walk with it, keep sagehood, remain human, yet find the point of sane equilibrium between both conditions.

316

He will maintain a proper equilibrium between being aware of what is happening in the world, remaining in touch with it, and being imperturbable towards it, inwardly unaffected and inwardly detached from it.

317

Sahaja is the final phase and, in striking contrast to the first phase, the Glimpse, lasts as long as corporeal life lasts. In this he brings the light into every day's thought, speech, and behaviour. It is the phase of Application. So, little by little, disjointedly and at intervals, he gets established in a calm awareness of his connection with, and relation to, the Overself.

318

It is that perfect unconsciousness of self which confers complete natural-ness, ease in relationships with others, and which radiates or, better, ema-nates peacefulness.

319

In deepest contemplation, the *Nirvikalpa Samadhi* of the Indian yogis, both egolessness and blissful peace can be experienced. But it is a tempo-rary state; return to the world must follow, so the quest is not finished. The next step or stage is *application*, putting into the active everyday life this egoless detachment and this satisfying calmness.(P)

320

When he lives in this godlike being with the background of his mind and in the world's activity with the foreground of it, he lives in the fullest sense.

321

You have to feel the rich peace of suddenly letting go of everything, of all your cares and tasks, all the knot of affairs which has tied itself around your ego, and then sinking back to where there is seemingly nothing.

322

It is not enough to become detached from the world, not even enough to meditate intermittently on the Overself. A man must *remain* every hour, every day, established in the fundamental attitude produced by the other two.

323

Mahadevan himself admitted to us that meditation is not essential if *gnana* is sought and properly followed. Therefore we are entitled to com-ment that *Nirvikalpa Samadhi* is not enough. The qualities needed for *gnana* practice, including detachment, must still be developed.

324

He has to work his way farther into *Sahaja*, and then settle down in it.

325

He who can stay in the world and keep his calmness in all conditions—whether they are attractive or repulsive—who can move in society with-out falling victim to the desires, attachments, or greeds which afflict it, who never lets go of the still divine centre within himself whether alone and quiet or with others and active, he is the real yogi and is experiencing the true *samadhi*.

326

He attends to his daily affairs with an awareness that the long-familiar ego is absent, that the divine Void is always present.

327

In *sahaja* we'll possess an imperturbable temperament; we'll possess human feeling but not be subject to the vicissitudes, excitements, and oscillations of human feeling. The mind will always be composed, because it will be held by the divine presence.

4

SEEK THE DEEPER STILLNESS

When the personal ego's thoughts and desires are stripped off, we behold ourselves as we were in the first state and as we shall be in the final one. We are then the Overself alone, in its Godlike solitude and stillness.(P)

2

One feels gathered into the depths of the silence, enfolded by it and then, hidden within it, intuits the mysterious inexplicable invisible and higher power which must remain forever nameless.

3

A life with this infinite stillness as its background and centre seems as remote from the common clay of everyday human beings, and especially from their urban infatuation with noise and movement, as the asteroids.

4

This stillness is the godlike part of every human being. In failing to look for it, he fails to make the most of his possibilities. If, looking, he misses it on the way, this happens because it is a vacuity: there is simply nothing there! That means no things, not even mental things, that is, thoughts.(P)

5

The spirit (Brahman) is NOT the stillness, but is found by humans who are in the precondition of stillness. The latter is *their* human reaction to Brahman's presence coming into their field of awareness.(P)

6

That beautiful state wherein the mind recognizes itself for *what it is*, wherein all activity is stilled except that of awareness alone, and even then it is an awareness without an object—this is the heart of the experience.(P)

7

The Stillness has so much to give mankind, yet mankind ignores or neglects it.

8

The Mystic who penetrates to this depth of meditation is momentarily lost to the world, lost indeed to everything except himself.

9

This glorious interlude of blissful peace, when thoughts come to rest and speech is silenced, ought to be valued at its proper worth.

10

It is true peace because he is inwardly at peace with himself, with his fellow men, and with God.

11

What he experienced in those quietly rapturous moments is to be used as a standard of comparison with what he experiences in everyday life. This will teach him, better than guides or books. It will show him his spiritual shortcomings and give him his right direction.

12

The Overself is first and last felt or experienced as a deep peace within oneself. Hence the larger meaning of the greeting used in the Orient and in early Greek Mysteries that "Peace be with you!"

13

When he first awakens to this great stillness, ordinary life seems a mere agitation and fuss.

14

In the ordinary person, consciousness remains only at his periphery, but in the adept it can be drawn at any moment and at will to this centre.

15

The Stillness may speak directly to a man's heart in clear feeling or leave its value and existence to be inferred from subtle clues provided.

16

It is not the kind of silence which shuts anyone else out rudely: it is too benevolent for that, too concentrated in seeking the inner reality to be so negative.

17

It is all the difference between living at the still centre and on the bustling circumference, at the mysterious core and on the prosaic surface.

18

"With an untroubled soul, abiding in himself he enjoys extreme happiness. This tranquillity may be described as resembling sweet sleep, or a lamp which in calm air burns without flickering. So, as time goes on, fixing his soul in itself, eating little, inwardly purified, he sees the soul in himself."—*Mahabharata*

19

It is in these deeper moods that life seems to pulse more quietly.

20

There is a silence born of ignorance and another born of knowledge—mystical knowledge. The right interpretation comes only through the intuitive faculty—not through the intellect.(P)

21

With such a perspective as can be gained on the mountaintop of the ultimate, commanding the entire scene as it does, every stage of the shift from ego to Centre can be seen.

22

The ordinary man, living his simple existence uncomplicated by questions about the abstract meaning of that existence, not troubling his head about yoga, religion, God, and such matters, enjoys his own kind of limited peace, one which the quester has forfeited.

23

There is no need for sensational psychic phenomena; because consciously or unconsciously you love being Being, therefore you have taken to the Quest.

24

Essence of Mind is more important than the temporary stages on the way to discovery of its ever-presence.

25

What men of our modern age, bewildered by tremendous world-wide happenings, crushed by the forces of an apparently uncontrollable destiny, deafened by the noises of a scientifically mechanical civilization, are really yearning after is simply Stillness. This, which would seem to be the simplest of all things, is inwardly the hardest to find of all things. This is what Jesus spoke of when he said, "Few there be that find it." Why is it so hard to find? The answer is that a price must be paid, as with all things. That price is the giving up of self. For Stillness is *behind* the self.

26

It is far subtler than the first ecstasies of a newly made mystic, much more refined than the personal joys of a religious saint. It is deeper, quieter, more relaxed yet, withal exquisite—this peace.(P)

27

He can buy this rare peace only at a costly price. He can be immune to the miseries of life only by being immune to its elations.

28

The immobility of that higher plane of being frightens most people away from it. They are ignorant of the blessed peace that is conjoined with it.

29

We may hold talent—be it the craftsman's, the intellectual's, the artist's—in high esteem, yet not lose our hold on the stillness. It is a delicate balanced position, reached after risky attempts.

30

There is intense feeling in this experience but it is as quiet as it is deep. The sensational or the violent mystical raptures belong to the beginner and occur on the shallower level.

31

It is in this superb stillness that truth finds its origin and beauty touches the heart. It is here that love—not its poor substitutes—is at last known. Such precious treasures must be paid for. The price is high and the purchasers few.

32

We ought not judge a deeper and different plane of being by our reactions to the present one. Here, its limitations inevitably cause boredom, impatience, and dullness if we have to sit unoccupied for a few hours. There, those limitations are non-existent and consequently we may sit for a whole eternity, yet in its stillness feel only contentment, serenity, and the sensation of being unutterably alive.

33

If he goes into the silence enough, he will become accustomed to the obstacles that bar entry and learn by practice how to deal with them.

34

Each man must create his own inner peace by his own struggles with himself, with his ego. It is attainable but the price must be paid.

35

In the stillness may be the Truth, but it has to come to him through his emotional beliefs, through the prejudices instilled in him by family and society, and through the limitations of his lack of higher education, his inability to grasp metaphysical statements above his simple elementary level.

36

The Sufis even use the term "veiling" when referring to ecstatic mystic experiences and discussing them with students sufficiently advanced to profit by this advice. Indeed one of the Sufi masters, whose name was Junaid and who lived in the ninth and tenth centuries, wrote that his ecstasies vanished altogether as he advanced to a higher stage.

37

The wise seeker after Truth will not lose himself in mystical and magical

symbolisms. In the end they become obstacles, screens between himself
and that which they ought to represent.

38

There is an immense realization of abiding at last in the complete truth
about life, the final word about reality. There is a perfect inner silence,
broken only when presently shapes from the environment come into the
field of awareness again or sounds from the external surroundings make
themselves heard. There is an utter emotional calm when desire and fear
lie quite still. There is a sense of reality, a reality that ever was and ever will
be, and of the surface-illusions having stopped at last.

39

In this deep stillness wherein every trace of the personal self dissolves,
there is the true crucifixion of the ego. This is the real meaning of the
crucifixion, as it was undergone in the ancient Mystery Temple initiations
and as it was undergone by Jesus. The death implied is mental, not physical.(P)

40

The city's uproar and the brain's turbulence die down. The desires and
troubles slip slowly away. There is a renewal of calm as consciousness
settles deeper and ever deeper until an utter void is reached.

41

He feels that he is now in the very centre of his being, that he has shifted
identity there. The ego no longer covers it over and occupies his whole
view. Rather is it now transparent to the light radiating from this centre.
This transparency is peace.

42

Subtle and, in the beginning, almost imperceptible is the growth of that
exquisite inner peace.

43

Learn to be satisfied with this gift, this grace of the Stillness. Do not ask
for more or for something more striking and dramatic. This is a common
error, and an ungrateful one.

44

The intensity of this experience, the deep tranquillity, separates it from
all other experiences.

45

The quester may reach a point when the aspirations and activities, the
practices and exercises, the meditations even, of the quest itself will fade
away as the grace invades him and the inner silence takes over.

46

Not seldom this high phase of the Quiet is accompanied by great light, of which this "Divine Body" is made and by which he may feel great ennobled awe.

47

Sitting there in deep contemplation, shut off from the world, detached and unconcerned in every way, he becomes the incarnation of stillness and silence.

48

Here is the final consummation of all his highest aspirations, as with bowed, humbled head he receives the mysterious bestowal of a supreme grace.

49

The most important kind of spiritual development is usually undramatic and unexciting. It is found and felt in a deep peace.

Quiet the ego

50

Peace is a quality which man must extract for himself by himself and within himself.

51

The seeker after stillness should be told that the stillness is always there. Indeed it is in every man. But he has to learn, first, to let it in and, second, how to do so. The first beginning of this is to remember. The second is to recognize the inward pull. For the rest, the stillness itself will guide and lead him to itself.

52

The presence is always there, always waiting to be recognized and felt, but inner silence is needed to make this possible. And few persons possess it or seek it.

53

There is an area of peace hidden within every man. Its presence is the gracious gift of God but his task is to discover it.

54

There is a stillness in the depth of each man, but he has to find it for himself, a work demanding patience and humility.

55

Whatever method of meditation is used, the last phase must always be the Great Silence.

56

He must begin this meditation by isolating himself in thought not only from the world but also from other people. He is not to be afraid of being inwardly alone. Only so can he find the great Friend who shall appear and speak to him out of the stillness.

57

That is that ultimate solitude to which all human beings are destined.(P)

58

"Seek lonely happiness," taught the first Shankara, "and concentrate the mind on *Paramatma.*"

59

The higher he climbs, the lonelier he becomes. The crowds forgather at the base; the chosen few scatter around the peak.

60

The feeling of oneness with others will not last if he is carried farther by this indrawing force. They seem removed from him, receding, and then vanishing.

61

Far from the arguments of mind-narrowed men, he will find himself without a supporting group in the end. He is to meet God alone, for *all* his attention is to be held—so fully that there is nothing and no one else. Thus the three become two, who in turn become the One, which it always is. Truth is no longer needed; its seeker has vanished. The great Silent Timelessness reigns.

62

Although other human voices cease to speak to him, he must now look only to, and be alone with, God, for the Silence itself will thenceforth speak to him.

63

He must learn not only to be alone and like it but, even more, to love it. For in the great silence of being shut in with his higher self he can find great satisfaction, serene fulfilment.

64

This is his private secret place. Here he must keep out of the world. Here he stands *alone* in the divine presence.

65

Each personal existence has its place to fill here in life and its development to undergo, but it is given a higher meaning than the animal's only as it is sought and found. Neither psychology nor physiology, neither metaphysics, religion, nor mysticism can each by itself sufficiently explain the human being. If, however, they work together in harmony they come much nearer to this goal; but their totality is still incomplete. The last turn of the key is philosophy. Thereafter the final revelation must come by itself, by grace, for man has then removed the obstruction, the tyranny of his own little self. If the ego remains to live and act in the world, whether busy in doing or lost in meditation, it is a purified, a surrendered being. But it has not surrendered to other egos. Even the gurus, however reputed and respected, can teach and lead others only by the path along which they themselves came. Their work can be helpful, valuable, encouraging; but at a certain point, when apprenticeship must give way to proficiency, it can become repetitive and restrictive. After that, the courage and strength to obey the Voice of the Silence, sought and given by the Silence itself, must alone lead him.

66

This aspiration must be his one master-feeling, the single key that fits all the ciphers of his destiny.

67

You get sidetracked into thoughts about various persons. Think only of one person—the true self or the guide. Apart from that, drop all thinking and dwell in his stillness alone. The thoughts about others must be reserved for some future date *after* you have thoroughly established yourself in the thought-free state of utter stillness.

68

The silencing of our thoughts and the inward concentration of our forces bring a rare stillness, a remarkable peace to us.

69

The Quest will come to an end when he turns away from teachers and teachings and begins to receive instruction from within himself. Previously all that he got was someone else's idea; now he is acquiring firsthand knowledge.

70

When the quiet receptivity is deep enough, we enter the stillness. When the stillness is deep enough, we cease to think, to desire, and to will anything.

71

Without leaving his room he finds out Truth! He simply sits still! This is the source of his knowledge and strength. The conclusion is: learn to sit still, *but* not only bodily; it must also be mentally. Yet not only that, not only for half a minute or so, but to sit still patiently. He must wait the situation out. So much—if not most—of the world's evil and misery and wrong action is due to the inability to do it.

72

To produce a result, one usually has to perform an action. But here is a non-action which produces an intangible result, one that cannot be photographed or packed or shown to someone else. Yet it is there, all the same, a marvellously satisfying harvest of peace unutterable, of inner support impregnable.

73

Let the personal will relax in this gentle peace.

74

"It is only because the sage does nothing that he can do everything. Nature never makes any fuss, and yet It does everything. If a ruler can cling to It, all things will grow of themselves." These are Lao Tzu's words. His advice to "do nothing" as the way to the best accomplishment simply means that ordinarily whatever we do is done at the ego's behest. It cannot therefore lead us into any happiness that will not be illusory in the end, any accomplishment that will not be destroyed in the end. To continue action in the old way is to perpetuate the ego's rule. But to refuse to do so, and to "be still," is to create the inner vacuum which allows the higher self to enter and work through us. This is inspired action.

75

Once he has touched this stillness briefly, learned the way to it, and comprehended its nature, his next task is to develop it. This takes time and practice and *knowledge*. Or, rather, the work is done on him, not by him. He has to let be.

76

In this condition, with the self quieted and the thoughts collected, patient waiting may bring on the inner stillness. Here, the world and its ways, the person and his desires drop out of the field of interest and attention; the Overself absorbs all the energies, its presence rendering him utterly humble, his consciousness now put on an ethereal plane.

77

He does not, can not, fabricate this inner silence, but he provides the correct conditions of relaxed concentrated listening which allow it to be discovered as a presence within himself.

78

By this simple act of unlearning all that you know—all that you have acquired by thinking, by remembrance, by measurements, by comparison, and by judgement—when you return to the mere emptying of the consciousness of its contents of thoughts and ideas, and when you come to the pure consciousness in itself, then only can you rest in the Great Silence.

79

He must not only give up the slavery of passion, but also the slavery of intellect.

80

Shiva Yoga Dipika: "Listen, I shall mention to you the method of worshipping Shiva who is made of Intelligence. It is a secret—the essence of the Sastras and the bestower of instantaneous freedom. . . . Thoughtlessness is the contemplation of Shiva; Inactivity is his worship; Motionlessness is going round him in veneration; the realization of the state 'I Am He' is prostration before him; Silence is singing his glory; knowledge of what ought to be done and what not, is good character; looking on all alike is the supreme pleasure."

81

When we dig down into the under-surface conditions which give rise to such a question, we find that the question itself vanishes and so there is no longer any need to try to find an answer to it. For it depended upon the mind's agitation, turbulence, curiosity, or imbalance, and when the mind's activity died down, when above all stillness lulled ego, the question died down with it.

82

The mind must constantly give itself up to the idea of its own infinity.

83

In her book *Mysticism* Evelyn Underhill writes: "The psychic state of Quiet has a further value for the mystic, as being the intellectual complement and expression of the moral state of humility and receptivity: the very condition, says Eckhart, of the New Birth. 'It may be asked whether this Birth is best accomplished in Man when he does the work and *forms and thinks himself into God*, or when he keeps himself in Silence, stillness and peace, so that God may speak and work in him; . . . the best and noblest way in which thou mayst come into this work and life is by keeping silence, and letting God work and speak. When all the powers are withdrawn from their work and images, there is this word spoken.'" She goes on to quote Eckhart further on the same theme: "And thus thine ignorance is not a defect but thy highest perfection, and thine inactivity thy highest work. And so in this work thou must bring all thy works to nought and all thy powers into silence, if thou wilt in truth experience this birth within thyself."

84

Chinese philosopher Lieh-tse wrote: "Avoid action, and keep the silence; all the rest is commentary."

85

Every outer activity is to be brought to an end; every inner one is to be stilled.

86

Thinking is mental action, just as moving is physical action. The admonition "Be still and know that I am God" refers not only to the body but also to the mind. Both are to cease from activity if the higher consciousness is to be attained.

87

Thinking can put together all sorts of theories and speculations and even discoveries. But only when it dies down and lets the pure quietened mind come to rest in the very essence of consciousness, at peace with itself, with nature, with the world, only then is there a deep sense of utter fulfilment.

88

When thinking comes naturally to its rest, either because he has felt his way through intense reverence to the higher power or because he has apprehended the truth by the subtlest and sharpest perception, then stillness is born. It would be an error to continue either the feeling or the thinking beyond this time. The utter stillness must take their place, and he must humbly yield to it. At such a moment, the ego is withdrawn; the knowing intuition, the great Peace, alone remains.

89

The process acts with the sureness of a chemical combination; if you quiet the ego, the Overself becomes responsively active.

90

Where the heart goes, there soon or late the other faculties will follow. This is why it is so important *to let* the Overself take possession of the heart by its total surrender in, and to, the Stillness.

91

The more he can keep his personal will passive and his personal mind still, the more shall wisdom and peace flow into him.

92

It is nice and noble to talk about becoming an instrument in God's hands, a channel of the Overself. But this is still an inferior relationship. It is not the highest kind. It is still occupied with the ego. Ascend to a higher level, give yourself completely to, and talk about, the higher power alone.

93

This centre of his own being never moves. It is forever in stillness.

94

To the extent that a man keeps inwardly still, to that extent he unfolds himself and lets the ever-perfect Overself shine forth.

95

Whether they are positive or negative, let all thoughts die. Then there will remain only Mind, which is always there, which is the Real.

96

He does not know why the grace is present, only that it is. He does not use the intellectual machine to find out. There is contentment, acceptance, peace. It is enough just now to take no precise scientific measurements but to stay with the Stillness.

97

In the Stillness he can renew his lost forces, re-find his store of wisdom and, if it is accompanied by solitude, find his innermost being.

98

An understanding based on logic alone, on the faculty of the intellect alone, may produce seemingly solid and sound ideas, but with time it may also produce counter-ideas which effectively oppose the earlier ones. For as it itself changes with the years and with the body, the ego may shift its standpoint, may accept what it previously rejected and reject what it previously accepted. If stability is to be found, it must be found at a deeper level and that is the changeless Overself.

99

Men try to fill the heart's emptiness with things and other persons when, if they would only let it alone ("Be Still!"), grace would enter and fill it for them.

100

Putting aside one's own internal and personal pressures is a precondition which sooner or later lets in the Overself's peace.

The still centre within

101

How beautiful, how comforting, and how profitable are those minutes of withdrawal from the world into the blessed stillness in the deeper layers of the mind and heart. Here one can enjoy oneself, one's self, one's inner self, one's Overself.

102

However dark or blundering the past, however miserable the tangle one has made of one's life, this unutterable peace blots it all out. Within that seraphic embrace error cannot be known, misery cannot be felt, sin cannot be remembered. A great cleansing comes over the heart and mind.(P)

103

The more he gives himself up to this element of stillness within and lets it work on him, the less destructive will his character and tendencies be.

104

The past has become a vanished phantasmal world. He can stay in peace.

105

There will be a zone of peace around him which some feel but others cannot. It seems to put him quite at his ease and free him from any trace of nervousness.

106

It is not generally known that Florence Nightingale drew her inspiration and courage for her Red Cross work in Crimea from her meditations in silence.

107

In that silent centre there is immense power and rocklike strength.

108

The Stillness is its own enthralling inner gain, sufficient in itself to pay for the time or effort given, but with return to activity there is a varied outer harvest.

109

This beautiful peace is both the reward of his efforts and the atmosphere surrounding his higher nature.

110

In this deep stillness the worst sinner feels that he is like a reformed, reborn man.

111

Whether from his study of inspired books or from meditations in the silence, he will draw understanding and strength for his life in the active, busy turmoil of the world.

112

There are situations which may seem beyond endurance and circumstances beyond sufferance. It is then that those who have learned how to withdraw into their interior being, how to return to their source, may find some measure of help and strength.

113

From this deep source, he nourishes the continuous tranquillity of the atmosphere he carries about with him; from it he gains the solid assurance that the quest is worthwhile and its goal very real.

114

When you have trained yourself to empty your consciousness of its thoughts at will, your worries will naturally be emptied along with them. This is one of the valuable practical fruits of yoga.

115

This is the refuge to which he must turn when troubled, this is the place of divine beatitude. Let him go into the silence; there he will find the strength to conquer.

116

In this wonderful atmosphere of unimaginable intense peace, all that was negative in the past years is effaced so radically that it becomes as nothing.

117

Even if there were no joy in the realization of the Overself it would still be worth having, for it would still be richly loaded with other treasures. But the joy is also there and always there.

118

Profundity and serenity become his great strength.

119

He can return from these visits to his innermost being richly laden with gifts, precious and uncommon.

120

Out of these deep silences he will gather wise decisions and originate new progressive inclinations; from them he will come with, first, the love of God and, second, the knowledge of God.

121

The quietness of this deep daily initiation into the Overself may seem a small and flat thing against the thrilling raptures that religious mystics and babbling evangelists have described. But its life-guiding and life-changing power, its truth-revealing light, will be of a much higher voltage.

122

In the end, as in the beginning, it is best to defer a grave decision to the Stillness.

123

The Overself remains always the same and never changes in any way. It is the hunger for this quality, thought of as "peace of mind," which drives men to seek the Overself amid the vicissitudes of health or fortune which they experience.(P)

124

To complain that you get no answer, no result from going into the silence indicates two things: first, that you do not go far enough into it to reach the intuitive level; second, that you do not wait long enough for it to affect you.(P)

125

In seeking the stillness and the beautiful inner equilibrium which comes with it, he will learn to find a new way of life.

126

It is as though he had an inner, separate consciousness which was forever fastened to a central point of his being.

127

He who has attained this stage will be ready to forgo all those worldly activities, benefits, and assets which the bidding of his higher self may call for.

128

This reached, he reaches the true source of power, evicts all confusions, and becomes inwardly clear.

129

According to the intensity of his concentration and withdrawnness will be the sharpness of his realization that: *This is the truth!*

130

The stillness is not experienced in the same way as a mere lazy and idle reverie: it is dynamic, creative, and healing. The presence of one man who is able to attain it is a gift, a blessing, to all other men, though they know it not.

131

No problems vex the mind here, because none can arise. All problems are now seen to be fictitious because they arise out of a wrong view of the world.

132

The Stillness possesses a power to purify the heart, to heal strained nerves and sick bodies.

133

He who can gain this deep buried state will gain the attributes of supernal power and untroubled calm which go with it.

134

This will change your life and give you real peace. You will know that you have touched truth, and henceforth problems of the whys and wherefores of human existence can come no more to vex your head and pain your heart.

135

This peace is not to be confounded with lethargy and inertia, for it is a dynamic condition. It is the peace that comes after storm. It puts tormenting desires to rest. It brings the confused mind into surety. It heals the wounds caused by other people, by our own selves, and by a harsh destiny.

136

Out of the Stillness what is true may come forth with high certitude.

137

Out of this stillness will come the light he seeks, the guide he needs, the strength he requires.

138

The first way of finding peace when harassed by a hard problem or situation is to turn away from the tumult of thoughts and look for the still centre within. When it is found and just when it leaves, or must be left, ask it for the guidance needed. Let it correct those thoughts.

139

From this inner stillness the highest truths have come forth and passed into human knowledge.

140

The more still it becomes, whatever the mind knows it knows more clearly, and hence truly.

141

The stillness does for you what you're unable to do for yourself, and therefore it can be said to manifest grace. For by yourself you can only use your will, the ego's will.

142

As a serious Quaker, John Woolman was, as he himself wrote, "a man taught to wait in silence, sometimes many weeks together, until he hears God's voice."

143

All questions can find some kind of an answer in this mental silence; no question can be brought there often enough without a response coming forth in time. It is needful to be patient and to have faith during the waiting period. The inner monitor is certainly there but we have to reach it.

144

The Stillness is the only magical panacea, applicable always in all situations.

145

Amid the trouble and clamour created by one's own weaknesses and other people's misunderstandings, it is better to remain silent, to rest content with entering the stillness and turn the problem over to the Higher Power.

146

There comes a time when out of the silence within himself there comes the spiritual guidance which he needs for his further course. It comes sometimes as a delicate feeling, sometimes as a strong one, sometimes in a clear formulated message, and sometimes out of the circumstances and happenings themselves. Not only does it tell him and teach him, but sometimes it does the same for others. Such is the effect of the Divine Life now working increasingly within him.

147

The certitude of truth and the plenitude of reality—with their coming a great peace falls onto man.

148

In that peace-filled oblivion of the lesser self there is renewal of life and rebirth of goodness in, and by, the Overself.

149

The more he finds his way from the tumultuous surface of his consciousness to the quiet mystery of the centre of his being, the more he finds the steady comfort of truth and the better he understands life.

150

Just as a man who has escaped from the inside of a burning house and finds himself in the cool outdoors understands that he has attained safety, so the man who has escaped from greed, lust, anger, illusion, selfishness, and ignorance into exalted peace and immediate insight, understands that he has attained heaven.

151

When he has achieved the capacity or gotten the Grace of sitting in the unbroken stillness of a perfect contemplation, he will feel a loving sweetness indescribable by human words and unmatched by human joys.

152

Bliss begins only when the point of contact with the Overself is approached and reached. For at this point the mind begins to be taken possession of, and the ego to be absorbed. Naturally the experience is most intense, most vivid, and most rapturous during meditation, for then there are no other distractions to share attention or get in the way.

153

He will find that this tremendous peace puts all his desires to rest, that the great love it engenders overpasses all his other loves.

154

If there is a paradise anywhere it is here, deep deep within a man, where he is absorbed forever into a state of utter desirelessness, of complete negation of living, of unruffled contentment in habitual contemplation.

155

It is a sweet peace gracious beyond all telling.

156

One arrives at a blessed state where all lesser desire comes to an end, because it is Satisfaction itself; where all will ceases to be active, because there is nothing that needs doing; where the little and limited love which depends on someone else, whether for receiving or giving, dissolves into an infinite ocean of pure love.

157

The peace overwhelms everything else. Nothing seems to matter any more. There are no problems, no difficult decisions to make, no trying situations to endure. There is only this loving benignant Power holding them all, more important than them all.

158

Such is the enchantment of the Stillness, that one would like to stay in it forever.

159

"I, the Homeless, have My home in each person's heart." This is what the Great Silence told me.

160

Friction and opposition cannot exist on this higher level where all is at peace.

161

The Tamil poet and sage Tiruvalluvar calls this sublime state of Yoga "the vision of the supremely beautiful," reminding us of similar language in Plato.

162

How sweet is this tranquil relaxed state by contrast with the inevitable struggle of day-to-day living!

163

To sit in this delicate tender exquisite stillness, aloof from all that is ugly, coarse, violent, or brutish, is a lovely experience.

164

In the depths of meditation, when one is sitting still and enchanted, all egoism gone for the moment and all care suspended, it is possible to understand what the word "Heaven" really means.

165

From this peace which is always within him now he looks out, as from a citadel, upon the world's disharmonies and distresses.

166

In its beautiful soothing peace he lets his hurts lapse from memory, his troubles evaporate from mind.

167

The peaceful feeling which comes over him shows more vividly than words what the desireless state means.

168

The freedom which he attains is in the background of consciousness, as it were. For here he rests tranquilly in the mind-essence alone. No separate ideas exist here, whereas the foreground is occupied by the ordinary ideas involved in human existence. He perceives now that the value of all his former yoga practice lay in its capacity, when success crowned it, to enable him to approach behind the stream of ideas to the bed on which it flowed, that is, to the mind-stuff itself.

169

The harmony of the highest state is unbroken by thoughts. It is like a song without words; it is the perfumed essence of stillness, the deepest heart of silence.

170

There are times when the white sheet on the desk before me remains untouched minute after minute, for words will not come to express the inexpressible mood, the strange presence, the incredible loss of memory which makes me forget where I am, what I am, what I am trying to do, and which mysteriously merges me into That which *is*, but is not any particular thing. Only after I return to normality do I discover that during that mood I was no longer the writer or even the thinker, for there were no thoughts. It was a mood of release and a benign one.

171

When one comes into the real, deep stillness, every mental and emotional activity comes to an end.

172

The Stillness is both an Understanding, an Insight of the mind, and an Experience of the being. The whole movement or vibration comes to a stop.(P)

173

When he temporarily achieves this lofty condition, he ceases to think, for his mind becomes inarticulate with heavenly peace.(P)

174

The effort should be to find inward stillness through a loving search within the heart's depths for what may be called "the soul," what I have called "the Overself." This is not the soul thought of by a judge when he passes the sentence of death and asks the Lord to have mercy on the condemned man's soul. It is the Holy Ghost of Christian faith, the diviner part of man which dwells in eternity. The nearer we get to it in our striving, the greater will be the mental peace we shall feel. It can be found and felt even whilst thoughts continue to move through the mind, although they will necessarily be thoughts of a most elevated nature for the baser ones could not obtain entry during this mood.(P)

175

The whole of one's aim should be to keep the mind in an unbroken rest permanently, while using the intellect whenever necessary in an automatic manner to attend to external duties. "Does not that destroy the efficiency of the intellect?" it may be objected. No—only its selfishness is destroyed. Do the hands lose their efficiency because we use them in a purely mechanical manner? Just the same, when one unites with God he regards himself as greater than mere intellect, which becomes for him only an instrument to deal with the external world.

176

Here, in the divine centre, he can turn at will and rest completely absorbed for a while and completely lost to the world. No thinking will then penetrate its stillness. Here is peace indeed.

177

This is the Great Silence. While he is under its spell, words will not come to his lips or pen, nor thoughts to his brain. They would only be disturbances.

178

That deep silence has a melody of its own, a sweetness unknown amid the harsh discords of the world's sounds.

179

Both the dreamer and his dream, the thinker and his thought, will merge into this sublime stillness.

180

As the peace settles over him, he becomes as still as a stone. He does not wish to move, to speak, or even to think.

181

Ideas which are thought, emotions which are felt, and physical experiences which are lived fall away when Stillness is entered.

182

One may sink inward to the point of being tightly held by the delicious Stillness, unable for a while to move limb or body into activity.

183

It is the quietest part of the mind where all the stir and babble of the day's clamorous thoughts are left behind.

184

In this practical workaday business of living, thinking is a useful and necessary activity. But on a higher level, the transcendental level of an awed quietude, there is no need or place for thinking or words—only being.

185

When all thoughts move far away and then are gone, when mental pictures fade off, then the whole being rests in the Stillness of THAT WHICH IS.

186

In that beautiful silence, no words form themselves, no intellectual activity goes on.

187

It is the secret undercurrent which flows beneath all his mind's activity.

The Great Silence

188

One who has cultivated the inner life and learned to sit quietly without creating or demanding endless talk of a trivial kind, finds that fuss, nervousness, or fidget will be his companion less and less.

189

Too often people are afraid of sitting in silence. Each thinks he or the others should be continually talking, continually throwing sentences at each other. If the silence does fall and remains a little while, they feel awkward, uneasy, as if they were not doing what was expected of them. It is a sign of human weakness that a person feels he or she must continuously be vocal should someone else be present.

190

Sufi remark: "If what you come to tell me is less beautiful than the Stillness, keep it to yourself."

191

Why should silence be such a social sin?

192

We spoil the silence with our talk.

193

The strange result of going deeper and deeper into the Real is that silence falls more and more as a curtain over his private experience and private thought. The strong urgency of communication which the missionary and the reformer feel, the strong need of expression which the artist and the writer have, trouble him no longer. The inner voice is tight-lipped, or speaks to him alone. He begins to see how much apostolic utterance is merely the overflow of personal emotion, how much artistic achievement is motivated by personal ambition, how much spiritual service is simply another phase of the ego adoring and serving itself. Thomas Aquinas came to such an insight late in life and he, the author of so many books dedicated to the glory of God, could never again write another line. Those who stand on the outside may consider such a severe restraint put upon oneself to be harsh and fanatical, perhaps even antisocial. But it is safe to say that all these critics have never tracked the ego to its secret lair, never had all movement of their individual will stopped by the divine Stillness.

194

Whoever enters into this perfect peace must emerge from it again in the end. When he returns to his fellow men he will find it hard—if he is a novice—to keep silent about his wonderful experience, but easy if he is a proficient. This is because the novice is still egoistic whereas the adept is truly altruistic. For the one is concerned with his own experience whereas the other is concerned with whether his fellows are ready to leap so high.

195

It is not easy to translate this sacred silence into comprehensible meaning, to describe a content where there is no form, to ascend from a region as deep as Atlantis is sunk today and speak openly in familiar, intelligible language; but I must try.(P)

196

The truth which leads a man to liberation from all illusions and enslavements is perceived in the innermost depths of his being, where he is shut off from all other men. The man who has attained to its knowledge finds himself in an exalted solitude. He is not likely to find his way out of it to the extent, and for the purpose, of enlightening his fellow men who are accustomed to, and quite at home in, their darkness unless some other propulsive force of compassion arises within him and causes him to do so.(P)

197

We have heard much about the sayings of Jesus, nothing about his silences. Yet it was from the latter that they came and in the latter that he himself *lived*.

198

Let him first attain this insight, and then talk about the selfishness of being silent about it if he still feels like doing so.

199

The man who found his divine soul will not, unless he is divinely enjoined to do so as part of a special beneficent mission, publicly advertise the fact.

200

"Be ye as shrewd as serpents," Jesus warned the disciples. Therefore, avoid arguments and verbal traps. Keep answers to two or three words, even to the extreme of being evasive. Specimens are: "Perhaps," "A hard problem," "Yes," "No," "I do not know." Do not make statements on your own initiative—better to be silent, refer questioner to others as authorities, such as "Professor X" or "His Holiness the X."

201

Out of that grave silence there will come to his mind the declaration of truth. And out of that in turn will come his argument with others about it.

202

In keeping silent about his spiritual status and inner activities, he is not trying to be wilfully obscurantist but is rather imitating the mode of being he finds in the Overself. For what could be more hidden, more elusive than that?

203

It is not advisable to break the stillness in order to give inner help to other persons. Such an activity should be reserved for a special time. One should not disturb the benediction of one's own stillness, one's own being alone with God, for any reason of this kind.

204

Many persons in different parts of the world and in different centuries have had glimpses of that other order of being which is their highest source, but how few are those who have succeeded in establishing themselves in continuous communion with that higher order, how rare is the feat? And who, having established himself therein, can find enough words to express what he now perceives and experiences? Words fall back; this is a plane not for them: this is a vast universal silence impregnated with consciousness which swallows every individualized being, for individuality cannot exist there. The established man can turn to it in this great silence and must himself remain silent to do it the honour it deserves. All language is so limited that it must seem blasphemy when put side by side with this awed reverent stillness which is the proper form of worship here.

205

Truth lies hidden in silence. Reveal it—and falsehood will creep in, withering the golden image. Communication by speech or paper was not necessary.(P)

206

The complete silence which he finds in the centre of his being cannot be conveyed in words to others without passing into the intellect, which originates and arranges them. But to do this is to leave that centre, to desert that silence, and to step down to an altogether lower level.

207

No one has ever brought a full report when he emerged from tunnelling in that mystic silence, and no one can.

208

The deeper he penetrates into this inner being, the more will he feel inclined to keep the development quite secret. It is becoming too holy to be talked about.

209

We are vocally benumbed on entering the presence of embodied spiritual attainment, for the intellect is silent and abashed at feeling so acutely its own inferiority, its own futility. And it is the intellect in which we mostly live, not the intuition.

210

He carries his secret as a woman carries her unborn child. Its importance is supreme.

211

The Chinese Master Ekai (thirteenth century) wrote: "Words cannot describe everything. The heart's message cannot be communicated in words."

212

There are some inner experiences which seem too holy to be talked about in public, too intimate even to be talked about with intimate friends, too mysterious to be mentioned to anyone else except a student or a teacher who has passed through similar experiences himself.

213

Is it not strange that the highest experience of an inner nature open to man is a completely secret one, a fully hushed one, and almost an indefinable one? Looking back upon it afterwards, knowing how profoundly beautiful and deeply moving it was at the time, he will find it difficult to speak about it to others.

214

Thoughts can be put into words, spoken and written; but the truth about Reality must remain unworded, unspoken, and unwritten. All statements about it which the intellect can grasp are merely symbolic—just clues, hints. Only in the great stillness can it be known, understood.

215

At this point, communication by words must stop: the seer lapses into himself, into his own silent experience of the Ineffable where there is no second person.

216

It is this inner work in the Silence which reaches the deepest level and in the end achieves the greatest effects. The world does not understand this, and hence its noisy and superficial activities which have produced the chaos and disorder of our times.

217

How extraordinary is this stillness that it can convey meaning without making use of words! For the communication is made through feeling, not through intellect. But inevitably, when the stillness ends, the mind begins to work, and the intellect begins to work upon the experience and translates it into words.

218

When the Great Peace is felt and thoughts utterly stilled, there are two possible but different mistakes which he may make. One is to start analysing what is happening. If he wishes to do this either to instruct intellect or to communicate it to others, he must wait until it is no more and for a day longer. Otherwise he cuts it short or diminishes its quality, besides losing the secondary benefits of its afterglow. Nor do words give it to others at the time of its presence, for it gives itself, silently.

219

The reason why this silent, inward, and pictureless initiation in the stillness is so much more powerful *ultimately*, is that it reaches the man himself, whereas all other kinds reach only his instruments or vehicles or bodies.(P)

220

Truth may be written or spoken, preached or printed, but its most lasting expression and communication is transmitted through the deepest silence to the deepest nature in man.(P)

Index for Part 1

Entries are listed by chapter number followed by "para" number. For example, 7.295 means chapter 7, para 295, and 6.119, 137, means chapter 6, paras 119 and 137. Chapter listings are separated by a semicolon. Please note also that, for the reader's convenience, the first number in the right-hand running heads throughout the text indicates chapter number.

Index for Part 2

Entries are listed by chapter number followed by "para" number. For example, 2.90 means chapter 2, para 90, and 3.287, 317, means chapter 3, paras 287 and 317. Chapter listings are separated by a semicolon. Please note also that, for the reader's convenience, the first number in the right-hand running heads throughout the text indicates chapter number.

The 28 Categories from the Notebooks

This outline of categories in *The Notebooks* is the most recent one Paul Brunton developed for sorting, ordering, and filing his written work. The listings he put after each title were not meant to be all-inclusive. They merely suggest something of the range of topics included in each category.

1 THE QUEST

Its choice —Independent path —Organized groups — Self-development —Student/teacher

2 PRACTICES FOR THE QUEST

Ant's long path —Work on oneself

3 RELAX AND RETREAT

Intermittent pauses —Tension and pressures —Relax body, breath, and mind —Retreat centres —Solitude — Nature appreciation —Sunset contemplation

4 ELEMENTARY MEDITATION

Place and conditions —Wandering thoughts —Practise concentrated attention —Meditative thinking — Visualized images —Mantrams —Symbols —Affirmations and suggestions

5 THE BODY

Hygiene and cleansings —Food —Exercises and postures —Breathings —Sex: importance, influence, effects

6 EMOTIONS AND ETHICS

Uplift character —Re-educate feelings —Discipline emotions — Purify passions —Refinement and courtesy —Avoid fanaticism

7 THE INTELLECT

Nature —Services —Development —Semantic training — Science —Metaphysics —Abstract thinking

8 THE EGO

What am I? —The I-thought —The psyche